THE REFERENCE SHELF

SOUTHERN AFRICA

edited by **GRANT S. McCLELLAN**
Editor, CURRENT Magazine

THE REFERENCE SHELF
Volume 51   Number 3

THE H. W. WILSON COMPANY
New York   1979

THE REFERENCE SHELF

The books in this series contain reprints of articles, excerpts from books, and addresses on current issues and social trends in the United States and other countries. There are six separately bound numbers in each volume, all of which are generally published in the same calendar year. One number is a collection of recent speeches; each of the others is devoted to a single subject and gives background information and discussion from various points of view, concluding with a comprehensive bibliography. Books in the series may be purchased individually or on subscription.

Library of Congress Cataloging in Publication Data

Main entry under title:

Southern Africa.

(The Reference shelf ; v. 51, no. 3)
Bibliography: p.
1. South Africa—Race relations—Addresses, essays, lectures.   2. South Africa—Economic conditions—1961–   —Addresses, essays, lectures.   3. South Africa—Foreign relations— 1961.   —Addresses, essays, lectures. 4. Africa, Southern—Race relations—Addresses, essays, lectures. 5. Africa, Southern—Politics and government—1965–   —Addresses, essays, lectures.   I. McClellan, Grant S.   II. Series.
DT763.S745   301.1′68′06   79-15138
ISBN 0-8242-0633-9

11S / 79

PRINTED IN THE UNITED STATES OF AMERICA

PREFACE

Southern Africa is a land of great beauty and even greater natural wealth. It is also the last place in Africa where whites rule blacks in the old colonial manner. The colonial pattern dominated all parts of Africa until shortly after the Second World War; there were few places in the continent not ruled by the colonial administrators of France, Britain, Portugal, or Belgium. However, in the twenty-five years since the war, almost thirty former colonies have won their independence and formed their own national governments. Only in the area called southern Africa has the tide of independence and majority rule been slowed; only here, in three of the four countries, does a small minority of whites still control government, economy, and society to the virtual exclusion of the blacks.

Change, however, is the order of the day even in southern Africa. Racked by guerrilla warfare and under pressure from both the United Kingdom and the United States, Rhodesia, a former British colony has taken the first steps toward granting majority rule—steps, however, that have been tentative, grudging, and possibly not fast enough to allow for a peaceful transition. The Republic of South Africa itself, monolithic, enormously wealthy, industrially powerful, and dominated by the Afrikaners, descendants of the original Dutch settlers, is also under pressure to moderate if not end its system of racially-based social exclusion known as *apartheid.*

The third country in southern Africa is Namibia (South-West Africa), a former German colony that was mandated to South Africa by the League of Nations after World War I. The United Nations has required a reluctant South Africa to allow free elections in Namibia by July 1979. The results of this election may determine whether independence and majority rule can be established quickly

5

and peacefully or whether Namibia will have to face the kind of guerrilla conflict that has torn Rhodesia apart.

The last country, Botswana, the former British protectorate of Bechuanaland, is a politically independent black African state—the only one in southern Africa.

The articles in this compilation attempt to describe the situation in each of the four countries. Part I is devoted to South Africa and *apartheid,* the supreme expression of racial domination; Part II concerns Namibia, Rhodesia, and Botswana; the articles in Part III have to do with the economy of South Africa, whose industrial strength (and weaknesses) may be the key to the future of the whole area; finally, Part IV explores the range of national and international pressures and interests at work in southern Africa; all striving to achieve some sort of solution.

The editor wishes to thank the authors and publishers of the selections that follow for permission to reprint them in this compilation.

GRANT S. McCLELLAN

May 1979

CONTENTS

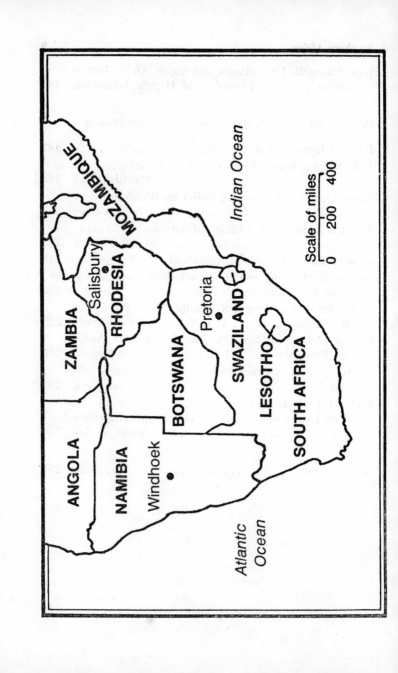

I. SOUTH AFRICA: LAND OF APARTHEID

EDITOR'S INTRODUCTION

Whichever aspect of South Africa one considers—political, economic, or social—the question of race is fundamental and unavoidable. Everything in the nation is geared to the Afrikaners' control of the black majority. *Apartheid,* which means separateness, is the iron rule, a rule carried so far that blacks and whites cannot even live in the same townships. The ultimate "separateness" is the creation of the *bantustans,* tribal homelands, where blacks can enjoy—so the Afrikaner theory goes—freedom and independent development.

In the first selection, Tom Wicker of the New York *Times* discusses the deep-rooted basis for this racial policy. Next, Roger Omond, South African correspondent for the *New Statesman,* suggests that the new generation is not nearly so committed to *apartheid* as its elders.

The conditions in a bantustan are described as a curse in an *In These Times* article, but in the fourth selection, Connie Mulder, the white Minister for Plural Relations in South Africa, presents the official view of the bantustan as an opportunity for independence and separate development for blacks.

The next two articles in this section are first-hand accounts of civil deprivations decreed under *apartheid*—the first from *Foreign Affairs* is by Donald Woods, an exiled South African newspaper editor; the other from *Commonweal* is by Representative Thomas J. Downey of New York, a member of a Congressional Committee on South Africa.

The growing response of black students to apartheid, in

the form of black consciousness, is described by Helen Zille of the *Chronicle of Higher Education* in the final article of the section.

THE AFRIKANER'S CLAIM TO SOUTH AFRICA[1]

Visitors to South Africa usually get their news from the English-language newspapers. But while these journals are vigorous and outspoken, the Afrikaner press more importantly reflects and influences the Afrikaner government.

I took it as significant, therefore, when a half-dozen Afrikaner editors and commentators with whom I recently lunched in Johannesburg agreed that change in South Africa's repressive racial arrangements was necessary and inevitable. I suggested that, in view of the Afrikaners' position as part of a minority of less than five million whites in a country with nearly 19 million blacks, the basic Afrikaner need was to master the arts of minority-group politics.

A look of shock and pain crossed the face of Dr. Willem de Klerk of *Die Transvaaler,* South Africa's most influential journalist.

"No," he said after a moment, "I cannot accept that. This country is ours."

And that, I believe, is the root of the problem in South Africa. The Afrikaners, who have been in unchallenged power since 1948 and appear in no danger of losing that power by any means short of violent upheaval, are not colonial interlopers. Their history dates back more than 300 years to the founding of the Cape Colony by the Dutch East India Company; and it is a singular history that gives them a mystical sense of their right to rule, a paranoid fear of subjugation and cultural disappearance, and a fierce independence.

---

[1] Article entitled "This Country Is Ours," by Tom Wicker, columnist. New York *Times.* p A19. D. 26, '78. © 1978 by The New York Times Company. Reprinted by permission.

Afrikaner history cannot adequately be retraced in a short article, but two of its most important episodes were the Great Trek (1836–1838) and the Boer Wars with the British (1880–81, 1899–1902), the latter more recent than the American Civil War and at least as traumatic in Afrikaner memory.

The Great Trek was a northern migration of the Afrikaners (of Dutch, German and Huguenot descent) after the British seized the Cape Colony at the end of the eighteenth century. At the Battle of Blood River, a few hundred "Voortrekkers" defeated thousands of Zulus—after trek leaders had asked Divine help and promised, if given victory, to rule the land as God's domain.

After the Afrikaners founded the Transvaal Republic and the Orange Free State, the British moved in again— this time after the discovery of gold and diamonds in the Afrikaners' inland territory. The hard-fought Boer Wars (in which the Afrikaners claim a bit loosely to have invented modern guerrilla warfare) brought the two republics forcibly into the Union of South Africa and the British Empire. The present Republic relinquished dominion status in 1960 and withdrew from the British Commonwealth in 1961.

"This Country Is Ours"

The Afrikaners' lasting suspicion of the English-speaking whites of South Africa obviously derives from this history. And older Afrikaners today can remember when they and their parents were a downtrodden minority rather despised by their colonial masters. After Afrikaners regained political power in 1948, owing to a split in the English community, they ruthlessly set out to keep that power against all challengers. When "coloreds"—persons of mixed black and white descent—were disenfranchised, for example, it was less for overt racial reasons than from fear of a political alliance between English and colored voters.

The series of desperate conflicts with the Zulus and the

British, all against seemingly overwhelming force, makes more understandable the Afrikaners' profound fear that their unique culture and heritage and language—all existing nowhere else—may somehow be wiped out. Their survival despite these conflicts, and their ultimate triumphs over blacks and British, contribute to their sense of mission. The essence of the violent Afrikaner history is defiance, self reliance, independence.

When such a people are told, therefore, that their rule must yield to the majority of South Africans—a black majority at that—every Afrikaner instinct cries out in protest. Subjugation, cultural disappearance, the breaking of the Blood River pledge—all seem implicit in the idea of majority rule; and would not easy submission to such a prospect be a betrayal of those ancestors who time and again fought stubbornly against impossible odds, only to win final vindication? Might not such vindication yet crown the contemporary struggle?

The Afrikaner also has more than his share of the world's endemic racism and contempt for black capabilities —an attitude he shares in varying degree with most English-speaking South Africans. But it is Afrikaner power and Afrikaner history that most fearfully complicate the racial situation in South Africa today and make an equitable solution so hard to predict.

Despite the Afrikaner journalists' agreement on the need for change, for example, there was little agreement around the luncheon table on *what* change, let alone how much. And the consensus among these intelligent and obviously well-intentioned men was that the real problem was to devise some political means for the Afrikaner minority to avoid being "overwhelmed" and forced "to live by black standards," so that Afrikaners could continue to maintain themselves "as a nation and as a culture."

That does not bode well for far-reaching change by peaceful means. . . . Even Afrikaners know that the kind of change most amenable to them probably would be regarded by the growing black majority as no change at all.

WILL THE AFRIKANERS FIGHT IT OUT?[2]

It's almost blasphemy to ask the question, but: will the Afrikaner fight? Or will he, grudgingly and almost certainly too late, concede the absolute power that he has maintained at the expense of every other group for three decades?

Most parties interested in the South African impasse base their policies and tactics on the belief that the white ruling class will fight to the bitter end—a belief encouraged by Pretoria, in the hope that the prospects of an all-out war will discourage its opponents. But there are some faint signs that white intransigence and determination to fight it out are not as solid as is believed generally in some London and Washington circles, the committee rooms of the African National and Pan-Africanist congresses, Moscow, the UN and even the streets of Soweto.

Several factors indicate this. One is that 59 percent of young white South Africans asked for exemption or deferment from military training in 1976. Another comes in the thoughts of the political scientist Andre Du Toit. In a brilliant paper, he suggests that pragmatism could win over ideology when the chips are really down, and draws some kind of parallel (which he says is far from exact) between the surrender of the Boer forces in 1902 and the situation that may soon face Vorster and Co. In his dissent from the contemporary wisdom about the inevitability of an Afrikaner last-ditch stand, Du Toit is joined by a number of other Afrikaner intellectuals.

A further factor suggesting that white South Africa may realize one day that fighting for apartheid is akin to hara kiri is the military arithmetic: there are just too many blacks, supported by a wide range of outside forces, for the whites to win.

[2] Article by Roger Omond, South African correspondent. *New Statesman.* 95:808-11. Je. 16, '78. Copyright 1978. By permission of the author.

This contradicts the despairing white liberal's usual argument that the apartheidists are locked into a situation giving them no escape but to go down fighting and that they lack the imagination or political courage even to conceive another option. It is a view that cannot be ignored— one that I have argued before in the *New Statesman*. But it may be unduly pessimistic. The white liberal is surrounded daily with evidence of his impotence and with Afrikaner Nationalist intransigence, cruelty and stupidity. It is difficult not to despair, which is why many use their impotence as an excuse for doing nothing or little, why some join revolutionary movements (and generally end up in jail) or why many emigrate.

Most of us have gone through the range, or at least considered the second option and then decided on the third. Emigration is both more comfortable and more tormenting. The advantages of a free society are many and varied —not least being able to write an article like this. And in a country where a white opposition vote is restricted to near-impotence, there is some satisfaction in having voted with your feet: at least Vorster will not be able to claim *my* support in his claim that he speaks for all right-thinking South Africans when that means compliance with his authoritarian ideology.

But it is no longer (if it ever was) the liberal—despairing or otherwise—who will force radical change on South Africa's rulers. Change will come not if apartheid's opponents opt for patient intellectualizing (that has been tried for years with no success) but only if the various pressures on Pretoria—political, economic, moral, military and sporting continue to be applied. Looked at objectively, what few changes there have been in South Africa in recent years have resulted from pressure, however reluctant the white *pro tem* rulers may be to acknowledge this fact. In just one area, that of sport, South Africa today is a rather different place than ten years ago when Vorster banned Basil d'Oliveira [a black cricket player] from touring with [a team from] the MCC [Marylebone Cricket Club of Great

Britain] because he was a mixed race of South African. Peter Hain showed how anti-apartheid campaigns can create a climate for change.

In a rather different way, Donald Woods' call for the economic isolation of the country could have a similar effect. The question is whether when all the political, economic, moral and military pressures have been applied, the Afrikaner will still fight to maintain his power and privilege. The optimists say no, and that those making the most bellicose noises now will be among the first to fold.

Some comfort may be drawn from history. In 1902 the Boers were faced with the decision of whether to continue a hopeless struggle against the British Army or whether to surrender and work for a new Afrikaner dawn. Eventually they chose the latter. The difference between then and now as Andre Du Toit has pointed out (in his paper to the University of Cape Town summer school last year) is that then the Afrikaners were virtually powerless. Now they are not. But Du Toit sees some similarities between the debate among the Boer signatories to the Peace of Vereeniging [the treaty of 1902 that brought to an end the Boer War] and the crisis now facing Afrikanerdom.

Du Toit distinguishes between two parties in these debates the radical bittereinders and the conciliatory bittereinders: those who saw the maintenance of the two Boer republics as equivalent to the continued existence of the Afrikaner nation versus those who perceived that republican independence was not necessarily the same as national existence. He quotes the South African Republic's Acting President Schalk Burger as then asking:

The question is whether it is better to continue until the people are exterminated, man, woman and child, than to try to come to terms. Or, on the other hand, to continue until they obtained what they wanted, only to find that the people were extirpated. For whose benefit would the struggle then have been carried on?

The conciliators won, peace was signed and, as Du Toit says, the Treaty of Vereeniging "was not the end of the

Afrikaner people, but can now be seen rather as the prelude to the emergence of a revitalized Afrikaner nationalism and the establishment of Afrikaner hegemony in South
Africa."

Pretoria's present rulers seem committed to the all-or-
nothing approach of the radical bitereinders of 1902. But,
Du Toit says, what was decisive in victory for the conciliatory bittereinders during those debates were the desperate
conditions and prospects of the non-combatants, most in
the British concentration camps or facing abject poverty.
Reason and not just emotion was urged on the Boer delegates—and reason eventually won.

Pragmatism for the Afrikaner now means little more
than making cosmetic changes to the face of apartheid: relaxation of some so-called petty apartheid measures and
changes in terminology like the renaming of the Department of Bantu Administration and Development (widely
abbreviated to BAD) to the Department of Plural Relations. But these are early days yet: there is some way to go
before the debate in Afrikaner government leadership
reaches the point of discussing whether the survival of the
Afrikaner rests on the maintenance of apartheid and repression.

Du Toit and many other verligte Afrikaners implicitly
endorse the thesis of American political scientist Herbert
Adam who says in his book *Modernizing Racial Domination* that the view of the Afrikaner as a solid, immovable
character ignores the spoils of three decades of absolute
power, the corruption through control of the fleshpots of
state capitalism and the thinning religious veneer.
". . . The majority of the 2½ million 'mini-despots' has
now become as unprincipled, opportunistic and pragmatic
as their shrewder, profit-grabbing English speaking an-
tagonists," says Adam. Their conflict becomes negotiable "if
confronted by equal forces."

And there's the rub. What constitutes equal forces? To
what extent will the Afrikaners be prepared to negotiate?

At what stage will Pretoria opt for conciliation? Will Afrikanerdom remain monolithic? Will the English-speaking people continue to give their Afrikaans-speaking rulers electoral support and continue to be prepared to let their sons die in defense of apartheid? How many Afrikaners will let their sons die for the same unwinnable cause?

Even at this stage, there does not appear to be much overwhelming desire to fight: in 1976 a total of 63,104 young men were called up for Defence Force duties and of these 37,518—a staggering 59 percent—applied for exemption or deferment. Only 9.9 percent were granted exemption but 87 percent got deferment, one of the most usual causes being university study. (They will still have to serve later though.) In the same year 3,814 men failed to report for military service and 507 were convicted. There are no figures for the number of men who left the country to avoid the draft. But the case of two Natal conscripts who sought refugee status in Britain because they were determined not to "fight for white supremacy in a civil war created by apartheid" attracted wide publicity in South Africa.

A military official in the predominantly English-speaking city of East London has said privately that he has more trouble tracking down Afrikaans-speaking draft dodgers than English ones. Conversely, an increasing number of middle-class English-speaking parents of male teenagers who will be due to fight for apartheid in a couple of years time are inquiring about emigration.

All this, and especially the application rate for deferment or exemption, hardly indicates young South Africa's burning desire for confrontation on the battlefield or in the streets of the black townships. There is a large degree of compulsion about military service backed up with heavy penalties: another indication, perhaps, that Pretoria is not as confident of its white backing as it claims. Just about every white South African boy is now being called up for compulsory two years national service. In contrast, during World War II when South Africa provided one of the

largest volunteer armies per size of population to fight the
Nazis, there was no conscription.

Conscientious objection to fighting for apartheid is
only marginally more popular than the cause of communism, long banned in South Africa. Old blood-and-thunder
[Prime Minister] P. W. Botha hastily amended the already-
restrictive Defence Act three and a half years ago after the
South African Council of Churches called on Christians to
consider whether Christ's call to identify with the oppressed did not involve becoming conscientious objectors.
The new Act made it even more difficult to discuss conscientious objection, let alone counsel troubled teenagers
about to go off fighting for apartheid. Maximum penalty
for contravention: a £3,000 fine or six years in jail.

Just over a year ago the Catholic Bishops Conference
asked for alternative forms of national service for those who
viewed their call-up as participation in unjust oppression.
The government maintained a frosty silence.

Conscientious objection to killing is not recognized in
the Defence Act as grounds for exemption, although those
who can prove their religious bona fides usually serve in
non-combatant roles. But those whose scruples do not allow
them to put on uniform are jailed. Botha's treatment of
those who differentiate between a just and unjust war does
not seem to indicate much confidence in the morality of
apartheid.

On the other hand, defense is a top priority and the
politicians have found that whipping up a war psychosis
can be useful electorally. Last year's election campaign was
fought largely on the supposed threat to white identity by
overseas forces and "internal agitators": the white electorate obligingly gave the government the biggest-ever Parliamentary majority (now 135 seats or 82 percent), versus
the combined opposition total of 30. Botha himself displays
what a fellow-Afrikaner, Progressive Federal Party MP
Van Zyl Slabbert, once called "a blood lust that would
make Count Dracula look like a Highveld mosquito." The
Defence Force takes a major slice of the national budget:

£1,000 million in 1976, representing 19 percent of the total and 5.1 percent of the gross domestic.

While the financing for defense is there, an imponderable in any decision to continue fighting for apartheid would be the extent to which South Africa would tolerate high casualties among the white forces. The country has had it relatively easy on the battleground: in the two years from April 1975, 33 security force members were killed, according to a Defense Department White Paper on fighting in the "operational area" of Namibia against SWAPO [South-West Africa People's Organization] guerrillas. Initially victims of the war were given heroes' funerals: now there are too many deaths and Pretoria seems to have appreciated that massive publicity for every serviceman killed could become counter-productive. Significantly, no figures are ever given for wounded and South African newspapers are barred from reporting about the maimed.

Rhodesian white intransigence began to melt when the cost in white lives of the war against the black nationalists was appreciated: 403 security force members and 113 white civilians killed from 1972 up to 20 October last year [1977]. Given a war of Rhodesian intensity, Pretoria would have to figure on a vastly-increased death rate. Historically, the Boers, because of their small numbers, avoided pitched battles with the British Army during the two Anglo-Boer wars and were horrified by Britain's readiness to tolerate high casualties for minimal advantages. Now the battle order has changed and it is SWAPO guerrillas who are avoiding open battle. But many speeches by the Nationalist politicians remind their listeners that "South Africa is a small nation." It could be that a too-high death rate would not be tolerated by white South Africa. Already there have been some murmurings among white parents on just how their children have died: military censorship and at least one cover-up effort have not reassured parents.

Occasionally restive, too, are some members of the top military brass. A few of the more senior and self-confident generals talk vaguely about the dual role necessary to win a war in which many, if not the majority of black South Africans will be on the opposite side. These military men talk about the need to win the proverbial hearts and minds of the people. Mao's dictum about guerrillas (or "terrorists" as they are now almost universally called) being like fish swimming in a friendly environment appears fairly regularly in the generals' speeches.

Vaguely in the back of some white liberals' minds is the possibility of a military coup—or at least the stage being reached when the senior career officers tell [President John] Vorster and Co. that a war in defense of apartheid cannot be won. . . . Certainly the military should have more sense than the politicians who found a war psychosis so useful in last 30 November's general election. Military coups are an African tradition, runs one despairing liberal argument clutching for a far-fetched hope. Why should the tradition stop at the Limpopo River?

Not many Afrikaners are thinking that way. Nor are the thousands of English-speaking whites who supported the National party in such numbers last year and who are junior partners in the political power structure. Curiously, however, it is some Afrikaners who are doing most of the new thinking, despite the rigidities imposed on them by the party bosses. The mini-debate about the future of the Afrikaners is usually sparked off by a troubled academic and although Afrikanerdom is still generally monolithic, the dissent indicates some strains. In May 1976 Rhodes University psychology professor Dreyer Kruger said there were reasons not only to expect the downfall of the Afrikaner but actually to welcome it. Nine months later he called on Afrikaners to bring about radical change, even at the risk of being arrested. At the same time Pretoria historian F. A. van Jaarsveld (once considered the leading Afrikaner historian with a distinct pro-Nationalist leaning in his writing) said that apartheid had brought the Afrikaner to the end of the road. More recently self-exiled author Laurens van de Post said he feared greatly for the future of his people: "Unless he realizes that the future can only be assured by sharing power, the Afrikaner is doomed."

Intellectuals like these are supposed to breathe faith into Nationalist ideology and to provide the moral base of apartheid. When they deviate, the reaction from the politicians is fierce: they are portrayed as hensoppers (literally handsuppers) if not verraiers (traitors). The dissidents are growing in numbers, despite the best efforts of men like hardline Nationalist MP Daan van der Merwe who said people like he were the only true Afrikaners and the "rich intellectual types" were manipulators of Afrikaner religion.

The ferocity with which the intellectual rebels are greeted betrays deep unease. So does the fact that blacks are being brought into the Defense Force in greater numbers: Coloureds (mixed race) and Indians will have compulsory national service in the not-too-distant future. The Chief of the Defense Forces General Magnus Malan, has revealed that more than 20 percent of the forces in the "operational area" are blacks.

The blunt fact, of course, is that four million whites—even if all were convinced of the moral rectitude of fighting for apartheid—cannot do battle with the allegedly communist inspired guerrillas on the borders while policing a restive black population at the same time. Even P. W. Botha can do his arithmetic, despite the deep reservations of having to depend on blacks to protect white lives.

Equally important is that the Bothas of South Africa are almost classic cases of psychological insecurity who feel (perhaps correctly) that when the chips are down they will be on their own. The strident appeals to the West that South Africa is protecting the Cape sea route and that it has minerals vital to the free world have fallen on deaf ears. The rhetoric along these lines has been replaced with Vorster's ill-considered election challenge to the West to do its damnedest. But behind this bluster and talk of the Jews committing suicide in ancient times rather than surrendering (the clear implication being the delightful prospect of a twentieth century Afrikaner repeat performance), lies deep unease. The Afrikaner beat ill-armed blacks in a series of nineteenth century wars and held off the British Army for some years at the turn of the century, but this time the situation is different. Now the Afrikaners face the world. And they are a small nation.

Although constant appeals are being made to Afrikaners to remember their past military successes, history is being misused for propaganda purposes. No mention is made of the fact that the Afrikaners are not as immobile in adversity as is claimed. The Great Trek was prompted by unwillingness to accept what they considered unpalatable government. And when Natal, for example, was annexed by the British, they trekked again. After the first and second Anglo-Boer wars, hundreds if not thousands abandoned "their" country for Rhodesia, Kenya, and South America.

More recently a group of extreme Right-wing Herstigte Nasionale Party supporters sent a team to Bolivia to investigate resettling there in the event of Vorster selling out the white man, as they quaintly put it. For a nation that protests it has no other home but South Africa (and uses this as the rationale for repression) the Afrikaners can be curiously mobile.

What worries many Afrikaners (even in the National party)—and which may become a more important factor when it comes to *die volk's* decision whether to fight for apartheid or not—is the isolation of the leadership from the rank and file. The leadership, particularly at cabinet rank, tends to move in a closed circle of like-minded Afrikaners. Their lives are confined often to their plush homes in Pretoria; their offices of state in the Union Buildings; the parliamentary session in Cape Town where the presence of more than 100 ambitious backbenchers is enough to stall any qualms; a couple of party congresses where they are greeted as heroes and bedecked with ornate buttonholes by over-awed schoolgirls; riding around in chauffeur-driven black Cadillacs or Mercedes-Benzs to an exclusive Afrikaner club and Broederbond meeting. The party has become an end in itself; the maintenance of power being no less important than the wellbeing of *die volk daar buite* [people not in the party]. If Nixon was an imperial President, Vorster and Co. are not far behind. Allegations of corruption in high places are being made more frequently, the Rhoodie highhandedness in running the Department of Information another indication that the leaders have developed a contempt for standards accepted even by the obedient caucus.

And it may be having an effect. Psephologists (particularly on the opposition side) pointed in April to the Spring's by-election result that saw a large swing away from the National party when it was least expected as an indication of some more Afrikaner restiveness.

The optimists—there are not many left in South Africa now—feel that on this evidence and just a gut-feeling, that when the crunch comes, South Africa will develop its own version of white Rhodesia's chicken run. They may just be right. But in the interval there will be more bellicose rhetoric and more deaths on both sides. Vorster will continue to fudge the issues in South Africa as the problems of Namibia and Rhodesia dominate the headlines. There will be more "concessions" on petty apartheid and Pretoria will use its new constitutional plan to include tame Coloured and Indian leaders in a sham decision-making process as a propaganda weapon. . . .

The key to solving the South African impasse is the maintenance of pressure from as many sources as possible until Pretoria is confronted by . . . [equal forces]. It is impossible to say just when that stage will be reached. But when it is, the Afrikaner, as the senior partner in the white political power structure, may indeed decide that the conflict is negotiable and opt for pragmatism—which will mean the surrender of absolute political power although the maintenance of some economic muscle—rather than go down fighting.

SOUTH AFRICA'S BANTUSTANS[3]

At 5 P.M. in any South African city, you can see a stream of blacks moving towards the train station. From there, they go out to their homes in black townships, often two hours away from the whites-only areas where they work.

In Pretoria, South Africa's capital, the blacks are not simply going to a township. They are actually leaving South Africa for another country—though they, too, will return in the morning, ready for work at seven. They live in GaRankuwa, part of an independent country called BophuthaTswana; if border controls were strictly observed, the GaRankuwa railroad station would have to process 90,000 passports an hour during Pretoria's peak rush hours.

Two years ago, Pretoria's workers were still South Africans. But last December, BophuthaTswana's Chief Lucas Mangope took the plunge: his country became the second of South Africa's bantustans [tribal homelands] to accept independence from the rest of the Republic.

Of course, BophuthaTswana has had some difficulty presenting itself as an independent country. To begin with, no one outside of a few Nationalist party officials knows exactly where its borders are; the country includes six or seven large bits and several black dots, all separated by pieces of South Africa, and no one knows which the bits are. Most of its population had never lived in Bophutha-Tswana; South Africa's white regime assigned them to the bantustan because of their tribal origin.

BophuthaTswana is trying hard. It is poor. Most of its gross national income is earned outside its borders, in South Africa's mines, factories and industries, and in cities like Pretoria: South Africa's Ministry of Foreign Affairs

[3] Article entitled "Independence for Black Bantustans a Curse, Not Cure," by the southern Africa correspondent. *In These Times.* 3:8-9. D. 6-12, '78. Copyright © 1978 by the Institute for Policy Studies, Inc., 1509 No. Milwaukee Ave., Chicago, IL 60622. Reprinted by permission.

supplies some 70 percent of Chief Mangope's government budget.

But BophuthaTswana is doing its best to build up its resources; just last month, Mangope's ministers announced a new development plan, based on tourists from South Africa. The big attraction? BophuthaTswana, using aid from South Africa, is about to install an artificial wave-making machine in a large man-made lake, to simulate the beaches that can be found along South Africa's southern coast.

Dumping Ground

The nine bantustans—for that is what Bophutha-Tswana and Transkei remain, despite their so-called independence—serve as the keystones of South Africa's system of grand apartheid (pronounced apart-hate). Under the Nationalist party's policy of separate development for the different races, blacks are assigned to the bantustans—less than 13 percent of the land, for 87 percent of South Africa's people.

Until 1976, the ultimate goal of independence for the bantustans—or homelands, as the government has taken to calling them in the last decade—remained far in the future, when white South Africa deemed its blacks capable of ruling themselves. But since the Soweto disturbances, the government has speeded up the process. Two bantustans are independent, a third is about to be, and the rest are under pressure to accept independence in the near future.

Many South Africans believe the speedup is the result of a government decision to push separate development as far as it can, so that the nation's blacks will be fragmented and unable to claim any hold on the country's wealth.

Ever since the Nationalists came into power in 1948, South African blacks have objected to the bantustan policy. None of the bantustans is a viable economic unit; they contain no natural resources, no industry, and little arable land. In 1976, the nine bantustans together had an average annual per capita domestic product of R64: about $6 a month. If you exclude white residents of the bantustans, the figure dropped to a monthly product worth $5 per capita. The people who live on the bantustans survive on almost nothing—unless a member of their family has obtained a pass to work in South Africa, and can send wages back to them.

Poor islands in one of the world's richest countries, the bantustans were created as a dumping ground for unwanted laborers, a method of population control and a way of defusing black protest. South Africa's infamous pass laws give it the right to send any black back to the bantustan to which he or she has been assigned; the unemployed, the blacks who are too old or too young to work, and the politically active can be removed from white areas without appeal—sent back to starve, or to serve as a reserve of cheap labor for white South Africa.

Tribal Opportunists

The men who have accepted independence for their bantustans are fairly unsavory characters, and are widely hated by South African blacks. Because the bantustans are supposed to be organized along tribal lines, the government appointed chiefs, claiming to follow traditional patterns. In fact, the tribal base is as ridiculous in itself as the bantustan system, since over a third of South Africa's blacks live in urban areas, and many are about as connected to their tribes as an Italian-American is linked to the village his grandfather came from.

Chief Mangope, like Chief Kaiser Mantanzima in Transkei, is a ruthless opportunist; in both Bophutha-Tswana and Transkei, the opposition has been disbanded or jailed, and government officials are free to use their positions for personal gain. In both countries, too, about half the legislature is directly appointed by the chief, making a farce of the democratic process in the only parts of South Africa where blacks can vote for their national government.

A similar sitaution is developing in Venda, which is slated for independence early next year. Just after the pre-independence elections last month. Chief Patrick Mphephu detained more than 50 members of the opposition, without charges or trials. The opposition had just gained 31 of the phu, 42 other members are government-appointed chiefs, but apparently he felt that margin was too close for comfort.

Pretoria seems to have agreed. The Venda detainees were picked up by South African police, and held in South African cells. And throughout the uproar that followed the jailings, South African government officials continued to describe Mphephu's move toward independence as "the kind of democratic, peaceful change that should serve as an example for the rest of black Africa."

Holding Out Against Independence

One bantustan leader, KwaZulu's Chief Gatsha Buthelezi, has stood firmly against independence, and since 1976, he has begun to suffer for it. He has said repeatedly that he will not sell his people's birthright—he will not let the Zulus cut themselves off from the rest of their country.

Until recently, Pretoria allowed Buthelezi to speak freely, pointing to him as an example of South Africa's free speech.

But for the last two years, it has put increasing pressure on him to accept the kind of independence given Transkei and BophuthaTswana. The subsidy that Pretoria gives Buthelezi, who governs the most populous of the bantustans, is substantially smaller than that given to any other bantustan leader; last year, KwaZulu's entire subsidy was barely three-fourths the amount it needs to run its school system, which is only one of the four departments the subsidy theoretically covers.

Buthelezi has been forced to levy additional taxes on his people; not surprisingly, they are beginning to grumble. There are indications that Buthelezi will be forced to accept independence or be thrown out by his own people—a

situation that his more radical critics have predicted since
he accepted the bantustan post.

Along with the push to speed up independence has
come a redoubled effort by South Africa's regime to remove blacks living illegally in white areas. The well-pub-
licized raids on Crossroads, a squatter township outside
Capetown, have been repeated in other townships throughout South Africa, as policemen sweep through whole cities
of corrugated iron and cardboard houses, looking for
blacks who are not legally employed. Crossroads was remarkable only because its inhabitants organized resistance.
(Incidentally, Crossroads also showed up the absurdity of
the tribal basis of the bantustans: when Transkei refused
to accept those Crossroads residents assigned to live there,
the South African government simply reassigned them to
Ciskei, the homeland for another, though related, tribe.)

Ten Children Die Each Day

Dawn "crime swoops," in which the police and army
block off a black township and move through it checking
passes, have also become commonplace in the last year;
since 1976, it has become too dangerous for police to patrol
the townships regularly, and the swoops are the only kind
of police protection offered urban blacks. But the swoops
only catch one kind of criminal, the pass offender. Where
once blacks without the proper permit might, with luck,
hope to avoid arrest, now they are almost inevitably faced
with "endorsement" back to unemployment on the bantustans.

The pass raids and crime swoops seem to have been
prompted by a combination of factors. In addition to increased black unrest over issues like the system of bantu
education, black unemployment has reached an all-time
high. No official figures exist, but estimates range as high
as 16 percent in Johannesburg to 40 percent in the bantustans. As a leader of Black Sash, an organization of liberal whites, said recently, "Black unemployment is being
pushed out to the homelands," where the regime need not

concern itself with unemployment relief or medical aid, where the only work is subsistence-level agriculture, and where any political unrest will not disturb the structure of apartheid.

Blacks who are sent back to the bantustans may spend years in resettlement camps set up by the South African government, waiting to be sent somewhere else. Conditions in Thornhill, in Ciskei, are probably typical. Last year, the only doctor working for the camp's 10,000 residents revealed that ten children a day were dying of malnutrition and complications. She was transferred. This year, a typhoid epidemic broke out at Thornhill; the medical facilities were enlarged to meet the emergency, and the camp now boasts a six-bed hospital and a full-time nurse.

Everyone from South Africans to the Organization of African Unity to the United Nations has long recognized that the policy of separate development has meant development for South Africa's whites and underdevelopment for its blacks. But as the regime speeds up the independence process, and as more passes are exchanged for passports, more of South Africa's blacks will find themselves in positions similar to that of BophuthaTswana's citizens: migrant workers in a foreign state, aliens who have no claim over their country's wealth or political process, laboring for white South Africa and living in poverty and powerlessness.

A NEW DEAL FOR BLACKS[4]

The principle underlying the policy of independent development in South Africa is rooted in the evolution of a workable form of co-existence for the population. This will allow every race and group to live a full life while contributing to the larger welfare of the country.

In considering the situation of blacks in our area, one

[4] Article by Dr. Connie Mulder, minister for plural relations and development in South Africa. *Business Week.* p 23. O. 9, '78. Reprinted from Business Week by special permission. © 1978 by McGraw-Hill Inc.

has to guard against the temptation to over-simplify the issues. Thus a new five-year plan is being investigated as a way to avoid the pitfalls in balancing and scheduling the whole question of how race relations should be developed and advanced in the all-important period ahead.

Meanwhile, the position of the blacks in the white metropolitan areas is the subject of particularly intense discussion, as it is crucial to the evolution of the non-discriminatory concept as a whole. In this discussion, South Africans are becoming more aware that the solutions lie in their hands and are to be found through consultation.

Such consultation and discussion has already led to a form of self-government in black rural areas and in certain black urban residential areas. In the urban areas, this has been achieved by establishing community councils. These councils liaise with government institutions at various levels and are expected to bring closer cooperation between blacks and other groups. It is recognized that the various representative groups cannot function independently. There must be collaboration, cooperation and an identity of interests.

One should add, however, that if the approach to improving group relations in the country involves constructive cooperation and mutual understanding, it also demands a reserved response to activist elements with ulterior motives that are not in the best interests of the majority. There is no question but that all sections of the population of the country are receptive to changes aimed at peaceful coexistence on the basis of group autonomy. Their interests must come before those of activists who want change by violence.

The Role of Community Councils

Official policy aims at maximum autonomy in geographic areas in which groups that differ ethnically and culturally can manage affairs and matters of their own concern. The community councils will perform an important role here.

One recent innovation introduced by legislation during the 1978 parliamentary session, is the right of 99-year leasehold in the urban black residential areas. Blacks who qualify for residential rights on a family basis will benefit most.

The relevant legislation, namely the Black (Urban Areas) Amendment Act No. 97 of 1978, gives blacks wider rights to erect buildings in their urban areas for residential purposes or to conduct businesses or professions; to encumber the right of leasehold by mortgage bonds and to let, sublet, transfer, sell or otherwise dispose of their rights.

To assist in this, the scope has been broadened for blacks to obtain loans direct from financial institutions for the construction of houses and other buildings. There is no restriction on the purposes for which loans may be obtained and registered as bonds against the registered rights of leasehold. Thus capital can be found for the further development of new black businesses or professions.

It is expected that the investments of blacks in building societies alone will total some $170 million in the initial stages. Moreover, apart from financial institutions, employers will assist black employees with loans.

It seems logical that the development of a responsible middleclass black community will be encouraged by such moves. In turn, this should lead to a more stable and contented black community.

The broad objective is that people of all races should have a proper stake in the country's economy, while also enjoying autonomy in the government of their own affairs. This seems the right way to engender a loyalty to the common goal of stability and self-determination.

SOUTH AFRICA'S FACE TO THE WORLD[5]

More than any other nation today, South Africa's foreign relations are linked indissolubly with the internal

[5] Article by Donald Woods, former editor of the South African newspaper, the East London *Daily Dispatch* and author of the book *Biko* (1979). *Foreign Affairs.* 56:521-8. Ap. '78. © Donald Woods, 1978. Reprinted by permission of the author.

workings of its society. Maintaining the country's present
degree of interdependence with European and American
private enterprise depends on the preservation of an image
of internal "stability." In addition, deflecting further international sanctions requires the muffling of Western anxieties about racial injustice and potential racial conflict. Thus
the most important aspect of South Africa's foreign policy
must be a public relations campaign directed toward the
governments and citizens of the industrial democracies. The
chief underlying theme of this propaganda campaign is
the implicit alliance between white, Christian, democratic
and anti-communist South Africa and the "free world."

For example, the South African government often appeals to Britons and Americans for support by arguing that:
"We fought on the same side in World War II." In fact, the
country's ruling National party supported Nazi Germany
in World War II. At that time the National party was in
opposition to the governing party of General Jan Smuts,
and bitterly opposed South Africa's alignment with the
Allies. The result was that Smuts was never able to commit
all his forces to the war against Hitler, having to keep some
of them at home to deal with the Nationalists and their
fringe organizations.

Such effrontery is no surprise to those of us in South Africa who oppose apartheid, because we know that South Africa's external policy is based on tactics to ensure that the
Western world will not probe its facade too deeply. Pretoria's campaign has two basic aims: (a) to obscure as far
as possible the true nature of the apartheid regime, and (b)
to present an external image of moderation and pragmatism.

A main theme on which Nationalist propaganda is based
is that the 25 million people of South Africa do not constitute one nation but a number of "national units" each with
its own language, culture and territory. The full absurdity
of this is only apparent to those who know South Africa
well. The so-called cultural differences between the black

ethnic groups are not only minimal but are rejected by most of the blacks themselves as a political factor.

The five million Zulus and five million Xhosas, for example, have a common culture, and the Xhosa and Zulu languages are strongly similar. It would be more accurate to say that there are cultural differences between an Alabaman and a Nebraskan than it would be to talk of cultural differences between a Zulu and a Xhosa. As an English linguist, I can differentiate between the Alabama accent and the northern accent within a few words. As a Xhosa linguist, I sometimes cannot tell for several sentences whether a person is speaking Xhosa or Zulu.

The truth is that the South African government is less concerned with "cultural differences" than with the age-old political device of divide and rule. Being a white minority of five million in a country of 25 million, they simply wish to divide the black majority into smaller units comprising Zulus, Xhosas, Swazis, Tswanas, Vendas, Sothos, Coloureds (mulattoes) and Indians. To avoid according them basic civil rights, they are giving to each of these alleged "separate ethnic units" absurdly small territories along the fringes of the country within which to exercise such rights. These Bantustans or "homelands" total 13 percent of the country's territory whereas the whites, who comprise less than 20 percent of the population, claim 87 percent of the territory—and that 87 percent happens to include the gold and diamond mines and all the developed industrial and metropolitan areas and harbors.

But that is not all. The rationale for this policy is based on two further myths. One is that the "homelands" are the "traditional territories" of each "national unit." The theory is that the white settlers arrived in South Africa at about the same time as the blacks, and settled the white 87 percent at the same time as blacks were settling "their" 13 percent. This allegation, however, has been disproved by radiocarbon dating tests showing that there were negroid communities in South Africa as far back as the fifth century, long before the first white settlers arrived in 1652. The Xhosas, for example, were well established as far south as the Gamtoos River area by the fifteenth century (considerably beyond what is now the Xhosa homeland, the Transkei). And the blacks did not live in static "areas" but were nomadic peoples, cattle-herders, moving throughout South Africa in search of ever more grazing land.

Another notion upon which Nationalist propaganda is based is that the blacks "want" territorial separation.

The truth is that they have never been allowed any choice in the matter. There has never been a nationwide poll of blacks by way of referendum on the issue and all the evidence suggests that the entire concept of "homelands" would be overwhelmingly rejected in such a referendum. For evidence of this, we must, as Governor Al Smith used to say, "Take a look at the record."

All the nationalist leaders of black South Africa, the leaders of the banned African National Congress, Pan Africanist Congress and Black Peoples Convention (Chief Albert Luthuli and Nelson Mandela, Robert Sobukwe and the late Steve Biko) have consistently rejected the "homelands" policy. Not only that, even the "homelands" leaders themselves, such as Chief Gatsha Buthelezi, Chief Kaiser Mantanzima and others, have also made it plain that they would reject it if given an alternative. Like all the apartheid laws, territorial apartheid is a white creation for the political convenience of whites. Abraham Lincoln spoke of "government of the people, by the people, for the people." Apartheid is government of the blacks, by the whites, for the whites.

Another frail plank of the Nationalist propaganda platform is the claim that the Nationalist regime is a bastion of Western values against communism.

On the contrary, the Vorster regime is communism's greatest recruiting ally in southern Africa. Many young blacks of South Africa, increasingly embittered by the West's refusal to sever links with the Vorster regime, are turning to the East for aid. They point out that Russia has no investments or trade and no diplomatic links with South Africa—and that only the Western states veto strong steps against apartheid in the UN Security Council.

South African pleas for Western solidarity are particularly ironic because government spokesmen have several different lines on this issue, turning one face to the West and another to their internal constituencies. In the recent all-white elections in South Africa, the Nationalists launched the most vicious attacks against the Western states, and in particular America. America, a government minister proclaimed in one speech, was more of a threat to South Africa than was the Soviet Union.

Another commonly heard South African argument is that South Africa is freer than most African countries and that South Africa has a free press.

Neither of these claims has validity. Apart from a small handful of African countries, including Amin's Uganda and Bokassa's Central African "Empire," Pretoria has the most repressive regime on the continent of Africa. The South African government: imprisons people without trial; restricts political dissidents to specific areas of the country; ordains where people may live and work, and what categories of work they may do, according to skin color; forbids marriage between persons of different race groups; reserves the vote to the ruling white minority.

In spite of all the rhetoric, the basic fact that neither the Prime Minister nor the Foreign Minister can refute is that in South Africa not one of the more than 20 million blacks can vote for the central government of the country. Finally, the mainstay of the South African economy, the system of migrant labor, breaks up family life for millions of blacks. Under this system blacks are only tolerated in the so-called white areas for their labor, and for many of them this involves acceptance of contracts that keep them effectively separated from their families for 11 months out of every 12. As Minister of Information C. P. Mulder revealed in a speech in February 1978, the ultimate aim is that every single black man and woman in South Africa be regarded as a citizen of one of the "homelands" and therefore a "foreigner" in the "white" area. In a country with more than 20 million blacks, there is not to be a single black citizen. The question of freedom becomes moot where citizenship is denied.

How many other African states proclaim residential areas according to skin pigmentation? How many African states forbid people of one color to marry or to live with or to play sports with people of another color? How many African states have job reservation based on race?

As to freedom of the press, can the government explain how, if the press is free in South Africa, I came to be banned without trial, accusation or explanation, or how Percy Qoboza came to be detained and how his newspaper, *The World,* came to be closed down overnight without any reasons being given? The truth is that press criticism of the government in South Africa is only allowed if it is ineffective—and the same goes for political opposition.

The parliamentary opposition is only tolerated because it has so few supporters. This is so because in South Africa only whites may belong to the token parliamentary opposition; it is forbidden by law to form multiracial political parties. There is no doubt in my mind that if by some electoral miracle the parliamentary opposition in South Africa gained enough support among whites to threaten the regime with defeat at the polls, it would be outlawed by a stroke of the pen—as so many critics of the government have been.

I wish I had the opportunity to challenge Pretoria with the facts of my own banning. Foreign Minister Roloef Botha is reported to have said that I was banned for "reasons other than journalistic reasons." There were no specifics. Now there are many hundred of laws in South Africa prescribing severe penalties for any activity connected with opposition to apartheid. Surely if I had done anything to contravene any of these many complex and wide-ranging laws (several of which place the onus on an accused to prove his innocence instead of on the state to prove guilt) the obvious course of action would have been to prosecute me. With all

these statutory aids behind them, could not the government representative accuse me in open court? Did they feel
I might prevail against a state prosecutor and a state-ap-
pointed judge? Or are they once again relying on secret
recommendations by secret police?

Punishment without trial in South Africa has reached
massive proportions, and the list of people acted against
after no other process than secret police recommendation
now numbers in the thousands. These include hundreds of
detainees, of whom at least 45 are known to have died in
the hands of security police—most notoriously, of course,
Steve Biko, whose savage treatment has now been revealed
to the whole world. Of these 45 deaths in arbitrary detention, no less than 27 have occurred since the Foreign Minister stated in 1974 that the regime would "move away from
racial discrimination."

The most important purpose of the South African
propaganda is to preserve the economic links with the West
that prop up the apartheid regime. Only by preserving these
economic links with the West can the whites of South Africa
keep suppressing the black majority. Their central argument here is based on one main proposition—that severance
of such economic links would harm blacks in South Africa
more than whites.

As usual, this claim is based more on white preference
than on evidence of what South Africa's blacks themselves
feel. Albert Luthuli, Nelson Mandela, Robert Sobukwe,
Steve Biko—all have been unequivocal on this point. They
have consistently maintained that black South Africans
are no strangers to worse sufferings than fringe unemployment, and would prefer this to a continuation of the economic links that help to maintain the system that oppresses
them. Those advocating preservation of those links are either Nationalist ministers, white industrialists or Bantustan
leaders.

Ideally, the best way to prove what most of the blacks
of South Africa really want in this regard would be to let
them vote on the issue after a campaign in which all spokes-

men could participate—but unfortunately Luthuli and Biko are dead, Mandela is imprisoned, and Sobukwe and hundreds of other black leaders are banned or detained. It is important to remember, in view of statements to the contrary by Pretoria spokesmen, that no Nationalist claim as to authentic black majority opinion has ever been tested by vote among blacks in South Africa—not in more than 300 years of recorded history.

Let us strip away all the obfuscations and rhetoric and look at the basic reality the Nationalists refuse to confront. It is that five million whites have to come to a realistic accommodation with the legitimate civil rights demands of more than 20 million blacks—in short, that the white minority has to accept that it is a white minority. Government ministers appear to refuse all realistic acceptance of this fact because they see it as amounting to "losing their white identity." Accordingly, they act as if their identity were the main consideration in the whole equation. Clearly, this cannot be justified. If it were, then the Welsh would have the moral right to enslave all Britons for fear of losing their Welsh identity as a numerical minority.

But it can be argued that perhaps even the Welsh, after all, have a territory within which to "preserve their identity." More to the point, then, why don't the Afrikaner Nationalists initiate negotiations with the black majority with a view to gaining their own "homeland"? Provided their territorial ambitions are less greedy, in fact considerably less greedy than the scale of 87 percent, as at present, they might find the blacks disposed to be generous in this regard. Arguably, South Africa's centrally located Orange Free State or a comparable extent of territory would be as appropriate a "homeland" for Afrikaner Nationalists as the Transkei would be for Xhosas. But that is not the present argument of exponents of apartheid. The Nationalists' position in effect decrees that they can have their territorial cake and eat it too, while monopolizing all the decisions related to the having and eating thereof.

And if they claim they have to do all these things to

stay where they are because they "have nowhere else to go," this is also untrue. They have no more claim to permanence in their areas of South Africa, or for that matter anywhere in South Africa, than any other community there. I would say that if the whites can only preserve their identity by opposing and killing others, it is their duty to emigrate from South Africa. If they are unwilling to accept the realities of life on the African continent (most Africans being black) they should go and live where people are predominantly white—as in northern Europe. If they should reply that their people cannot afford to emigrate, my reply is that they therefore cannot afford apartheid. If they belong in Africa, as they claim, then they must accept their fellow Africans who are blacks as fellow citizens in every sense of the word.

And if they point to "what has happened to whites in the rest of Africa," my reply is: "What indeed has happened to whites?" The Mau Mau killed fewer whites in Kenya (36) than the Nationalists have killed blacks in detention in South Africa. More whites have died in the civil war caused by the policies of Ian Smith's government in Rhodesia than have died under black governments in Zambia, Tanzania, Kenya, Malawi, Mozambique, Angola, and even Uganda, together. I exclude only the former Belgian Congo from this claim, and even in that case it is surely accepted by now that the Congo erupted into antiwhite violence precisely because the Belgians had for decades done what South Africa's whites are now doing—withholding from blacks all meaningful political rights.

But the final indictment of the apartheid regime is this: just as the Nationalists refuse to confront reality in their own country, so they pose and reply externally to issues that are spurious and irrelevant. No one in the West has demanded of the Afrikaner Nationalists what South Africa claims is demanded—the "suicide" of their people. Thus, when they say the West should "get off their backs" on this score, they are setting up for themselves a paper tiger that can be heroically defied.

What the West is really saying to Pretoria, what Africa is saying to Pretoria, and what most South Africans are saying to Pretoria is: "Talk to your own people. Negotiate with the real leaders chosen by your country's blacks. Determine your own future by peaceful negotiation with your own black majority. If you begin to do this, and stop imprisoning them, banning them, detaining them and killing them, there will be no more talk of sanctions, ostracism and pressure."

That is the challenge Pretoria should answer—not the ones the Nationalists themselves have devised for propaganda purposes. But if the South African government continues to evade their real challenges, if they continue to oppress the blacks of South Africa while continuing to present to the world an artificial facade of pragmatism that obscures such oppression, they will ultimately be responsible for the world's worst racial civil war, the effects of which will poison communities far removed geographically from South Africa. Such a racial conflagration will involve, to some extent, every country in the world where men of differing color live—not least of all the United States. It is therefore no longer invalid to describe apartheid as a threat to world peace.

Meanwhile, it is the moral duty of every person to whom the South African campaign is addressed to pull the entire debate over apartheid back from the vaguely theoretical to the directly practical and personal issues proceeding from it. During the time it took to read this article, five black babies in South Africa died of malnutrition in one of the richest countries in the world, with two-thirds of the world's gold, more than half the world's diamonds, more than three-quarters of the world's uranium, and the best agricultural land in all Africa. It is not only in detention that the victims of apartheid die.

JUSTICE UNDER APARTHEID[6]

On October 19, 1977, barely a month before Parliamentary elections in South Africa, security police there conducted one of the largest mass political arrests in recent years. Eighteen major black community, political and religious organizations were banned. Also banned was the Christian Institute, a prominent bi-racial civil rights group in South Africa. In addition, scores of churchmen, journalists and community leaders were detained under provisions of the South African Internal Security Act. *The World,* South Africa's most widely read black newspaper, was put out of business and its editor arrested along with several members of the newspaper staff.

South African Minister of Justice James T. Kruger characterized the banned groups as having "sweet-sounding names . . . (while) the aims of these organizations only serve as a smoke screen to cover their subversive activities." Kruger described the individuals arrested as "those persons whose activities endanger the maintenance of public order." The Minister of Justice assured South Africans that the country would "not be disturbed by a small group of anarchists."

Among the so-called "anarchists" arrested were the Reverend Smangaliso Mkhatshwa, Secretary General of the South African Catholic Bishops Conference, Reverend Drake Tshenkeng, Rector of St. Mary's Anglican Church and Percy Qoboza, editor of *The World.*

Since the October 19th crackdown, the South African government has liquidated the assets of several of the banned organizations and approximately $375,000 from their bank accounts has been seized by government officials. Recently, other religious and political leaders have been

[6] Article by Thomas J. Downey, Long Island congressman and co-ordinator of the Congressional Ad Hoc Monitoring Group on South Africa. *Commonweal.* 105:721-2. N. 10, '78. Copyright © 1978 Commonweal Publishing Co. Inc. Reprinted by permission.

detained, including members of the Young Christian Workers, a Catholic workers' organization.

Over the past 30 years, the ruling Nationalist party has enacted a string of restrictive legislation which, in effect, gives a blank check to government security officials seeking to act against political opponents of apartheid.

The Suppression of Communism Act of 1950, strengthened by the Internal Security Amendment, number 79 of 1976 gives the Minister of Justice broad powers to declare any organization unlawful if he believes that it promotes communism. Similarly, "communism" was widely defined by statute to include anyone working to subvert the state. The Terrorism Act of 1967 allows for the detention without trial and charge for an indefinite period of persons suspected of terrorism. No South African court can intervene to prevent the implementation of a detention order issued under terms of the Terrorism Act.

The New "Banning" Rules

Intermediate steps against individuals opposed to the white Nationalist government include "banning." The Minister of Justice may prohibit any banned person from attending a gathering of more than two people, whether of a political or social nature. Indeed, persons slapped by the government with a banning order are not even allowed to be in the same room with more than one member of their family. The most serious banning orders, which may last for years, amount to virtual house arrest. In addition, the writings and speeches of banned persons may not be published or made public without the specific permission of the Minister of Justice. Even past literary works or texts of speeches made before a banning order are affected retroactively by this law.

The wife of Reverend Theo Kotze, a Methodist minister arrested last October, explains what a banning order means. "He (Kotze) is prohibited from attending any gatherings of himself and more than one person . . . this includes the family, so that Theo and I cannot meet together with one of our children. He may not give any educational instruction . . . (and) he may not prepare, collate, publish, distribute, or dispatch any document." Breaking a banning order, in this case lasting five years, makes the individual liable for a prison sentence of up to five years.

Those persons who are detained or arrested under provisions of the Internal Security Act or the Terrorism Act are routinely subject to physical abuse, according to studies made by organizations like Amnesty International. Over the past two years, there have been 22 deaths among prisoners held by South African security police. Official explanations of these deaths range from "suicide by hanging," "jumped six floors down stairwell," "slipped on a bar of soap," to "stroke." Black civil rights leader Steve Biko's death in detention just a year ago was a result of head injuries. He is only the most prominent political prisoner to die in South Africa recently. On July 10, a black youth died while "plunging to his death from the fifth floor" office of the same Port Elizabeth security building where Biko allegedly sustained his fatal injuries.

In the face of mounting political repression in South Africa the Congress and the Carter administration have struggled to respond. Last fall the United States Ambassador to South Africa was momentarily withdrawn in protest of the October arrests. This year a flurry of bills have been introduced in the Congress which are designed to reduce or elminate US-South African political and economic ties until the Nationalist racial policies are reformed. The most important legislative initiative of the recent Congress is a measure to prohibit US Export-Import Bank loan guarantees to South African government corporations. But, many critics of apartheid argue that these and other initiatives are only a band-aid approach to the problem.

US Economic Investments

Our economic investment in South Africa is huge. Over 300 US corporations have over $1.6 billion invested in South Africa. In 1977 this country was South Africa's second biggest market for its goods and the US ranked first in the world in exports to South Africa. Our banks have extended $2.2 billion in credit to South Africa over the past few years.

Immediately following the November 30, 1977 South African elections, American industrialist Henry Ford Jr. paid a personal visit to inspect his large plants there. The Ford visit came on the heels of widespread foreign criticism of the mass political arrest just a few months before. Mr. Ford pronounced his company's investments in good hands and commented to the world press on the excellent business climate in South Africa. Shortly after the visit Ford, the largest US employer in South Africa, announced an $8 million expansion program. For the average South African the message of Ford's visit and the subsequent expansion was clear. Powerful US business interests are solidly behind the ruling government.

In reply to questions about their hiring and employment practices in South Africa, US companies often explain that they are a moderating racial force. American executives say that they are eliminating discriminatory wage scales and training blacks for management positions. Moves to reduce or eliminate US investment, they argue, will only negate their efforts and hurt the 80,000 blacks working for US corporations in South Africa. The figures say otherwise.

The Ford Motor Corporation employs 4,800 workers in South Africa. Their management staff of about 280 is exclusively white and of more than 1,500 other white-collar positions only 20 blacks hold positions. The largest financial employer in South Africa is Citibank with about 200 people on its payroll. Citibank has one black management employee. Approximately one-third of the US corporations in South Africa have signed the so-called Sullivan Principles. The principles were drawn up by the Reverend Leon Sullivan. Signing the code pledges US companies to begin to end economic and racial discrimination in their South African plants. In reality, US corporations can in good faith hold jobs open to both blacks and whites based on ability knowing full well that few, if any, blacks will qualify for highly skilled and highly paid jobs. Programs to train black South Africans for these positions are grossly inadequate.

Sadly, US foreign policy and American businesses have not been a force for change in South Africa. We have attempted to gently modify the Nationalists' repugnant racial programs while failing to address the main issue. The white Nationalist government is a part of the problem in South Africa, not part of the solution. Apartheid is enforced by repression on a massive scale, condoned or directed by the Nationalists. Given the intransigence of the current South African government, further US investment in South Africa only serves to prop up the white minority. The Congress and the administration must be willing to face this dilemma if we are seriously interested in avoiding a violent racial confrontation in South Africa. Step-by-step economic and political pressure on South Africa would represent a reasonable counterpoint to the current do-nothing attitude which prevails among top US political and economic policymakers. The United States is in no position to prescribe the solution to South Africa's racial problems. But, we are under no obligation to expand and strengthen ties with South Africa under the present circumstances.

THE ROLES OF WHITE AND BLACK STUDENTS IN SOUTH AFRICA[7]

In 1968, when student leader Steve Biko led black students out of the multi-racial National Union of South African Students, few newspapers considered the event worth reporting. The split was dismissed as a student squabble.

A few months later, when Mr. Biko and the black students formed the exclusively black South African Students'

[7] Article entitled "White Students' Union Struggles to Define Role in Divided South Africa," by Helen Zille, Johannesburg correspondent. *Chronicle of Higher Education.* 17:11. S. 25, '78. Copyright © 1978 by Editorial Projects for Education, Inc. Reprinted by permission.

Organization, the event was recorded in a few paragraphs on the inside pages.

Today, political analysts agree that the founding of the black-student organization was one of the most important political events inside South Africa during the past decade.

Mr. Biko, whose death in detention last year provoked a worldwide outcry against the South African government, had signaled the re-emergence of the black-nationalist movements that the government had cracked down upon in the early 1960's.

Under his leadership, black nationalism went a step farther than the movements that preceded it.

Black Consciousness

It formed a coherent plan of action aimed at making black nationalism an irresistible force of opposition to the South African government.

The black students' guideline was the "black consciousness" philosophy—pride, self-reliance, and a commitment to restoring a black African heritage in the white-ruled South.

This philosophy, and its rapid spread among urban blacks, shook the white political structure to its roots. Last October, the government acted, imposing a blanket ban on the black-student organization and on all the other black-consciousness organizations.

But the ruling National party, with its commitment to apartheid, was not the only white political group to find itself threatened by Black Consciousness.

White liberals, in particular, who had previously regarded themselves as "the voice of the disenfranchised majority," found themselves stripped of a role.

Black consciousness, in effect, told whites that they could not fight black battles. As a consequence, white liberals faced the classic identity crisis: They had to identify a role in South Africa and then pursue it.

That caused such deep turmoil in white opposition ranks that today—10 years after the founding of the first

black-consciousness organizations—it has still not been resolved.

One of the few anti-government groups that have worked
out new roles for themselves is the National Union of South
African Students, the white organization that Mr. Biko and
his followers rejected 10 years ago.

The union, which operates on most English-language
university campuses, has formulated its own policy of
"white consciousness," to complement, not contradict, black
consciousness.

White consciousness represents an attempt to prepare
whites for living in an Africa with a black majority.

For the liberal students who formulated the concept,
"white consciousness" grew out of the need of white students, who did not want to join the National party or emigrate, to come to terms with black consciousness and formulate a relevant role in a society polarizing between two
brands of nationalism.

The white-student organization was the first group in
South Africa to come face to face with the re-emergence of
black nationalism when black students rejected multiracial
student politics in 1968.

Racism in Reverse

At first, most members strenuously resisted the black
students' move, calling it "racism in reverse" and capitulation to the government's apartheid policy.

It took about three years for white students to recognize
that the step black students had taken was "historically necessary" and the only practical and effective step in the South
African political context in which multiracial political
groups were forbidden.

Eventually leaders of the white-student union came to
this interpretation of black consciousness:

—Blacks are rejecting multi-racial opposition to the government because all attempts in that direction have ended
with whites taking the lead.

—Black students also regard whites, no matter how liberal, as having too much at stake in the system to oppose it
effectively.

—Most important, blacks are excluded from the liberal
democratic institutions on which whites based their opposition. It was fine for whites to protest through the ballot
box, but it was absolutely useless for blacks, who had no access to democracy in "white" South Africa.

Blacks thus had to formulate an effective opposition
within a structure of racial group politics that they had
had no hand in creating.

The answer for them lay in forming one group, so that
they, like the ruling Afrikaners, could forge for themselves
a nationalist identity with its own pride and values, to bargain on an equal basis with white nationalists.

At the same time that white, liberal students were coming to accept the "historical necessity" of black consciousness, the government was preparing to crack down on the
white students themselves.

Radical Adaptations

Following the investigation by a Parliamentary commission of inquiry in 1973, the white students' union was declared an "affected organization" and forbidden from receiving funds from abroad. Eight of its leaders were banned.

Deprived of its role, its chief source of funds, and its
leaders, the National Union of South African Students was
forced to make radical adaptations.

The union took its cue from the American black-consciousness leader, Stokely Carmichael, who had told American whites: "Go home and educate your own people."

That concept became the cornerstone of the union's
concept of white consciousness. It adopted as its theme,
"Education for an African future."

Auret van Heerden, the current president of the student
union, explained that this meant getting whites to abandon
their "First-World bias"—the training and conditioning

that formed them to fit into a West European society, not an African one—and adopt instead a "Third-World bias," appropriate to their role in a developing African country.

Although he did not spell out the full implications for whites of being part of an African society, Mr. van Heerden said that they will be far-reaching.

"Whites can go a long way to making the inevitable as non-violent and acceptable as possible," he said.

To do that, he added, whites must employ their skills and education in an African context.

Restructuring Courses

"Whites, who have been educated with their First-World bias, will have to redirect their training. At the same time the education system will have to be restructured so that future white generations avoid the same mistake and acquire the necessary training for their role in an African society," he said.

On university campuses, the student union hopes to begin this process by restructuring courses so that students who want to study subjects relevant to underdeveloped countries, do not have to go overseas to do so. Among the specific proposals:

—In medicine, emphasis should be switched from highly sophisticated clinical techniques, involving expensive, modern equipment, to community medicine. Students are compiling a handbook on community medicine that they hope will become the standard textbook on the subject.

—In law, the present focus on company and tax law should be shifted to such areas as labor law.

—In engineering, the curriculum based on designing high technologies for urban communities should be abandoned in favor of one based on designing technologies appropriate to the needs of backward rural areas.

—In architecture, the curriculum should focus on rural development rather than modern urban structural design.

Leaders of the white-student union say that the program

is catching on, that students are becoming involved in projects aimed at taking their courses out of the classroom to the sectors of the community that need them most.

They are convinced the union is regaining its momentum after the crackdown in 1973, and that many of the students who previously rejected the union as representing "old-school liberal moralizing" have now begun to support the "relevant action program."

II. TOWARD MAJORITY RULE: NAMIBIA, RHODESIA, AND BOTSWANA

EDITOR'S INTRODUCTION

At present the eyes of the free world are on two countries in South Africa—Namibia and Rhodesia—each of which is in the process of political change. Each is hoping to achieve the goal of majority rule through the democratic process of election and not through violence.

Namibia, formerly Southwest Africa, although settled by Germans in the nineteenth century, is administered by South Africa. Bowing to pressure, the South African government begrudgingly held preliminary elections for a representative assembly prior to United Nations elections scheduled for July 1979, which must include all factions. In the first article in this section, Jonathan Kapstein of *Business Week* discusses the parties involved in the sham election and the opposing political parties. Next, Christopher Hitchens, writing in the *Nation,* underlines the conflict between the factions, SWAPO and the Democratic Turnhalle Alliance, even more vividly, and Richard Sklar of the Los Angeles *Times* fills in the details of the UN provisions for the projected election in July 1979. The fourth article, from the *Economist,* is optimistic about the success of majority rule in the elections.

"The Storm Before the Storm" characterizes the turmoil in Rhodesia, now called Zimbabwe–Rhodesia. In his *Esquire* article, Geoffrey Norman paints a frightening picture of guerrilla warfare plaguing the Rhodesian population. The next three articles from the New York *Times* and the *Christian Science Monitor,* present further accounts of the two groups of guerrillas, the Shona and Ndebele, their leaders, and age-old rivalries. Anthony Lewis of the New York *Times* discusses the aspirations and foreign connections of the two factions.

Terrorism and world economic sanctions forced Rhodesian Prime Minister Ian Smith to form a black-white interim government as reported in a *Time* article, but few regarded it as true progress toward majority rule. However, in a *New Republic* article written in October 1978, some merit was found in the move, which was seen as a step in the right direction and a deterrent to Communist intervention until the UN-sponsored election of April 1979. A *Time* magazine selection reports on the results of that election and the prospects for the new biracial government headed by Bishop Muzorewa, the first black prime minister of Rhodesia.

Of the three countries vying for independence, Botswana with the smallest white population is already on the road to democracy with a popular and effective black president. Still, as the next three articles from the New York *Times, To The Point,* and *Ebony* point out, the country is completely dependent for its economic life on shaky neighbors and suppliers and weakened by the existence of reverse discrimination.

A HEALTHY NAMIBIA BUT WITH PROBLEMS[1]

. . . It was a harrowing bird's-eye view of the world's newest nation, Namibia, the former South-West Africa, which came into being in early December—if you accept the legitimacy of elections held under the stern eye of South Africa, which has ruled the territory for years. The election —largely unrecognized by the rest of the world, boycotted

[1] Article entitled "A Healthy Namibia Has Some Problems," by Jonathan Kapstein, bureau chief covering Africa from Johannesburg. *Business Week.* p 24B-F. D. 25, '78. Reprinted from Business Week by special permission. © 1978 by McGraw-Hill Inc.

by three parties, and punctuated by bomb blasts and arrests —presumably turned over administration of the area to the multiracial Democratic Turnhalle Alliance (DTA). The DTA is widely regarded as Pretoria's puppet, and much of the world prefers to postpone Namibia's birth announcement until elections—promised but by no means certain—are held under UN auspices later on.

Nevertheless, few nations start out with such healthy economic prospects and such political headaches as Namibia does. For example, the Rössing uranium mine near Swakopmund, 46.5 percent owned by Britain's Rio Tinto-Zinc Corp., is heading toward full capacity and could make Namibia the world's fifth largest uranium producer. But the mine's chairman, G. A. MacMillan, will tell you cautiously: "Political uncertainties have not affected us so far, but our buyers are very concerned. We have to tell them we just don't know what will happen."

We had much the same feeling at the hands of our steely eyed pilot, Stafleu. As we skimmed the Namibian turf, one thing came clear: This new nation is not overcrowded. We saw such animals as gemsbok (oryx), kudu, springbok, rare mountain zebra—and sheep pastured at about one per 30 acres—but no people until we reached the coastal plain. This phenomenon is not surprising when you consider that water evaporates up to 18 times faster than it falls in areas of this arid hinterland.

The moribund port of Walvis Bay is something that South Africa wants to keep. Despite the nation's valid legal and historic claims, however, diplomatic sources expect that it will be handed over to Namibia as that country's port after exhaustive play as a negotiating pawn. In fact, Walvis Bay is an expensive proposition. The rich Benguela current appears to be fished out, and the catch dwindled from $115 million in export earnings last year to $70 million this year.

The Mining Industry

The export standby in Namibia for years has been metals mining, and the nation's largest mine is the Tsumeb, whose two biggest shareholders are the US firms Newmont Mining Corp. and Amax Inc. Canada's Falconbridge Copper Ltd. is a major copper miner, but in all, such base metals accounted for only 15 percent of last year's $460 million in mineral revenues.

Gem diamonds accounted for $230 million in export revenue last year, and uranium added $173 million more. One classification puts Namibia seventh in world mining importance by value of output, even though mining provides only seven percent of employment.

Uranium exports from Rössing alone probably will reach $300 million next year. That value will go even higher when General Mining's Langer Heinrich uranium mine comes into production using a unique chemical separation process. Diamond mining already pays a 61.5 percent tax bite, but Professor Wolfgang H. Thomas of the West German Institute for Science and Politics, the ranking economic expert on South-West Africa, expects that, at the very least, the bite will go still higher. "No independent black government will let them continue to make the profits they are getting," he says.

The question remains just how independent a government will emerge. The South African-sponsored election held on December 4–8 was a battle between two elements of South Africa's ruling party. The expected winner was the DTA, headed by white farmer Dirk Mudge.

The South-West African People's Organization (SWAPO), which has UN endorsement, denounced the election as a setup but conceded in advance that its effort to persuade voters to boycott the polls would fail. Internal SWAPO leaders in Windhoek assert that the army and police ensured voting. So did employers, who told black laborers to vote DTA, or rival Aktur, or be fired. Just before the election, Jason A. Angula, SWAPO's labor secretary, told me, "We are telling our people not to vote, but we are fully aware that they will have to." Angula's real fear: "We doubt that UN elections will ever take place."

A German Influence

Even white businessmen agree. Says Merrill Pike, man-aging director of the South-West Africa arm of the Johan-nesburg-based Barlow Rand conglomerate: "It would be easy for someone to stage an incident and regretfully post-pone the UN elections. It would be a mistake, too."

Axel Johannes, SWAPO's youth secretary, says, "We do not care who runs the elections, so long as it is not South Africa." Johannes looks emotionally shattered, and col-leagues attribute that to mistreatment while under arrest by South African police. He was arrested again on election eve, along with five other SWAPO leaders.

South Africa has administered the former German colony since 1916, but German influence remains strong. Even hotel waiters just off the tribal lands speak German as a second language better than they do English or Afrikaans. Of the 90,000 whites, 25,000 speak German as their first language, and many more tens of thousands can claim West German passports.

Meanwhile, the capital, Windhoek, is a garrison town. The tidy, modern, desert city is aswarm with young South African Defense Force troopers. The Kalahari Sands Hotel teems with staff officers. Suspicion flourishes. Everyone listens to other people's conversations—I nearly speared someone's ear with my fork while dining with Professor Thomas. Nevertheless, it seems that South Africa's racially based social barriers have largely come down—and with hardly a twitch.

Economic activity is at a standstill, however. The lone capital investment in manufacturing in two years is a $575,000 tire retreading plant opening this month under Barlow Rand auspices. Says Pike: "Even if SWAPO na-tionalizes the mines, they'll still need tires."

Anticipating an Upsurge

But while activity is at a standstill, there is no lack of interest. Caterpillar Tractor Co. has said it will offer off-shore financing for mining equipment purchases, recog-

nizing that South African financing may be undesirable.
Corporate lawyer John Kirkpatrick, of Windhoek, tells of
German government interest in both public and private
projects. "They don't even blink at 100 million Deutsch-
mark projects," he says. Economic planner George Low tells
of international agencies and mining groups eager to get in
on underwriting a $30 million geological survey.

His wife, Juliette Low, a commercially rated pilot with
a new Beech Aircraft Corp. franchise, hopes to break into
what has been the territory of Cessna Aircraft Co. and Piper
Aircraft Corp. Anticipating an upsurge in mining investment after independence, Beech has flown in a Super King
Air demonstrator plane. A group of five British and South
African engineering firms is conducting a self-financed via-
bility study for a new railroad.

Still, there may be several major unwanted side effects
from independence. For one thing, if a UN election does
take place, the embrace may be suffocating.

The UN Transition Assistance Group will have up to
9,000 soldiers and advisers in Namibia—one for just about
every 100 inhabitants. The UN group plans to lease 1,000
Land Rovers, 16 helicopters, and $30 million worth of other
aircraft, spending $300 million overall and undoubtedly
generating demand inflation.

Moreover, economist Low warns, "The biggest burden
to bear will be advisers." Low notes that a SWAPO-led
Namibia would not accept any from South Africa, but there
would be lots of East Europeans. And no matter who ends
up on top, concludes Low gloomily, "the business hustlers
are already gathering."

THE NAMIBIAN CONFLICT[2]

The town of Windhoek does not have much atmosphere; its tedious neatness recalls suburban white Rho-

[2] Article entitled "Namibia—Rhodesia Again?" by Christopher Hitchens,
foreign editor of the *New Statesman* (London). Nation. 227:725-6. D. 30, '78. ©
1978 by the Nation Associates, Inc. Reprinted by permission.

desia, and in Namibia, as in Rhodesia, it is often hard to "feel" the imminence of total change. But if you wander around Windhoek for a while, the signs of the Namibian crisis do begin to disclose themselves. Rather like Maigret, arriving in a sleepy and silent town, the visitor gradually begins to notice patterns and reminders of other places in other times.

For a start, the main street is called Kaiserstrasse, and down this strip run all the blue-chip businesses. Here is the office of the fabled De Beers Diamond Company and here, sharing the building, is the office of the "Democratic Turnhalle Alliance" (in translation, Drillhall Alliance; the combination of brutality and sentimentality in nomenclature is familiar), the party built up by South Africa to take over the territory next year. Walk a little farther and you can turn into Goeringstrasse (after the family of the notorious Hermann). Farther along is a row of streets named for every composer from Brahms to Wagner, and on Brahmsstrasse is the headquarters of a church organization that denounces the Turnhalle Alliance as "neocolonial and reactionary." This used to be a German colony, and in the bars and hotels the red-faced businessmen inveighing against "Kaffirs" are, as often as not, doing their inveighing in German.

The Germans withdrew, after conducting a war based on principles of extermination which they later adopted to European use. Helmut Bley, a German scholar specializing in Africa, has written a book arguing that German colonial policy was one of the roots of Nazi racism. Looking up the record, one can see why. The Herero tribe, now split between nationalists and South African collaborators, used to be the largest in Namibia. It is now a small minority, in consequence of an "extermination order" signed by General von Trotha earlier this century. History is hard to shake in this territory.

Over the hill, just out of sight of the capital itself, is a sprawling and sordid African township. It is named Katutwa, which means "those without a home." Here the nationalist force of the South-West African People's Organization (SWAPO) is exceedingly strong, and here the contract laborers from the north, who live in compounds under conditions of serfdom, plan for the day when they will get their country back. The United Nations has declared SWAPO the sole legitimate representative of the Namibian people, but its supporters are under no illusions —in this area the South African armed forces count for more than any number of General Assembly resolutions.

A Three Way Conflict

At the moment, the Namibian conflict divides three ways. On the one hand stand the black African majority, who have been fighting for a generation against illegal South African occupation of their country. Unlike their less fortunate Zimbabwean counterparts, they have managed to preserve a largely unified liberation movement which, although not without internal dissent, has contrived to keep military and political action unified.

Opposed to this movement, naturally enough, is the white oligarchy of Namibia, of which one-third is still German and the rest Afrikaner. Under pressure from SWAPO, they have modified the apartheid rules somewhat, and abolished the more irksome kinds of racial legislation (mixed marriage, for instance, is formally tolerated).

The Democratic Turnhalle Alliance rather resembles Ian Smith's Rhodesian Front, much as the December elections resemble Smith's "internal settlement." Dirk Mudge, the DTA leader, is a tough farmer with a long history as leader of a white supremacist party. He has imported some black figures into his coalition, but still relies chiefly on the South African and indigenous business interests who pay his bills (and have recently helped him buy up most of the newspapers in Windhoek). When I asked him if he was funded from South Africa he did not bother to deny it.

In the middle, between the black majority and the intransigent whites, are the Namibian white and black liberals and the five Western members of the UN Security

Council (Great Britain, France, West Germany, Canada and the United States). The UN constituent in this group is, alas, rather feeble. The Namibian National Front and the group of ex-SWAPO dissidents are at least firm on their multiracial opposition to South Africa's plans for the territory, while the Western Five, in the words of Mr. Tlhabanello, SWAPO's spokesman in Windhoek, are "apparently compromised by their close economic links with South Africa itself." The pretense that the December 8th election —boycotted by SWAPO and decidedly won by the Turnhalle Alliance—could be followed by others properly organized in 1979 does not really bear examination when you remember that the 20,000 or so South African troops will certainly be staying on. What we are seeing in Namibia is another Unilateral Declaration of Independence, only this time backed even more strongly by Pretoria because those involved are of South African, rather than British, stock and because the economic stake is more direct.

Indeed, as the establishment South African *Financial Mail* put it, Namibia's economy "is operated in colonial style with South Africa as the imperial power, and with most of the spoils of fishing and mining sucked out by foreign firms." That, really, is the heart of the matter. South Africa wishes to retain control of Namibian uranium and diamonds, and to use the country as a position from which to continue the destabilization of Angola. It can do so only by fighting a classic colonial war, especially in the heavily populated area of Ovamboland where resistance is concentrated. With the lessons of Rhodesia staring it in the face, the West should do better than maintain "evenhandedness" between the illegal occupier and the colonial subjects.

ELECTION RESULTS IN NAMIBIA[3]

The election results in Namibia (formerly South West Africa) held no surprises when they were revealed Friday, December 15, 1978, almost two weeks after voting began. Certainly the outcome is not expected to resolve any of Namibia's most controversial issues. In fact, despite a heavy voter turnout, the election itself is unlikely to change world opinion that the exercise was a charade.

A landslide victory gave the Democratic Turnhalle Alliance—South Africa's chosen political instrument—268,130 of the 326,716 votes cast in the widely criticized balloting.

The vote was held to choose a 50-man representative assembly. The DTA will hold 41 of the seats, the runner-up right-wing Aktur party will hold six, and one seat each will go to the other parties.

Over the last few months, even as voter registration continued, widespread condemnation of the entire exercise mounted. At one point, the United States, Canada, Britain, France and West Germany—the five nations working to effect a United Nations-supervised transition to independence for Namibia—jointly branded the election outcome "null and void."

The United Nations, for its part, demanded that the scheduled balloting be canceled and that a planned UN-supervised election be held later in the year. All three major opposition political parties—the South-West Africa Peoples Organization (SWAPO), the Namibia National Front and the SWAPO Democrats (a group that broke away from SWAPO)—refused to participate.

The people of Namibia, which lies just north of South Africa on the continent's west coast, look back upon a history of colonial oppression that has been severe.

[3] Article entitled "In Namibia, They've Counted Votes, But the Verdict Is Undecided," by Richard Sklar, political science professor and member of the African Studies Center, UCLA. Los Angeles *Times*. Pt. V, p 2. D. 17, '78. Copyright 1978 Los Angeles Times/Washington Post News Service. Reprinted by permission of the author.

At the turn of the twentieth century, two indigenous African peoples—the Herero and the Nama—vigorously resisted German colonization. By 1908, both had been defeated.

An immense, largely arid country twice the size of California, Namibia is home to scarcely more than one million people—approximately 90 percent black and 10 percent white. Because the country is wealthy in uranium, copper and other metals and is the richest source of gem diamonds in the world, those who control its resources will wield political power.

Germany lost this sparsely settled colony as a result of her defeat in World War I. The League of Nations then assumed jurisdiction over recolonized South-West Africa, authorizing the Republic of South Africa to govern by mandate. Ever since, Namibians have been forced to labor on farms and in mines owned by Europeans, and to live in segregated towns under conditions of virtual wage-slavery. Today, after 58 years of South African rule, Namibian economy still depends on regimented black labor.

In 1966, the UN General Assembly terminated South Africa's mandate to govern Namibia. This decision was upheld by the International Court of Justice, but rejected by the Republic of South Africa. However, South Africa has been compelled by pressure from many countries, including the United States, to grant it independence.

In 1975, the South African government convened a constitutional conference in Windhoek, Namibia's capital city, that was attended by 11 ethnic delegations—10 black and one white. Meeting in an old German gymnasium called the Turnhalle, the conference took 18 months to produce an impractical document that was soon discarded. But the participating groups did form a political association, the Democratic Turnhalle Alliance.

Its principal leader, Dirk Mudge, is a prosperous farmer of German extraction. German whites, who comprise about 30 percent of the white population, appear to identify with the emergent Namibian nation more readily than do the more numerous Afrikaner whites. Most Afrikaners (the predominant white ethnic group in South Africa) who live in Namibia now support a rightist party that does not belong to the Turnhalle Alliance.

The Role of SWAPO

In Namibia, as elsewhere, repression has been the father of revolution. The forces of revolution have been harnessed by SWAPO, led by Sam Nujoma. This movement is mainly supported by the Ovambo people of northern Namibia, who constitute 46 percent of the country's population.

SWAPO has operated from bases in neighboring Zambia since that country achieved independence 14 years ago. When Angola became independent in 1975, some 1,000 miles were added to the length of SWAPO's northern sanctuary for guerrilla incursions into Namibia. During recent years, SWAPO established a close relationship with the Soviet Union.

From the time of its inception in 1960, SWAPO has been opposed by a rival nationalist organization, the South-West Africa National Union (SWANU), supported mainly by the peoples of central and southern Namibia. Today, SWANU is the core of the Namibian National Front which includes at least eight black political groups in addition to liberal whites.

Having bowed to the inevitability of Namibian independence, the South African government wishes, above all, to prevent SWAPO from assuming power. Hence the South African administrators in Namibia planned elections that would lead to the formation of a Constituent Assembly fully aware that SWAPO would not be ready to conduct an effective campaign within the country by December. The Democratic Turnhalle Alliance—South Africa's chosen political instrument—also favored elections this month, but the United Nations refused to endorse a one-sided election that would leave SWAPO out in the cold and justify its continued recourse to violence.

Last August, UN Secretary-General Kurt Waldheim advised the Security Council that a fair election under effective UN supervision could be held by April 1979 but no earlier. SWAPO and the National Front concur in this view—shared by the five Western nations working under UN auspices to help achieve independence for Namibia. Under pressure from those countries, South Africa agreed to minimize the significance of the election held two weeks ago, claiming it might be a mere "warmup" for the real contest to come, whereupon the Western nations toned down their objections. But both SWAPO and the National Front called upon their supporters to boycott the vote.

Hardly anyone believes that South Africa held merely a practice election and has no ulterior motive. Shortly before the voters went to the polls, in fact, South Africa insisted that the decision to hold any future election would be strictly up to the newly elected representative body. And throughout the election itself, South Africa repeated its intention to retain authority in Namibia until after the supervised election, now scheduled by the UN for July.

The Pretoria government particularly resents the neutralization of its military and police power in Namibia that the United Nations would enforce prior to an election under its auspices. If the UN plan is implemented later, the South African army in Namibia would be cut to a token force of 1,500. At that point, the UN would bring in a peacekeeping force of some estimated 7,500 troops and 2,000 civilians, including police officers.

This UN plan has met opposition from both ends of the political spectrum. SWAPO worries about the undefined role of the South African administration, which is supposed to function under UN supervision during the transitional period. It also bemoans UN failure to reject South Africa's claim to Walvis Bay, Namibia's main port.

While the Security Council agrees that Walvis Bay is an integral part of Namibia, it has decided to leave that question for negotiation once Namibia has become independent. But SWAPO contends that South Africa, if it controls Walvis Bay, will have an economic stranglehold on

the new nation and negotiations will therefore be meaningless.

However, SWAPO may not win a clear majority in an
election held under UN supervision. In that event, the two
anti-SWAPO political alliances—the Namibia National
Front in alliance with the SWAPO Democrats and the
DTA—would probably bury their ideological differences
and form a coalition government. If the election has been
conducted fairly and impartially, SWAPO would have to
abide by the result.

World opinion would make it very difficult for any of
the parties or powers concerned to defy a genuine expression of the popular will. Regrettably, the recent election in
Namibia was no such thing.

NAMIBIA AND SWAPO[4]

Optimism about anything to do with southern Africa
is in short supply these days. But there may now be good
reason for hoping that the western powers' solution for
Namibia is actually going to get somewhere. This is because the two main contending parties, the South African
government and the South West African People's Organization, SWAPO, both seem to have reached the conclusion
that they can win a United Nations-sponsored election.
Both sides cannot be correct. But if both keep on believing
it, the way opens for the election which the UN wants to
hold in the second half of next year.

During the past 21 months, the five western countries
involved—America, Britain, France, Germany and Canada
—have painstakingly tried to move the territory towards
independence. Time after time, just as the last obstacle
looked about to be overcome, a new difficulty, real or manufactured, presented itself. Now there is at last a change of
mood.

[4] Article entitled "Positive Thinking," by the South African correspondent.
Economist. 269:32-3. D. 30, '78. © The Economist Newspaper Ltd. (London),
1978. Reprinted by permission.

South Africa's current confidence—and that of the Democratic Turnhalle Alliance (DTA), the group it favors in Namibia—rests on the result of the five-day election held at the start of this month. Not only was an 80 percent turnout recorded, but the DTA won overwhelmingly, capturing 41 of the 50 seats in the new constituent assembly. It was an impressive result, even allowing for the presence of South African soldiers and policemen and claims from SWAPO, which was boycotting the election, that severe pressure was exerted on people to vote, and vote DTA.

The newly elected assembly met last week in Windhoek, the territory's capital. South Africa's prime minister, Mr. P. W. Botha, and its foreign minister, Mr. Pik Botha, were there to carry out their undertaking, given to the big five, to "persuade" the assembly to take part in a UN election. As a result, South Africa sent two letters to the UN secretary-general, Mr. Waldheim, at the weekend. It is significant that there were two letters, because the contents of the one conveying the assembly's views, if applied by South Africa, would effectively wreck any prospect of co-operation with the UN: it challenges UN recognition, financing and encouragement of SWAPO as the representative organization for Namibia, raises thorny problems about political detainees, and as a precondition for an election calls for all sides involved to renounce violence.

The other letter, in contrast, promises South Africa's own co-operation in the speedy implementation of the UN's Security Council Resolution 435 on Namibia, clearing the way for the UN-supervised election. It adds that there will be no reduction in the number of South African troops in the territory until violence ceases, that questions such as the size and composition of the UN military component can be resolved with the South African-appointed administrator-general, Mr. Justice Steyn, that maintaining law and order will remain the responsibility of South Africa's police force, and that the election date should not be later than September 30th [1979]. Each of these statements. plus a reference to the monitoring of SWAPO bases in neighboring countries, could become a major obstacle. But the guess is that the South African government has taken the decision to go ahead with a UN election, and that whatever is still contentious can be negotiated.

SWAPO, in turn, has declared its own readiness to go ahead with the election: a statement issued in Lusaka by its secretary for information and publicity, Mr. Peter Katjavivi, says: "We want to make it clear that SWAPO is on record as having accepted the UN plan and stands for its full implementation." Six SWAPO leaders inside Namibia, who were arrested after bombings on the eve of the election, were released this week.

Now it remains to be seen whether Mr. Waldheim will accede to South Africa's request that he order his special representative, Mr. Ahtisaari, to return to Windhoek to complete consultations during next month. Mr. Waldheim is likely to consult the five western powers, and a number of African nations. If all agree that the remaining differences can be reconciled, then the new year can see some rapid progress.

RHODESIA: THE STORM BEFORE THE STORM[5]

On the morning of the Air Rhodesia crash, I drank tea in the lobby of Meikles Hotel and watched while a Rhodesian couple walked through the room with the poise that comes from prosperity and much travel. When they reached the front desk, the man handed over his Belgian FN, an automatic rifle, to be checked. He was a rancher come to the city to relax, and he had carried the weapon along in his car in case he was ambushed.

"Quiet ride," the man said. "A bit dusty though."

I read the front page of the *Herald,* Rhodesia's daily. A four-engine Viscount, a reliable turboprop, was down on the northwestern frontier with 56 people aboard. The

[5] Article by Geoffrey Norman, roving editor. *Esquire.* 90:98-107. N. 21, '78. Copyright © 1978 by Esquire Magazine Inc. Used by permission.

wreckage had not been sighted. It was the first crash in the history of the airline, one more calamity for the outlaw nation.

Upstairs in my room, I unpacked and went to bed. I had been traveling for two days and was still sick and cramped from a gamma globulin shot. An hour or so later there was a knock on the door.

"Yes," I said, still groggy.

"Please to stay away from window, sir. There is a bomb scare."

"Thank you," I said, feeling a little absurd.

Five minutes later, there had been no explosion but a lot of shouting. I went to the window. Cecil Square, across from my room, had been evacuated, and the street in front of the hotel was empty and barricaded. An armored Land Rover was parked across from me and a soldier in camouflage and a beret disappeared behind it. I lay back on the bed and waited.

It was a mild explosion; a single hard shock with less force than a hand grenade. It barely rattled the windows. I looked at the street again. A suitcase was propped against a parking meter, split and torn at the seams. The soldiers had blown it up as a precaution, and papers were blowing out of it and fluttering harmlessly down the street and across the park. A few sheets hung in the branches of shrubs. Two soldiers carefully picked up the paper while others opened the street to traffic. A few curious pedestrians, mostly black, stopped to marvel at what a small charge of plastic can do to a suitcase. Ever since a bomb killed eleven shoppers in Salisbury's Woolworth's last year, all abandoned parcels are blown up on the spot, even innocent suitcases.

The maid knocked again. "All clear, sir."

"Thank you."

I dressed and went downstairs. The lobby was busy. The bomb scare had been an annoyance, nothing more. I bought a special edition of the paper, ordered the local beer and read about the crash. The burned-out wreckage of the

Vicount had been located, and eight survivors were in the hospital. Just below the headline, centered on the page, was a picture of the pilot, Captain John Hood, and his bride, taken at their wedding three months earlier.

That afternoon, I walked in a park where you could see a nearly perfect mix of all the ingredients of colonialism: endless space, abundant labor, and a compulsion to build on the frontiers reminders of home that are more beautiful and stately than home itself. The vivid purple jacarandas were in bloom. Also the orange camel's foot. And dozens of dazzling, fragrant shrubs. The lawns were mowed, the hedges trimmed, and the sidewalks swept spotlessly clean. The park took up acres in the center of the city and stretched out in all directions under a high, blue, eternal African sky. I watched a black wedding party gather in the park and buy ice cream from a vendor. The bride was in white, and her maids wore dresses as bright as the planted flowers. The groom and his ushers wore conservative blue suits. When they finished their ice cream, they walked away laughing, down a long slanted walk that ran under a canopy of green.

You do not see oppression in Rhodesia. Sometimes you can feel it or glimpse it in a small episode. I saw a stern white man glare at a black security guard for fifteen seconds after the guard had been abrupt with the man's wife. It was a look that demanded, and got, a craven response. The black man lowered his eyes and shuffled his feet before the white man walked on, satisfied. Waiters and bartenders are condescended to, and they in turn are obsequious. I saw a white soldier and a black beggar collide on the sidewalk. The soldier shouted at the black man, who said something apologetic back. The soldier walked away muttering, "Bloody black thief." But the brutal, institutional segregation of South Africa, apartheid, is not in the British style, and Rhodesians want you to understand that.

"We don't hate our blacks," I was told by a young businessman killing time at a bar until the discos heated up.

"We think of them as children, you see. And we love them, really. But they are lazy and happy, and they don't understand the importance of work. If you have a job for one of them, you have to explain very clearly what you want done and tell him that he won't be paid until the job is finished. That is the only way with them. They're not responsible, you see."

In La Fontaine, the hotel restaurant, Jack Dent played the piano for white people that night, as he had done across the continent for some forty years. He is from Kenya, but he has played everywhere. He said he liked Rhodesia and that the people were all right, "but they live in the past. All the songs they ask for were popular fifteen years ago."

The Storm Gathers

The Rhodesian crisis is almost fifteen years old, but the origins of the crisis go back nearly one hundred years to Cecil Rhodes, who believed his will and his energies were larger than Africa. The British colony of Rhodesia was his most perfect creation, his vision made real.

In 1965, the end of his vision was deferred and assured at the same time when Rhodesia, a self-governing Commonwealth nation for over forty years, declared its independence. It would not submit to British demands that it transfer power to the blacks who were in a huge majority.

After UDI (Unilateral Declaration of Independence) in 1965, the British declared that Ian Smith led a "rebel government." Rhodesia was also declared illegal by a vote in the United Nations, and economic sanctions were imposed. But the Rhodesians were safe for a while in the geographic folds of southern Africa. The friendly Portuguese colonies, Mozambique and Angola, lay to the east and west; and the titan of sub-Saharan Africa, the Republic of South Africa, to the south. Trade went on. For the first few years of its existence, the outlaw state was able to find markets for its large agricultural surplus. Foreign exchange was assured, and necessary imports came in despite sanctions. But the

whites did have to fight a few guerrillas and deal with legal
domestic opposition from blacks who outnumbered them
by some twenty to one.

But the whites did not bend. They were determined to
rule Rhodesia. It was their country; they had built it. If
there was a time for compromise, the late Sixties was that
time. Then, the whites could have dealt from strength.
Now it is too late, and whites look back on those years of
possibility with regret.

Time passed and pressures increased—pressures from
within as well as from nations that white Rhodesians
looked to as natural allies. They could not believe that
Britain and the United States would abandon them. Or,
indeed, actively oppose them.

The guerrilla war widened, and South Africa sent men
to help patrol the northwest Rhodesian border against infil-
tration. The Portuguese dictatorship collapsed, and Mozambique and Angola were free and no longer friendly.
Mozambique became hostile, in fact. Rhodesia was left to
rely on itself and on South Africa. But South Africa had
its own problems and could not afford to be dragged down
by the defense of a quarter of a million Rhodesian whites
to the north against some six million blacks living inside
the country and God knows how many more—some armed
and trained—across 1,700 miles of unfriendly borders. After
1975, Rhodesia was on its own.

It had been a British problem for ten years, but then
Henry Kissinger turned his attentions to it. The Russian-
backed faction had won a civil war in Angola, and it was
time for the West to salvage what it could in southern
Africa. So Kissinger used his celebrated shuttle techniques
to put heavy pressure on Rhodesia's one remaining ally,
South Africa. In a few weeks, he had forced Ian Smith to
agree to black rule after a two-year interim government.
He flew home and left the details to the British.

A Geneva conference, sponsored by the British, ended
in a shambles. The British invited every nation that would

be affected by the settlement to send a delegation. The conference turned into a propaganda sideshow, and Smith flew home wthout an agreement. The war intensified.

The administration changed in America, and Kissinger was gone. Andrew Young appeared to be making policy for the United States, and he was a supporter of the guerrillas who were fighting Smith's forces. Smith was cornered and down to a last few maneuvers. He was never a bright nor appealing man. A veteran Royal Air Force pilot whose face was rebuilt after a crash in North Africa, Smith was long on stubbornness and short on imagination. But he was not afraid to act.

In March 1978, he formed a coalition government with three popular black leaders—two of whom had spent several years in his jails—and declared that Rhodesia would act on its own to bring about majority rule. The army was integrated. There would be an election before the end of the year, and for the first time, blacks would vote. There would be a new constitution; Rhodesia would actually become a new country, called Zimbabwe, after an ancient southern African empire. Whites would be guaranteed some seats in parliament for ten years, so the solution fell a little short of strict one man, one vote. But there would be majority rule. Blacks would vote and govern the country. Smith hoped that the British and Americans would accept his plan. They did not. But Smith and the black leaders he had brought into the government were still trying to influence opinion in England and America, still hoping for a change of policy when the plane, the Viscount, went down on Sunday, September 3, 1978.

The Tribal Reality

On Tuesday morning, it was announced that ten passengers who had survived the crash had been found and murdered by black guerrillas. A soldier had seen right away that it would happen. "When we got the message, I looked at my map. If they were only ten minutes from Kariba, then

they had to go down where the 'terrs' was operating."
White Rhodesians will not dignify their enemies by calling
them guerrillas. They are terrorists, or "terrs" for short.

The Viscount had broken in two on impact. The forward section had exploded and burned. Eighteen people
in the tail section were bruised, shaken, and terrified, but
alive.

Five of the survivors left to find help and bring water.
The remaining survivors moved away from the tail section
when it caught fire. Later, some of them went back to the
wreckage for blankets, and that was when nine black men
dressed in work denims and carrying SKS rifles arrived.
They were calm and friendly at first. They moved all the
survivors still further from the crash site; then, without
warning, one of them said, "You have taken our land," and
all nine opened fire. Three passengers ran and escaped over
a low sand ridge. The terrorists bayoneted some of the
bodies and looted the crash site. Two young girls were
killed by the terrorist fire. One was eleven years old; the
other, four.

In Salisbury, a memorial service was scheduled for later
in the week; meanwhile, life and commerce went on. In the
basement bar of Meikles, a tough-looking kid who might
have been an off-duty soldier drank beer and said, "Bloody
black butchers. If we don't hit them hard now, then it's
time we all left."

That night at a disco, black and white soldiers argued,
pushed, then pulled guns. They were separated before anybody got hurt.

Across the border, in Zambia, Joshua Nkomo claimed
that his men "brought that plane down, but it is not true
that we killed any survivors." There was an extra shock in
this news, another level of outrage and irony. Before the
Viscount crash, the important news in Rhodesia had been
of a secret meeting between Nkomo and Ian Smith. Nkomo
leads one of the two guerrilla organizations waging war
against Smith's government. By all accounts, he is more
moderate and pro-West than Robert Mugabe, who leads the

other guerrilla army fighting in Rhodesia and who has promised to execute Smith and the three black leaders who joined his government.

Nkomo and Mugabe are allies. Their organizations are united under the Patriotic Front and supported by five African nations that call themselves the Front Line States because they are on the front lines of the war against white oppression in southern Africa. African politics, however, are not that neat. Mugabe's men have fought battles with Nkomo's where their operations have overlapped. "Oh, yes," an army major says, almost delighted. "They've stepped on each other's toes quite a few times now. We've come across the bodies."

The origins of these anonymous fire fights are not ideological but tribal. There is almost too much to be known about tribalism in Africa, so the original European solution was to ignore it or suppress it or negotiate with it as a last resort. The borders drawn across Africa for the convenience of white men had nothing much to do with the essential African reality: the tribe. But those are the borders that the world recognizes to this day.

African nations are not ruled by parties, but by tribes or tribal nations. When Rhodesia becomes Zimbabwe—and the blacks rule over this European abstraction with the name of a dead empire, either the Matabele nation or the Shona nation will be ascendant.

Most of Nkomo's men are Matabele, descendants of the Zulus, Africa's most fearsome warriors. They made the deal with Cecil Rhodes that created the state of Rhodesia. They were in a position to make deals because they had suppressed every other tribe in the area including the far more numerous Shona, whose descendants are Robert Mugabe's men. Agrarian, peace-loving, and accustomed-to-being-subject people, the Shona have nevertheless put the most guerrillas in the field. Their leader, Mugabe, has also made the most warlike speeches and statements.

In their bitter dreams, white Rhodesians see a prosperous nation abandoned by those who built it and fought over by rival tribes who will take the country back in an orgy of blood. The war will be fought with modern arms, but its passions will be as old as man and, at bottom, primitive. Ideology will not count, only blood and ancestry. It will be an irreducible, savage war that the whites will watch from their new homes in exile with cold satisfaction.

The Bush War

The day after Nkomo claimed the Viscount, the Rhodesian cominister of transport and power said that "any chance of an accord was ended." He also said there was no evidence that the plane had been shot down. The official Rhodesian position was that the guerrillas did not have the ability to bring down their airplanes but they would certainly murder survivors of a crash. Nkomo insisted that the plane was a military target in an operational area. The Rhodesians, he said, had been using Viscounts to ferry troops and supplies and added, "The world expresses shock and dismay over the death of a few whites but fails to notice that thirty blacks are killed by the government every day."

Three days after the crash, a Rhodesian soldier showed me a captured launcher for a shoulder-fired, heat-seeking missile: a SAM-7. I asked if it could have brought down the Viscount. He thought the plane was out of the weapon's range; but it was certain the guerrillas had used SAM-7s before. One had been fired at a spotter plane flying over Lake Kariba. It never locked on, and after it missed the plane, the missile landed in a new luxury hotel and casino, starting a fire that burned it to the ground.

Missiles, though, are the exotica of an African war. The guerrillas carry AK-47s and SKSs, the automatic rifles that are standbys in the arsenal of revolution. They use Chinese stick grenades, RPG-7s, B-40s, antipersonnel mines, and all the usual, fundamental weapons.

Tactically, the guerrillas are less than basic. They are elemental. The theory of guerrilla war is that when the occupying forces have been sufficiently weakened, the guerrillas will mass and defeat them by conventional military operations. Until then, the peasant population will be recruited and brought into line by propaganda and terror.

The victims of the Rhodesian war have so far been the black villagers scattered across the vast African savanna. Over 4,000 this year. The guerrillas' methods are brutal and direct. Sometimes they shoot people on the spot. Sometimes they bayonet them. One man had the back of his head bashed in with the sharp side of an ax. In his dead, open eyes, you could see total, uncomprehending shock. Villagers are often herded into a hut that is set on fire. Anyone who escapes the flames is shot. Sons have been forced to kill their fathers. Two or three years ago, it was common for a villager who was suspected of cooperating with the security forces to have his ears and lips cut off with a bayonet. The message was, "Say nothing, hear nothing." Sometimes the victim's wife was forced to cook the severed flesh and eat it.

"I can understand why they would hate the whites," a Rhodesian soldier said to me. "But why would they do that to their own people?"

It is an article of faith among white Rhodesians that the enemy is a coward. "They only hit soft targets," the soldier said. "If something is defended, they leave it alone. If one man with a rifle had been at that crash site, those terrs would have passed it by."

The Whites Mourn

The memorial service for the Viscount victims was held in the Anglican Church on Cecil Square, at noon on Friday. That morning it was confirmed that the Viscount had been brought down by a missile. The church was full and overflowing. It was hot and at least one woman was overcome and had to be carried out. Relatives of the dead sat in the front pews. Air Rhodesia stewardesses came in uniform to honor their dead. Outside the church, curious blacks looked on as Peugeots, Mercedes, and Datsuns drove by on the streets that were not blocked off. Their exhausts drowned out the singing of the choir. A slender, proud

woman with thin British lips read the gospel lesson in a
voice that trembled with the strain: "For it is written, I
will destroy the wisdom of the wise, and will bring to
nothing the understanding of the prudent."

At the flagpole where the Union Jack had first flown
over Rhodesia, mourners left wreaths. There were cards
with messages attached. Most were straightforward. "In
eternal remembrance of those who perished in the crash of
the Viscount." One or two were belligerent: "For our God
is a righteous God . . ." And some were doggerel: "Oh
do not cry for Tommy in the sky."

Passing cars slowed as drivers looked at the flowers.
From time to time, one would stop and get out to add another wreath to the pile. A young woman in a Fiat left a
wreath and slowly walked around the monument reading
the cards. Finally she put her face in her hands and shud-
dered. In another minute she got back in her car and drove
off into the traffic.

The flowers stayed around the monument all weekend,
wilting slowly in the heat. I walked past them and stopped
to read the cards. In the evening I went to the movies and
saw *The Wild Geese,* which is a celebration of the white
mercenary, made with South African money and distribu-
ted by Warner. (Will Jane Fonda and other committed
movie stars boycott Warner?) The original Wild Geese
were British mercenary Mike Hoare's men in the Congo
and the credits carried Hoare as the movie's technical
adviser.

The movie is implausible at every level. Richard Burton
as the mercenary leader is not even the least of the movie's
absurdities. There is a lot of shooting and dying as Burton
and his men fight their way through what seems like a
couple of regiments of blacks whose only tactic is to fron-
tally assault machine guns and die screaming horribly.
That, and hacking captured white men to death with ma-
chetes. The movie had been cleared as suitable by the
Rhodesian censor and the audience cheered and laughed
throughout.

There are no mercenaries in Rhodesia. The foreigners who are fighting there—including Americans—belong to the Rhodesian Army and are paid regular army wages. They go through the same training that every recruit goes through, even those Americans who have served in Vietnam. Some of them found it harder than they expected and deserted.

Futile Gestures

The Salisbury Symphony played Mozart on Sunday. There was jazz at the hotel. Cricket on the fields outside of town. Golf. Tennis. Lunch and matinee theater. The things that make up ordinary life go on . . . because to do otherwise would be to admit a kind of defeat.

Even the most determined whites admit that sanctions are finally hurting the country. But desperation does not show in the streets. Shop windows are full and the merchandise looks good. There are boutiques with names like Chic. Tailors who show excellent English worsted for making men's suits. Gift shops with ivory and exotic skins. I saw a beauty salon called A Cut Above and thought of the East Sixties. Correspondents who had flown in to write about the crash and its aftermath said that it was always a pleasure to come to Salisbury where everything worked. Especially after the frustrations of other African cities. "It is just great," one said, "to be able to pick up the phone, dial a number, and get through. The *first time.*"

What they cannot get past sanctions, the Rhodesians are learning to make themselves. Wine and liquor. Appliances. Basic machinery. Small arms. You cannot find out just how badly the country is being hurt by sanctions or exactly what steps are being taken. "We don't want to expose our suppliers, you know," someone in the government told me. "After all, they're helping us out, and we don't want to bring their own governments down on them. So just don't ask about sanctions. If you see a helicopter, don't ask where the spares come from."

The Rhodesians are English and will have their sweets.

But their supply of cocoa from West Africa has been cut off. The shops still sell a locally made chocolate. "A bit chalky," one woman told me. "But under the circumstances, quite good."

To live normally has been the goal of the whites since British warships first blockaded the country. Harold Wilson was prime minister of England then and he predicted that sanctions "would bring down the rebel government in a matter of months."

In the days following the Viscount crash, a report was leaked in London. According to the report, a government-owned British oil company had secretly violated sanctions in order to supply Rhodesia. Harold Wilson, according to the report, knew about it but did nothing. Oil got through.

Wilson's conduct is typical of British policy throughout the entire Rhodesian ordeal. When Rhodesia declared its independence, the British government wrapped itself in the cloak of the United Nations and urged mandatory sanctions by all member governments. Then, Britain itself immediately violated those sanctions in secret while insisting in public that sanctions were the moral and effective course and that all civilized nations should go along.

If sanctions have had any certain effect up to now, it has been to encourage the guerrillas. And if the secret violation of sanctions by the British who came up with the idea has had any certain effect, then it has been to let the Rhodesians believe "well, they don't really mean it." So the British have encouraged one side with words and the other by deeds and made a little money on the side. Meanwhile the war has gone on.

Ian Smith made a speech on Sunday night, one week after the Viscount went down. The next morning, a woman stepped into an elevator and pushed the button for six. The elevator started for the basement. "Oh my," she said, "we're going down."

"That's what I said after Smith's speech," a man in the elevator said and they both smiled.

There wasn't much Smith could say. He promised a

limited form of martial law which merely ratified an existing situation in the area where guerrillas have been active. He also promised to reconsider the government's policy of allowing the guerrilla organizations to keep political offices in Salisbury. He hinted at some arrests of the guerrillas' active supporters.

Hard-liners wanted Smith to get tough in unspecified ways. More strikes at the guerrilla camps in Mozambique, perhaps. But the country is stretched thin as tissue and any provocative action might bring the Cubans in. The regular Rhodesian Army numbers less than 10,000 men. With reserves on duty, there are about 35,000 in uniform. That is equal to about two American divisions. Those forces are spread along some 1,700 miles of unfriendly borders.

There is more manpower available, but not the wealth to organize it. The Rhodesians have recruited blacks into the army and some units are up to 90 percent black. Just about every able-bodied white man in the country is called up for some duty each year. A young civil engineer told me he spends 170 days in uniform. Women have filled in to keep commerce going but the stress of the call-ups, sanctions, and terrorist attacks has begun to show. Whites are leaving Rhodesia for South Africa, Australia, the United States, and other countries. A few days after the crash, New Zealand announced that it would accept white Rhodesian refugees. Some Rhodesians traveled to Bolivia to inspect conditions there. They returned disappointed with the oppressive, corrupt regime. The farmland, though, had looked good.

When a Rhodesian leaves, he leaves almost everything behind. He can take $1,500 with him. More and more whites have decided that it is worth it and have, as they say in Rhodesia, "taken the gap." About 62,500 people have emigrated since the beginning of the guerrilla war. Others hang on, hoping for a settlement that will include economic aid that will compensate whites for property that is confiscated. The British have said that this is not part of their plan for economic aid to a black-ruled Rhodesia. They did, however, guarantee the pensions of Rhodesian civil servants, and the bureaucrats, who had threatened to leave the country, are soldiering on.

On Tuesday, the Union Jack flew over Rhodesia again. It was Pioneer Day, the 88th anniversary of the arrival of the first white settlers. A ceremony was held in Cecil Square. Smith spoke and bands played and a few descendants of the original pioneers were on hand to be honored. This was, everyone knew, the last such ceremony. Next year there would be no Rhodesia and the Union Jack would never fly over Zimbabwe.

Walking away from the ceremony, I was caught in a block that was cordoned and searched. A line of police Land Rovers pulled up suddenly and blocked both ends of the street. Policemen wearing blue and gray uniforms and carrying shotguns stood by while all pedestrians were searched. A tall, cheerful white officer searched all the men. There were two women officers, one white and one black. I expected them to frisk women of their own race but the black woman immediately began tapping down white women shoppers. A young blond aped and clowned through the procedure. Older, dowdier women looked past the black woman as she put her hands over them and tried to hang on to their dignity. It was over in ten minutes.

In a last try for American support for his internal solution, Smith visited the United States. There was a prelude to the trip that was typical of fifteen years of confused policy toward Rhodesia. At first the State Department was reluctant to give Smith a visa. The blacks in his coalition had been allowed to visit the country and lobby congressmen on behalf of the internal settlement. Mugabe and Nkomo had both visited the US also and Nkomo had been interviewed on a Sunday television program. Smith, however, was different. The British let it be known that if he attempted to change planes in London, he would be arrested.

Secretary of State Vance finally yielded to pressure from

a group of senators led by Hayakawa of California and allowed a visa for Smith. He made his case in his wooden fashion and Hodding Carter, the State Department spokesman, made it clear that there was no progress and not likely to be any. Smith agreed and said he was disappointed. He also said he would be willing to meet with the guerrilla leaders in a US-sponsored conference. If it happens, there is not much chance of the kind of success that Carter had with Begin and Sadat at Camp David. The issue is simple now. One side or another will rule the country. The guerrillas want their armed men to serve as the military and police and for the white-led Rhodesian Army to be disarmed and broken up. This is intolerable to whites.

Nothing about colonialism is uglier than its end. No real solution to the Rhodesian question seems possible any longer except the old African solution: blood.

OLD ENEMIES MEET AGAIN[6]

The fathers and grandfathers of the men fighting in and around Rhodesia today would understand what is going on there better than it is possible for those who live a long way off and haven't caught up on the history of that part of the world.

They would understand, for example, why a good many blacks are fighting with the Rhodesian whites and, particularly, why two prominent black leaders are cooperating with white Prime Minister Ian Smith in trying to set up a transition black-white government.

Bishop Abel Muzorewa and the Reverend Ndabaningi Sithole are on the side of Mr. Smith and the whites. And many of their supporters are enlisted and fighting in the Rhodesian security forces which last week staged probably

[6] Article entitled "Old Enemies Meet Again in Africa," by Joseph C. Harsch, columnist. *Christian Science Monitor.* p 23. O. 26, '78. Reprinted by permission from The Christian Science Monitor © 1978, The Christian Science Monitor Publishing Society. All rights reserved.

the biggest series of attacks of the war so far into neighboring Zambia. The sorties or raids lasted three days. Rhodesian reports say the attackers struck three major black nationalist bases in Zambia and another nine satellite camps.

The objects of those Rhodesian sorties into Zambia are the followers of Joshua Nkomo. They and Mr. Nkomo are members of the tribe of Mtabele [Ndebele]. The black leaders who collaborate with Mr. Smith back in his capital at Salisbury are members of the Mashona tribe. Most of the blacks who serve in Mr. Smith's armed forces are Mashonas.

Back in the middle of the last century when white men began pushing up from South Africa into what is now Rhodesia the Mtabele were the masters of the Mashonas. Rhodesia itself is divided roughly by a high ridge running north and south. The Mashona lived on the east side of the ridge, the Mtabele on the west. But the warrior Mtabeles considered and treated the pastoral and agricultural Mashonas as their slaves. They roamed into Mashonaland at will, taking the cattle for food and the young men for their armies.

The whites first settled in Mashonaland to the east of the ridge. They had a deal, arrangement, or understanding with Lobenguela, the last of the chieftains or kings of the Mtabele. He would let the whites live in Mashonaland if they would leave him alone.

But according to British historian J. V. Woolford writing in the magazine *History Today* (August and September issues), that agreement broke down over a misunderstanding. Chief Lobenguela was willing to let the white settlers live in Mashonaland, but it never occurred to him that this arrangement deprived him of the right to take what he chose from the Mashonas. When he sent his raiding, or "tax collecting," parties to the Mashona villages, the whites objected.

That is, the white settlers became the protectors of the Mashonas against the Mtabeles, thereby depriving the Mtabeles of an accustomed source of food and manpower. The result was a short, sharp war in 1893. White troops, supported by Mashonas, marched from Mashonaland into Mtabele land, captured the Mtabele capital of Bulawayo and drove Chief Lobenguela and his warriors to the Zambezi River. He died there in 1894.

When Joshua Nkomo was born in 1915 there would still have been many a Mtabele warrior around who had fought under Chief Lobenguela against the white settlers over the right to exploit the hard-working and more docile Mashonas.

Mr. Joshua Nkomo's Plans

Mr. Smith wants very much to work out an arrangement with Mr. Nkomo. He has talked with him a number of times, including a trip to Zambia in August when they met secretly there. But just as efforts of the first white settlers to come to terms with Chief Lobenguela failed, so have these efforts broken down. Mr. Smith, like his white predecessors, seems to be able to get along with the Mashonas. But Mr. Nkomo comes from a more militant background. As an Mtabele and, in effect, the successor to Chief Lobenguela, he would find it difficult to accept a role as just one of a multiple executive authority in Salisbury, no better than a Mashona.

Mr. Smith would be delighted to have Mr. Nkomo as a member of his Cabinet. But Mr. Nkomo is said to believe that if he waits long enough events will make him the head man in whatever government emerges eventually in Rhodesia. He predicted during the spring that he would be in Salisbury within ten months. Last week, after the raids on his camps in Zambia, he asserted that "we intend to get to Salisbury in the time given."

British and American diplomats are still trying to get Mr. Smith and Mr. Nkomo around the same table along with the other black leaders. But at any such a gathering Mr. Nkomo would be the lone Mtabele against the old and familiar, to him, combination of whites and Mashonas—who now outnumber his Mtabeles by four to one. That helps to explain why he prefers war to the ballot box.

A GUERRILLA LEADER SPEAKS UP[7]

Robert Mugabe, a major leader of the guerrillas who control much of the Rhodesian countryside, said today that his movement was heading toward military victory and was entitled to "the reins of government."

He said he would not negotiate with Prime Minister Ian D. Smith or the black politicians who have joined in Mr. Smith's "internal settlement" and added that the forces of Joshua Nkomo, the other key guerrilla leader and an ally of Mr. Mugabe, had done so little fighting that they "cannot reap the reward of victory."

Mr. Mugabe said that he now "expects aid from socialist countries that have not assisted us in the past." The Soviet Union has for many years supported Mr. Nkomo; Mr. Mugabe, whose forces are based in Mozambique, has received some Chinese backing and the support of other Communist countries. Both groups enjoy support from black African nations near Rhodesia as well as sanctuary for their military forces.

Seeks to Reassure Whites

Mr. Mugabe offered reassurance to Rhodesian whites that "we don't mean harm to them because they are white." He said that they would be welcome in a "nonracial" society where people would be valued by their skills.

Mr. Mugabe leads the Zimbabwe African National Union, whose offices are in this capital [Moputo], and he was interviewed there.

Declaring that any government his movement led would want foreign investment on a partnership basis, he said that he had already had a visit from representatives of an American company, Union Carbide.

In answering questions about the military situation, he seemed extremely confident, almost matter-of-fact.

[7] Article entitled "Mugabe, Sensing Victory, Declares He Ought to Rule Rhodesia Alone," by Anthony Lewis, columnist. New York *Times*. p A10. F. 7, '79. © 1979 by The New York Times Company. Reprinted by permission.

"Now that we are firmly entrenched in the rural areas," he said, "and Mr. Smith's ground forces are no longer a match for our forces there, the next targets necessarily must be the cities." He said bases now existed around the cities and that this gave his forces "a rear from which we can hit the enemy any way we like."

Bars Talks With Black Moderates

Mr. Smith has just won the approval of Rhodesia's whites for a form of majority rule in which whites would keep considerable influence. An election under the new constitution is scheduled for April, but guerrilla control in the countryside makes uncertain how many people will want to vote, or be able to vote.

If the election led to a regime headed by a black moderate, he was asked, would he negotiate with it?

"Of course not," he said. "All that will have happened really is a change of heads—a black head being substituted for a white but with the body still the same—the same armed forces, the same civil service, the same judiciary, the same economic structure. The position will be one of a head acting as megaphone."

On the question of Communist-bloc military aid, Mr. Mugabe said that his movement had had help from China and from Rumania, Yugoslavia and North Korea. Mozambique is also believed to have turned over some Soviet weapons. "We are now expecting aid from the rest of the socialist bloc," Mr. Mugabe said, using a common euphemism for the Communist countries.

Russian Help Might Be Signal

Asked when such aid had been agreed to, he answered: "We expect, I say. We are on very good talking terms, and we expect that the relationship we are trying to establish will lead to some concrete aid coming our way."

If the Russians should actually begin direct arms supplies to Mr. Mugabe's forces, they might be signaling that they see at least a good possibility that the movement will win. But they could go on supplying Mr. Nkomo, who was in Vietnam last week, seeking to strengthen his ties with the Soviet bloc.

Mr. Nkomo heads the Zimbabwe African People's Union, which operates from Zambia. He has generally been thought to have better-trained forces, but few of these have been committed to the guerrilla war. Together the two movements make up the Patriotic Front, but that is more a name than a working combination. The distance between the two groups was made clear by Mr. Mugabe when he was asked whether he would share power with Mr. Nkomo's forces if the guerrillas won the war.

"No one else has done as much fighting as we have done, has undergone as much suffering, and therefore is as entitled to the leadership of the people," he said. "That's the message, pure and simple."

"Those who have not fought cannot reap the rewards of a victory to which they have contributed nothing," he continued. "Those who are capable of fighting must join our forces in fighting. Then our victory will be joint. Then the sharing will be joint."

There has been much speculation that if Mr. Mugabe's forces neared victory over the current regime in Salisbury, Mr. Nkomo would commit his troops against them in a final struggle for power.

"I don't see anyone raising his fist against the people at that stage," Mr. Mugabe said. "In other words, I rule out the possibility of a civil war. I don't think Nkomo will go to the extent of pitting his forces against the will of the people."

As to Rhodesia's future when the war is over, Mr. Mugabe made clear that he was committed to a redistribution of wealth. But he emphasized that change would not come in a hasty or doctrinaire way, or in disregard of white people's interests.

Question of Land Crucial

Until now, half the country's land has been reserved for the three percent of the population that is white, and white-owned farms are large and productive.

The "dispossessed Africans" had to be helped, Mr. Mugabe said. In the long run, land should not be privately owned, though he said "its use can be individualized." Then he noted the African tradition of land "belonging to the community."

Mr. Mugabe said there was a large amount of good land that was not in use and that should be redistributed "before you interfere with the right of ownership of the whites who have chosen to stay. We're not going to snatch all the land overnight—of course not. It's not feasible."

He also said that any farmer whose land was taken should be compensated for development he had accomplished—"the fact that they have grown trees, established fixtures, built dams and roads." But he added that the owners should be required to compensate "the laborer who was underpaid for years."

Mr. Mugabe was asked whether he expected whites to flee Rhodesia and what he would do about it.

"Well they are already running away," he said. "We can't stem that. Many more will panic, and are doing so. But we will try to give reassurance that we don't mean harm to them because they are white. It is the system we are fighting."

He said a line had to be drawn between "the broad European community" and Mr. Smith and his colleagues. The latter were responsible for a fascist regime, he said, and "should certainly be brought to trial—a fair trial, where they can be judged and their defenses heard."

ETHNIC LOYALTIES ON THE INCREASE[8]

Rhodesian nationalist politics, both inside this country and in guerrilla movements based in neighboring countries, are becoming overtly tribal, moving toward what

[8] Article entitled "Rhodesia Finds Tribal Loyalties On the Increase," by Michael T. Kaufman, correspondent. New York *Times*. p A2. N. 24, '78. © 1978 by The New York *Times* Company. Reprinted by permission.

many analysts believe to be an unavoidable civil war between blacks.

For years the historical enmity between the country's
two major tribal groupings has been nominally subordi-
nated to the black struggle against the white domination
personified by Prime Minister Ian D. Smith.

However, since September 1977, Mr. Smith, under pressure from the West and from South Africa, has by stages
relinquished power in exchange for influence over black
leaders. A vacuum has developed; in their attempts to fill
it, black politicians, often against their stated principles,
are exploiting tribal allegiances.

The most blatant example of tribalism in the Rhodesian
situation came recently when Kayisa Ndiweni, 61 years old
and chief of the Matabele [Ndebele] tribe, resigned from
the transitional coalition he had served as co-minister of
internal affairs.

Chief Quit With Rancor

The chief, a revered figure for the one million Rhodesians who belong to the Matabele tribe, quit with evident
rancor because he decided that his people were being short-
changed in the negotiations for a constitution establishing
a majority-rule government.

What Chief Ndiweni had sought was a legal requirement that the 72 Parliament seats not reserved for whites
be divided equally between representatives of the country's
two tribes, the Matabele and the Mashona. But the Mashona outnumber the Matabele by a 6-to-1 margin, so their
resistance to the chief's position in the secret constitutional
talks was reportedly implacable.

After Chief Ndiweni resigned, he called for Joshua
Nkomo, one of the leaders of the Patriotic Front rebels who
are fighting a guerrilla war against the coalition government, to return home immediately.

At his base in Lusaka, Zambia, Mr. Nkomo, the patri-
arch of the divided nationalist movement, must have
winced at the chief's words. As the only leading member of

the Matabele among the rivals for power, Mr. Nkomo has consistently de-emphasized tribalism.

His Tribal Assurances Dismissed

Here in Rhodesia, many people believe Mr. Nkomo's statements against tribalism to be genuine, but they also believe that these will prove irrelevant. "Sure, Joshua is above tribe and wants his movement to be truly national, but when the political process begins in earnest, the leaders will take their backing wherever it comes from, and in this it will come from tribal units," said Marshall Murfree, a professor of race relations at the University of Salisbury.

What has happened, according to observers such as Mr. Murfree, is that the bulk of the people who have fled to Zambia to enlist in Mr. Nkomo's army are Matabele, while the preponderance of those who have gone to Mozambique, to join the faction of the Patriotic Front led by Robert Mugabe, are Mashona. Many other members of the Mashona are loyal to Bishop Abel Muzorewa, one of the three black leaders allied with Prime Minister Smith.

Nominally, the two armed camps led by Mr. Nkomo and Mr. Mugabe are allied, but that alliance, never more than paper thin, has been at its weakest point since the Mugabe faction learned about the secret meeting held in Lusaka two months ago between Mr. Nkomo and Mr. Smith.

The tribal considerations have also brought about a subtle shift that could isolate Mr. Nkomo, according to key analysts . . . and recent statements from British and American officials elsewhere.

Open Support From Zambia

For years, Mr. Nkomo had been openly supported by the Soviet Union and Zambia. He was less openly backed by Britain, South Africa and the United States. Even Mr. Smith and his white supporters have privately said that Mr. Nkomo could assume power most smoothly, since his movement is far more cohesive than the Mozambique-based and faction-ridden forces of Mr. Mugabe.

The Matabele tribe, although smaller, is unified and

disciplined, while the Mashona are divided into seven often-competing units.

Now, however, with Zambia's reluctant decision to open rail links with Rhodesia, the prospect of Soviet or Cuban backing of Mr. Nkomo in Zambia appears to have all but disappeared. The Russians are reportedly unhappy with Mr. Nkomo's inability to defend against Rhodesian air attacks despite having received much military equipment from the Soviet Union. Under pressure from Mozambique, the Russians may be inclined to increase support to Mr. Mugabe.

British and American diplomats have also been making increasingly complimentary statements about Mr. Mugabe, saying that later his movement will almost certainly attract to it most of the Mashona majority.

One white lawyer who has long maintained close ties to the nationalist struggle predicted, "The crunch will not come with white emigration. It will come when the black two-thirds of Smith's army mutiny and join forces with rival camps, the Matabele with Nkomo, the Mashona with Mugabe."

He continued, "I will not be so foolish to say when this will happen, but it will happen. The real politics of this country have always been tribal, and as the power of the whites ebbs, tribal clash and warfare are certain."

A STEP CLOSER TO BLACK RULE[9]

We're trying to put things right,
but the battle carries on.
What a time, what a time it's
been.

What a time, indeed. The current ballad by Rhodesian Singer Clem Tholet reflected the country's mood as Tho-

[9] Article entitled "One Step Closer to Black Rule." *Time*. 113:52. F. 12, '79. Reprinted by permission from *Time*, The Weekly Newsmagazine; Copyright Time Inc. 1979.

let's father-in-law, who happens to be Rhodesian Prime Minister Ian Smith, led his white countrymen one step closer to black majority rule. . . . [On January 30, 1979] at Smith's urging, white Rhodesians went to the polls to approve by a wide margin a new constitution under which rule is to pass from the country's 240,000 whites to its 6.4 million blacks. The transition will take place after the whites, along with 2.8 million black voters, approve a new government in another election scheduled for April 20.

Smith, who had spent two weeks touring the embattled country, professed to be delighted that 85 percent of the 67,000 voters had supported his position in the referendum. "I had faith in the Rhodesian people to face up to the realities of life," he declared. "The result is even better than expected."

In truth, however, it had been a somber campaign. Smith's audiences no longer expected the speeches about preserving the "Rhodesian way of life" that had once characterized his campaign style. As he traveled through guerrilla-hit cities, towns and farming areas, his message was unadorned: "We have no other choice. This constitution is the best deal we can hope for. I'd rate our chances of success at a little more than 50 percent."

Every audience had felt the devastating effect of the last six years of active guerrilla war. At the Sports Club in the farming area of Centenary where Smith spoke, the man who should have been the chairman, Gert Muller, had died in a rocket attack on his farm on New Year's Day. One woman told Smith that she had lost five relatives within six months. She was supporting him in this election, not out of enthusiasm so much as out of a grim and grudging acceptance of the inevitable.

Some of the sharpest criticism of Smith's policies came in the cities and towns, where terrorism is increasing. In Salisbury the Prime Minister was heckled by a group of ex-servicemen still committed to the idea of a military solution. Some critics called the referendum a "mandate for disaster," and one young veteran taunted Smith with the words of another current song: "Will someone tell us why we fight? / Why what once was wrong is now what's right?" Nobody tried to explain that, by fighting off political change for so many years, the Smith government had helped to bring Rhodesia to its present impasse.

One of Smith's immediate problems is to maintain some kind of unity in his interim government, in which he shares power with three moderate black leaders: Bishop Abel Muzorewa, the Reverend Ndabaningi Sithole and Chief Jeremiah Chirau. Many black supporters of these leaders have already expressed their displeasure over the amount of power that the whites will retain after a new government takes office following the April elections. The whites will still hold 28 of the 100 seats in Parliament and one-quarter of the Cabinet portfolios, and will retain a strong voice over the judiciary, the civil service, the police and army for at least ten years. Though they will obviously have far less power than in the days when they ran the whole show, they will not be doing too badly for a group that presently constitutes less than 4 percent of the Rhodesian population.

Even the proposed name of the country under the new constitution reflects the continuing white influence. Until now, it has been assumed that, when Rhodesia passes to black rule, the country would become "Zimbabwe." But the present plan is that it will merely become "Zimbabwe-Rhodesia," a hyphenated abomination that angers Smith's black partners in the interim government and many of their supporters. A few cynics in Salisbury have suggested renaming the country Amnesia, after all the promises that have been forgotten along the way.

Guerrilla War Persists

The gravest problem, however, is that Rhodesia is still wracked by guerrilla war, and there is no end in sight. Twelve thousand black and white Rhodesians have been killed in six years of fighting; of those, 500 died last month alone, making January the third worst month for casualties since the war began. Almost 90 percent of the country is under one form or another of martial law; most people travel by convoy, with or without military escort, and most are armed. The Patriotic Front, headed by Joshua Nkomo and Robert Mugabe, has 12,000 guerrillas inside Rhodesia and thousands more in neighboring Mozambique and Zambia. The prospect is that it will fight on as long as it thinks it has a chance of coming to power in Salisbury. Western governments and several other interested parties made overtures last year to coax Nkomo into abandoning Mugabe and joining the interim Rhodesian regime. The efforts failed. Dismissing last week's results and the April election as well, Nkomo scathingly told *Time:* "The people will have won the war by April."

Smith's hope is that the elections in Rhodesia may persuade the US, Britain and other Western governments to take the lead in ending the 13-year UN economic sanctions against his country. Once a new black government is accepted as legitimate by other nations, it might then be able to gain some military support, if only from South Africa and a few others, in fending off the guerrillas. A likelier prospect is that the guerrilla war will turn into a broader civil war as the various black factions, separated by tribal, personality and ideological divisions, battle each other for power. Small wonder, then, that more than 13,000 of Rhodesia's dwindling number of whites chose to emigrate last year, and that between now and the April elections another 10,000 are expected to leave.

AN AFRICAN TRAGEDY[10]

One would be hard-pressed to find a crisis with fewer reasons for hope than the current one in Rhodesia. When Trotsky made his oft-quoted remark about the bad luck of twentieth-century people who wish for quiet lives, he might have had Africans in mind. There is little in the

[10] An article from the *New Republic*. p 5-8. O. 28, '78. Reprinted by permission of the *New Republic,* © 1978, The New Republic, Inc.

recent history of black-ruled states on the continent to make one optimistic about the prospects for a democratic or even a humane African government of Zimbabwe. Nor is there much in the record of the white regimes, past and present, to suggest that Rhodesia's white government will find the good sense and good fortune to transfer power peacefully to the black majority. So far it has not. But neither has it found much help in the advice of those nations in the rest of the world—most notably the United States and Britain—who have taken an interest in the outcome of the current troubles. When the history of this period is written, there will be no shortage of people to blame, but among the guilty will be those in the Carter administration who have muffed every chance to avert a tragedy in Rhodesia.

There is always a chance, of course, that the events in Rhodesia will somehow lead to a happy conclusion. Western-style multi-party democracy is not even a remote possibility, but no one expected that outcome in the first place. The best one could reasonably hope for in Rhodesia is a society set up roughly along the lines of, say, Kenya—a dictatorial but essentially benevolent government that permits the exercise of fundamental individual rights, the existence of a large and healthy private economic sector, and the expression of opposing opinions. In Rhodesia the word "democracy" is nothing more than an incantation. What is more important, and what is more properly a concern of American foreign policy, is that Rhodesia have a government controlled by Africans and which respects the rights of both whites and tribal minorities.

The United States should be most concerned not so much with guaranteeing the best possible outcome as with ensuring against the worst: a bloody and protracted civil war between a black pariah state, headed by Africans but controlled by whites, and Soviet- and Cuban-backed guerrillas of varying ideological tints. The United States first should do whatever it can to prevent a bloodbath in Rhodesia. Beyond that, it should try to avoid giving any help to those elements in the conflict—most of whom apparently support Robert Mugabe, leader of the Zimbabwe African National Union (ZANU)—who would establish a Marxist totalitarian state allied with the Soviet Union.

On these objectives reasonable men will find little to disagree about. The disagreements come on how best to achieve them. One option was offered, not for the first time, by Ian Smith during his visit to Washington: that the US endorse his internal agreement and repudiate the two leaders of the Patriotic Front—Mugabe and Joshua Nkomo, head of the Zimbabwe African People's Union (ZAPU)—who have rejected it as a capitulation to Smith. The Carter administration has declined this option. The internal agreement represents a desperate holding action intended to keep whites in control of an outwardly black government. It includes, for example, a provision that prohibits "political interference" in the police, armed forces, and civil service in the ten years following approval of the new constitution. This innocuous-sounding clause in practice means that the new black government will not be able to dislodge the whites who have operated the government under Ian Smith. Those Africans who believed the internal agreement would give them control of the government were rudely disabused by Smith's firing in April of Byron Hove, the new black co-minister of justice, who had the audacity to call for reorganization of the nation's police force. Moreover, any basic change in distribution of power—any "constitutional question"—will require a three-fourths vote in a parliament whose 100 members will include a blocking force of 28 whites, including eight to be selected exclusively from Smith's Rhodesian Front party. The constitution for a supposedly majority-rule Zimbabwe will have to be initially approved in a whites-only referendum.

The First Step Toward Majority Rule

During his US visit, Smith has won a few converts in Congress, but none at all in the White House or the State Department. Still, his air of calm reasonableness has won him a lot of sympathy from Americans unfamiliar with his past, if only because he seems such a nice contrast to those African leadrs, most notably Idi Amin, they are used to hearing about on the evening news. No doubt some have swallowed his tale that, having at last complied with the American demands put forth by Henry Kissinger two years ago in Pretoria, he has been abandoned and betrayed by the new administration. Smith is an intelligent and persuasive man, and there is a real danger that he has managed to win a substantial measure of support among the American public.

There is probably no way to exaggerate the malignancy of Smith's 13-year rule of Rhodesia. His regime was created in the name of white supremacy at a time when no one could doubt the certainty of eventual black rule throughout Africa. His entire career has been built on a stubborn refusal to acknowledge the obvious: that black Rhodesians would not accept an oppressive white rule forever. Smith's professed conversion to the principle of majority rule has been much exaggerated. The last year proves once again his incomprehension of the paradoxical but crucial truth that only by giving blacks effective control of the government can he hope to retain any influence on behalf of Rhodesia's whites. This is most apparent in the internal agreement, perhaps the last hope for a peaceful transition to black rule, but a hope that Smith has done everything possible to snuff out.

Yet, Smith is becoming increasingly irrelevant with each passing day. One should keep in mind the serious flaws in the internal agreement, but one should not lose sight of its possibilities for providing the basis for a peaceful transition to black rule. It is conceivable that it may yet accomplish what the United States and Rhodesia's blacks want. Much has been made by the Carter administration of the widespread suspicion of the settlement among the African population. Certainly blacks in Rhodesia have every reason to suspect Smith's sincerity, and in fact anything with which is he connected. But there apparently is a good deal more skepticism than unequivocal hostility in the minds of most black Rhodesians. It may well be that most of them will support the new government once it has been handed over—even nominally—to black men. If Bishop Abel Muzorewa, who before he joined the interim government was easily the most popular nationalist leader, has lost some of his support from Africans who think he has been hoodwinked (or worse), he may well be able to regain it as prime minister of a black government of Zimbabwe.

Moreover, the objectionable provisions of the new constitution may not be as incontrovertible as they now appear. Once the first giant step toward majority rule has been taken, the momentum most likely will prove overwhelming and irreversible. Once black men take the reins of the government, there is no chance that whites will be able to wrest them away. The provisions against "political interference" in the police, military, and civil service, the obstacles to amendment of the constitution, all the other flaws—these will most likely be conveniently forgotten as the new black government moves to consolidate its power. For their part, whites will be able to do nothing about it, except to leave.

Persuading them not to leave, of course, is the reason behind the provisions diluting the power of the new black government—and a perfectly legitimate reason at that. Certainly the United States should not frown on carefully-drawn measures to avoid a mass white exodus from the new Zimbabwe, even if they require something less than a perfect one-man, one-vote system. Smith has a proper concern with protecting the rights of his white constituents; unfortunately, he also has an exaggerated regard for the importance of their special privileges. In any event, both whites and blacks have a vital interest in preserving the morale of Rhodesian whites, whose advanced skills are essential to the functioning of the economy. If they leave, Rhodesia's African population will suffer severely from the economic chaos that will surely follow. Some American observers—perhaps including some members of the State Department—might take satisfaction in seeing the whites get what could be seen as their just deserts. But retribution will gain the blacks nothing but hardship.

These possibilities of course are no reason for the United States to endorse the internal agreement. But they do serve to suggest that American officials such as Andrew Young should demonstrate more charity toward the interim government. The open contempt shown toward Smith and his black allies has been largely to blame for the United States's lack of influence in shaping or reshaping the agreement. A year ago there was hope that the negotiating parties—Smith, Muzorewa, Ndabaningi Sithole, James Chikerema, and Chief Jeremiah Chirau—might work out a way of turning real power over to blacks. There was no reason to doubt the sincerity of the black participants. Sithole, after all, had helped to launch the guerrilla war against Smith, before he was deposed as head of ZANU by Mugabe, and Muzorewa was an old foe of the regime, militant enough to be regarded once as the instrument of Soviet imperialism. Naturally, both had selfish reasons for entering into talks with Smith: Sithole had lost control of his guerrilla base (or most of it, anyway), and Muzorewa was the odds-on favorite to win any free election. But they also saw a negotiated settlement as the only possible way of forestalling a long and brutal civil war. Moreover, they agreed to haggle with Smith only after the leaders of the Patriotic Front refused to promise to hold free elections before independence.

The United States should have encouraged Muzorewa and Sithole in their efforts and should have kept an open mind about what the negotiations might produce. That way, the Americans could have used their leverage to shape the agreement to their liking. Instead, President Carter let Young and the Africanists in the State Department voice their ridicule of the settlement and their contempt of its authors at every gratuitous opportunity, thus squandering any influence the United States might have had. There is good reason to believe that, had the administration kept open the possibility of supporting the internal agreement, it might have been able to force substantial concessions from Smith. By choosing to remain pristinely chaste from such a role in the negotiations, it has forfeited any plausible right to pass judgment on the final product.

As for the Anglo-American plan offered as a substitute for the internal agreement, one can only say that it is long on high-mindedness and short on practical recommendations. . . . More important, it never had any realistic chance of approval by the parties concerned; the only way it could be imposed is by force—in other words, by a British military invasion. Given the refusal of the British to take such action when Smith declared independence in 1965, there has never been any reason to expect it now. That being the case, the internal agreement should have been—and should be now—accepted as a reasonable *starting point* for discussions of how to bring black rule to Rhodesia. An unfortunate and short-sighted error in the Carter administration's thinking has been its assumption that the terms of the internal agreement are set in concrete. In fact, shrewd diplomatic efforts might very well extract from Smith the changes that would give the agreement a chance of success. Certainly this course offers more realistic prospects than the utopian Anglo-American plan.

By insisting on their own version of a settlement, the United States and Britain have given the Patriotic Front far more leverage than they could have gotten on their own. It should be kept in mind that Nkomo and Mugabe originally dismissed the Anglo-American plan, and only changed their minds when their black rivals began to negotiate with Smith—seeing it as a convenient device for discrediting any internal agreement. Nkomo and Mugabe had their own reasons for not negotiating with Smith, which boil down to a pronounced lack of enthusiasm for free elections—Nkomo, because he knows he lacks the personal popularity and the tribal base to win. He is a Kalanga, once a

Shona-speaking tribe but now mostly absorbed into the
Ndebele; the two constitute only about a fifth of the African population. Mugabe isn't keen on elections because he
is an avowed Marxist-Leninist who has ruled his own organization with what one expert calls an "appalling record of
violence and repression." What the two want, in essence,
is for Smith to turn the government over to them before
any elections are held, so that they can guarantee the outcome.

The Strategic Outlook

On the military aspects of the current conflict and the
necessary ingredients for peace, there have been numerous
misconceptions. A guerrilla victory in Rhodesia is not imminent; nor is it a certainty even over the long haul. So far,
the Patriotic Front has had meager successes against the
highly mobile and remarkably efficient Rhodesian Army,
which is four-fifths black. The Russians and Cubans have
given some help to the guerrillas, but they apparently are
not willing to provide the all-out support required for a
quick victory. It is simply not the case that the United
States must accommodate the Patriotic Front because it is
sure to win anyway. At this point, the outcome of the military conflict remains highly uncertain.

The Russians and the Cubans remain the wild card in
the Rhodesian power struggle. There are strategic interests
at stake which ultimately may prove more decisive than
the internal politics of Rhodesia. A principal aim of the
Carter administration's policy has been to prevent a full-
scale civil war which would give the Soviets the chance to
tip the balance with Cuban troops, as they did in Angola.
By strengthening the hand of the Patriotic Front, however,
the United States has increased the chances for the sort of
conflagration that would serve Soviet interests. The Soviets
would like a satellite government in Zimbabwe because it
would give them access to its rich mineral resources and
greatly enhance their influence throughout Africa. More
important to their designs, though, is South Africa. A civil

war in Rhodesia, let alone a Marxist government, would demoralize South Africa's whites; it would also leave them without a single friendly neighbor and expose them to intensified guerrilla attacks. If the conflict in Rhodesia escalates, South Africa may have no choice but to intervene against the Russian/Cuban side to protect itself. That would leave the United States with a highly unpleasant choice between standing by and watching Soviet satellization of southern Africa, and intervening on the side of the racist South African government with arms and perhaps even soldiers.

Nor is it true that bringing the two guerrilla organizations into a settlement will assure peace in Rhodesia. Given the deep and frequently bitter divisions between the rival leaders and their supporters, civil war would remain a strong possibility even if the Anglo-American plan were implemented, with the losers in the elections taking up arms against the winner. There is also the very real prospect of civil war between the two factions of the Patriotic Front, which are divided along tribal lines and which have already clashed any number of times. What the Anglo-American plan offers is not a simple choice between the current war and a guaranteed peace.

By now it should be clear that the Anglo-American plan has only the most remote chance of being accepted and implemented. The realistic course of action for the United States is to take the internal agreement as a starting point and show Smith its willingness to seriously consider endorsing it if certain important revisions are made. The internal agreement is not a good plan, but it is not a hopeless one. If concessions can be won to make it what it is supposed to be—a transfer of power from whites to blacks—then it may be able to secure the support of Rhodesia's blacks and the neutrality of the front-line states in Africa that so far have backed the Patriotic Front. Confronted with a genuinely black government in Zimbabwe, its own African citizens and its black neighbors may see no compelling reason to prefer the Patriotic Front any longer. Only that way will any black government have a chance of surviving all the potential tumult in Rhodesia, and of averting the mass carnage of a full-scale civil war and the grim repression of a totalitarian dictatorship. These last goals should be uppermost in the minds of the United States and Britain, and they should seize any opportunity to further them. Right now, the only opportunity lies with those parties in Rhodesia who have chosen a peaceful road to black rule over a violent one.

NOW, ZIMBABWE-RHODESIA[11]

I do not want this new country to be a sham, a fraud, a hollow shell with the mere trappings of independence—a brand new flag, sleek limousines, black faces in Parliament and the UN. I do not want Zimbabwe ever to become another banana republic.

So declared Bishop Abel Muzorewa, one of the four members of Rhodesia's biracial "interim" government, in a stem-winding speech to a group of black and white voters at the close of the country's historic ten-week election campaign. His vision of his violence-racked land's future was important, for he is soon to become the first black Prime Minister of Rhodesia, or Zimbabwe-Rhodesia as it is henceforth to be known. Last week voting for the first time on the basis of a universal balloting, the country's black population elected 72 members of a new parliament; the other 28 seats had been filled by white balloting a week earlier. The elections were strongly promoted by Muzorewa, outgoing Prime Minister Ian Smith, the Reverend Ndabaningi Sithole and their other colleagues in the "interim regime." Their hope is that their version of majority-rule government will win international recognition and bring an end to the UN economic boycott imposed on Rhodesia after Smith made his Unilateral Declaration of Independence from Britain 13½ years ago.

[11] An article from *Time*. 113:36-9. Ap. 30, '79. Reprinted by permission from *Time*, The Weekly Newsmagazine; Copyright Time Inc. 1979.

The elections were strongly opposed by the black guerrillas of the Patriotic Front, who have fought against the Smith regime from sanctuaries in Mozambique and Zambia for more than six years and were determined to upset the voting. Nonetheless, the Salisbury government claimed at week's end that about 60 percent of the 2.8 million eligible blacks had chosen to vote, and hailed this as an endorsement of the so-called internal settlement.

Although the final tally was not due to be announced until this week, it seemed almost certain that the largest number of seats would be won by the biggest of the black parties, the United African National Council (UANC). As the party's chief, Muzorewa, 54, who is both an ordained Methodist clergyman and a leader of the majority Shona tribe, would be called on to form the new government.

Whether black majority rule will really have been achieved when that government takes office in June is a subject of heated debate. Muzorewa and Smith say yes. The black nationalists outside Rhodesia say no, and fight on. Certainly there is no doubt that under the new constitution the 212,000 whites will still have a special status. Though they account for only 4 percent of the population, they are guaranteed 28 of the 100 seats in the parliament, and for ten years will have control, through a complex veto provision, over such vital areas as the judiciary, the civil service and the security forces. The whites are also guaranteed at least five of the new cabinet posts, presumably including one for Ian Smith.

Conceivably, as Smith himself implied last week, some of the special protective clauses for whites may be dropped from the constitution after the new government takes hold. "Whether we like it or not," he told *Time* Johannesburg Bureau Chief William McWhirter,

minority governments are unacceptable to the rest of the world. I had always hoped we could avoid black majority rule in my lifetime. But you have to change your tactics in this game, and we came to the conclusion that if we didn't change, we couldn't survive.

His successor, Muzorewa, is a slight (5 ft.), mild-man-
nered man who is particularly popular with urban audiences. His garb can be flamboyant, at one campaign appear-
ance he wore black trousers with yellow, red and green
stripes and a coat of many colors. He is notoriously thin-
skinned in dealing with rivals. Says a former colleague:
"Muzorewa is at his best as a preacher and at his worst as a
Cardinal." Though a reluctant politician at first, he waged
a strenuous campaign, traveling around the country for an
average of five or six appearances a day. At these he would
hold forth on his ideas about building a new country
"without friction" and pass out buttons bearing the UANC
slogan WE'RE THE WINNERS.

The voting went surprisingly smoothly. To counter the
threat by the Patriotic Front to disrupt the proceedings, the
government mobilized 90,000 troops and in many cases
transported voters to the polls. Muzorewa and other cam-
paigners were accompanied by armed militiamen. Mobile
voting units were trucked, under army escort, to about
1,500 of the country's 2,000 designated polling places.

The most important issue by far was peace. The candi-
dates concentrated on the ways in which they would end the
war, bring majority rule, open new schools and clinics, and
help blacks find jobs. Muzorewa's top vote puller was a
promise of free education for every child up to the seventh
grade. Another important issue: ways to help enable blacks
to buy their own farms. The average white in Rhodesia has
75 acres, while the average black has five. As Joshua
Nkomo, one of the Patriotic Front leaders, has said, "This
is the source of all our bitterness."

Particularly in rural areas, people sometimes seemed
confused about what the election was all about. At the
polling place in one town near the Mozambique border, a
woman said: "We were told by the police that we had to
come here, and we didn't argue. We just came." Others had
a better understanding. Said Jonah Dangaremdzizi, a villager: "This is the first time we have voted, so it is natural
that some of us are nervous. Peace is really what we want."

Solomon Mauura, a chief's messenger, was more explicit about his expectations: "We have had the war because we had no African leader. Now that we are voting one in, we hope he will bring an end to the fighting."

Few outside observers give Muzorewa much chance of succeeding, however. Says a ranking Western diplomat in neighboring Zambia: "This next period is going to be violent, and the dimension of the violence is far greater than anybody has imagined." Joshua Nkomo's Zambia-based branch of the Patriotic Front currently has about 25,000 men under arms, including some 2,000 inside Rhodesia. The Mozambique-based branch, under Robert Mugabe, also has about 25,000 guerrillas, with 8,600 of them inside Rhodesia. The Rhodesian security forces' incursions into Mozambique and Zambia, where Nkomo's headquarters in Lusaka was raided two weeks ago, have made the guerrillas angrier than ever.

Zambia is particularly vulnerable to Rhodesian attack and President Kenneth Kaunda has approached the US about buying defensive weapons, but was turned down. He is already getting missiles from the Soviet Union and artillery and air force training from China, and the chances are he will soon be asking them for more. With both sides in the Rhodesian dispute so jittery, the prospect is for an acceleration in the fighting.

For the Carter administration, the election has posed a delicate question about US policy in Africa. Until now, the administration, as well as the British government of Prime Minister James Callaghan, has pretty much accepted the black African view that a new Rhodesian majority-rule government could effectively end the war only if it included representatives of the Patriotic Front. Accordingly, the US and Britain have long advocated an all-parties conference on Rhodesia leading to a Salisbury government composed of both "internal" and "external" Rhodesian black leaders.

But the Anglo-American initiative has fallen apart. At present, nobody is pressing for an all-parties conference. Muzorewa and his colleagues do not want one because they

expect to be running the show in Salisbury. The guerrillas
do not want one because they expect to win everything
through force. The result, as Mugabe once put it: "The
real conference will be in the bush."

The US Senate passed a resolution last year that if the
Rhodesian election was judged to be "free and fair" and
open to all factions and if the new government seemed
ready to talk to the Patriotic Front, then the administration
should recognize it and try to lift the economic sanctions.
President Carter has said that by the time the new government is installed, he will make a decision on recognition
that will be based on "a moral dimension and not legislative politics."

In the meantime, the Callaghan government has fallen.
... Margaret Thatcher and her Conservatives ... [won] Britain's May 3 election, ... [and] will undoubtedly alter British
policy in the direction of support for Muzorewa and Smith.
Some Tory advisers have pointed out that Britain's relations with its African allies, notably Nigeria, could be
jeopardized by an abrupt change in policy on Rhodesia.
The Commonwealth Prime Ministers are scheduled to
meet in Zambia later this year. If the African members
should still be angry with Mrs. Thatcher at that time, they
could embarrass her greatly by deciding upon some kind
of retaliation, such as an attempt to expel Britain from the
British Commonwealth.

The Carter administration has tried hard in the past
two years to forge new ties with black Africa. What it fears
now is a steady enlargement of the Rhodesian guerrilla
war, with the US caught in the position of reluctantly supporting the Muzorewa government and with the Soviet
Union and Cuba looming ever larger in African eyes as
the liberators of the oppressed Rhodesian majority. Some
observers are dreaming of unexpected solutions, such as an
alliance between Mugabe, himself a Shona, and Muzorewa.
But this is probably wishful thinking. As one official of
Nkomo's organization says, "This war will not stop. It is
not possible at this stage to talk about a reconciliation be-

tween those who are inside the country and those who are outside." Despite last week's balloting, or indeed as a result of it, the sad outlook is for more months of blood-letting.

BOTSWANA: A DEPENDENT DEMOCRACY[12]

One day last week, a Rhodesia DC-3 flew over three refugee camps in northeastern Botswana. With pinpoint accuracy, the plane dropped loads of leaflets from 600 feet into the camps. And in all three cases, the slow-flying DC-3, a World War II relic, got away before the surprised Botswana defense force could set up effective ground fire.

The leaflets urged the refugees to return to Rhodesia where, they were assured, majority rule is already in effect, and not to go on to Zambia, where only death awaited them. But the real meaning of the leaflet drop was more ominous—that the camps were defenseless, in case the Rhodesians decide to bomb them as they have already bombed black nationalist bases in Zambia.

Western and United Nations officials here say there is no reason for Rhodesia to attack the Botswana camps. Rhodesian blacks living in them have been disarmed; those who want to join organized Rhodesian nationalist forces are sent on to Zambia as soon as possible, and offensive operations from Botswana against Rhodesia are not permitted.

Still, the Rhodesians want to shut off the refugee flow and recruitment by the nationalist forces of Joshua Nkomo in Zambia. And the leaflet incident shows how carefully Botswana's President, Sir Seretse Khama, and his respected External Affairs Minister, Archie Mogwe, have to play their roles as leaders of one of the "frontline" states surrounding Rhodesia.

[12] Article entitled "Dependent Democracy," by Tom Wicker, columnist. New York *Times*. p A23. N. 28, '78. © 1978 by the New York Times Company. Reprinted by permission.

On the one hand, they have to support the black nationalist fight for control of Rhodesia; on the other, in a weak nation with less than a million people and a tiny defense force only 18 months old, they are all but defenseless against Rhodesian armed might—which commands much respect in these parts.

Botswana, moreover, produces almost nothing but diamonds (a new mine now being opened will be one of the world's richest) and beef. The latter has to be exported and almost everything the nation uses—including all its food except beef—has to be imported along a single rail line that runs just inside the country's eastern border from South Africa to Rhodesia.

The Rhodesian railways actually operate this line through Botswana. Thus it is vulnerable to a Rhodesian political decision to cut off Botswana's vital supplies, or—in the likely event of black nationalist civil war in Rhodesia after white rule ends—to military disruption from across the border.

Nor is Rhodesia the only threat. Most of Botswana's imports, particularly its food supplies, come up the rail line from South Africa. And the South Africans are fond of warning that "the first countries that will be hit by sanctions are Botswana and Lesotho," another independent nation, which is entirely surrounded by South Africa.

If, that is, worldwide economic sanctions should be imposed on South Africa, either for its internal racial policies or for its attitude on independence for Namibia (another territory bordering Botswana), South Africa might immediately shut down its exports to Botswana and Lesotho. That step could be taken either as return pressure against those imposing sanctions or as a necessary measure to protect South Africa's own consumers.

The Threat to Cut Supplies to Botswana

The threat to cut off supplies to Botswana in the event of sanctions may be only a South African defense tactic. But it suggests that the issue of sanctions is not so simple as it may appear to some nations. And since Botswana also opens its borders to South African refugees (of whom there are not so many now as in the months following the 1976 Soweto riots), it is another reason why Botswana's political position is precarious.

The vulnerability produced by its excessive reliance on imports is also a good reason why Sir Seretse and his economic advisers—including the American governor of the Botswana central bank, Brenton C. Leavitt of Wyoming—are trying to develop arable agriculture in Botswana.

That won't be easy. The Botswana traditionally raise cattle, an occupation that scorns farming. Many others cross into South Africa as migrant laborers—another link of dependency, since there would be no jobs for them in Botswana if South Africa sent them home.

Sir Seretse and his advisers have set a goal, moreover, of educating every Botswana up to at least sixth-grade level. That, too, tends to work against the development of agriculture, since education usually raises people's expectations rather than sending them back to the soil. And Botswana already has a worrisome influx of rural youth into the few towns and cities along the rail line to the outside world.

Gabarone itself was little more than a village at independence 12 years ago. Now it is a remarkably pleasant small city with a university, the government center and an easy-going interracial atmosphere. Whether that can be maintained, along with Botswana's flourishing democracy, depends primarily on its troubled neighbors.

BOTSWANA AND ANTI-WHITEISM[13]

Perhaps more than any other country in southern Africa, Botswana is a captive of its geographical situation. Hemmed in by South Africa, Rhodesia, Zambia and South West Africa, this large but sparsely populated country is

[13] Article entitled 'Rise of Anti-Whiteism' Threatens Multiracial Haven. *To the Point.* 7:37-8. O. 13, '78. © 1978 African International Publishing Company (Pty) Ltd., South Africa. Reprinted by permission.

not only economically dependent on its neighbors, but is finding itself increasingly involved in their conflicts.

During the past few years thousands of refugees from Angola, Rhodesia, South West Africa and South Africa have streamed into Botswana, putting a strain on its economy and creating new tensions with its neighbors. During the past two years clashes with the Rhodesian security forces have dramatically increased. Although the government has denied that there are terrorist bases in Botswana, it is evident that terrorists operating from Zambia have used Botswana as a point of entry into—and exit from—Rhodesia. Last year the Botswana government issued a statement documenting 41 incidents involving Rhodesian soldiers. It claimed that in 1976 alone there were five killings, seven kidnappings and two cases of arson.

Until recently Botswana was one of the few countries in the world without an army, but with the increasing tensions and conflicts of the sub-continent, it was last year forced to create a defense force. This has put further strain on the country's limited economic resources. Although it is still a relatively small force—between 1,200 and 1,500 men—the army has already cost Botswana $20 million, and according to a UN survey published last year, escalating conflict in the region is expected to cost the country at least another $60 million.

Botswana's modern history has been dominated by the attempts of its people to avoid the incorporation of their country into the more powerful neighboring states. The country—then known as Bechuanaland—became a British protectorate in 1895, after the Tswana chiefs had appealed to the British government to prevent the area being put under the control of the British South Africa Company. Although the Tswanas successfully resisted political incorporation, they could not prevent the economic integration of their country with South Africa.

When Botswana became independent in 1966, its leader, Sir Seretse Khama, was forced to recognize the constraints of the country's position within the sub-continent. While identifying itself with the aspirations of black Africa, Botswana has attempted to maintain a balance between the demands of the militant black African states and the white-ruled states to which it is geographically and economically bound.

Speaking after his installation as president, Khama made it clear that moderation would be the keynote to his country's policies and Botswana would do nothing to upset the delicate balance in southern Africa. His aim, he said, was the creation of an atmosphere in which "a white man can live side by side with a black man without racial friction." Under Khama's guidance, Botswana became one of Africa's few examples of a liberal democracy. The first elections were held shortly before independence in 1965. Khama's party, the Botswana Democratic Party (BDP), won 80 percent of the votes and 28 of the 31 seats. Since then Khama and the BDP have dominated Botswana politics, winning 27 of the 32 seats during the country's last elections in 1974.

But the situation in Botswana is rapidly changing. Even multiracialism, one of the mainstays of Khama's policy, is being challenged by the tensions generated by racial confrontation in the sub-continent. Addressing the annual conference of the BDP in 1975, Khama was forced to concede the "rise of anti-whiteism" in the country. Some civil servants had been attacked by opposition MPs "not because they are incompetent or unpatriotic but because they are white."

Deteriorating Race Relations

Since then race relations in Botswana have steadily deteriorated under the dual impact of military reprisals from Rhodesia and the political influence of the radical refugees and exiles from neighboring states. The extent of this deterioration was vividly illustrated in March this year when Botswana troops murdered three whites—two South Africans and a Briton—in the Tuli block in northern Botswana. Whites, particularly those in Francistown near the Rhodesian border, are finding it increasingly difficult to live in the country.

At the same time the country's liberal-democratic principles are being challenged. Developments in neighboring states and the presence in Botswana of foreign revolutionaries have clearly taken their toll. Tension has steadily mounted between the ruling BDP and the major opposition party, the Botswana National Front (BNF), a Marxist-Leninist party that favors closer links with socialist countries. In June this year the government withdrew the passports of 17 BNF members who were planning to attend a youth conference in Cuba. The government claimed that the youth conference was merely a front to allow young Tswanas to receive military training so that they could subvert the State.

In September students from the University College of Botswana clashed with the Gaborone police after a student demonstration against the arrest of an army officer implicated in the murder of the three whites in the Tuli block. The government blamed the student unrest on foreign influences and deported two South African academics who were teaching at the university.

Although the BNF won only two seats in the last elections, there are indications that it is steadily gaining ground. Escalating conflict, the involvement of Russians and Cubans in southern Africa and the possible installation of radical governments in neighboring states, would all favor its growth. Since its formation in the late Sixties, the BNF has advocated the introduction of socialist policies to Botswana and the immediate rupture of relations with South Africa. The ruling BDP has taken a more moderate, gradualist approach. It has advocated the gradual disengagement of the Botswana economy from South Africa. Until recently this policy has enjoyed some success particularly as Botswana has managed to attain a degree of economic independence through its rich diamond and copper-nickel mines. But the threat of conflict in southern Africa and the strain on the economy of the consequent military expenditure may change all this, forcing Botswana to abandon the neutral position it has held since 1966.

SIR SERETSE KHAMA OF BOTSWANA[14]

He suffers from diabetes and high blood pressure. The irregular beat of his heart is being steadied by a pacemaker implanted in his chest. And even indoors he wears dark glasses to protect his sensitive eyes from glare. Yet, despite such debilitating infirmities, Botswana's 57-year-old President Sir Seretse Khama—the former prince who three decades ago gave up his tribal throne in order to marry the woman he loved—has emerged as one of the staunchest, most unblinking foes of the *apartheid* policies of neighboring Rhodesia (Zimbabwe), South Africa and Namibia. While standing in the eye of a brewing hurricane which, many observers predict, will put an end to white arrogance and privilege in southern Africa, Sir Seretse vows, "We will continue to condemn *apartheid* and those who believe in it and try to perpetuate it in our region."

Putting his money where his mouth is, President Khama has given asylum to some 13,000 political refugees who have poured into his Texas-size country (pop. 719,000) to avoid arrest under South Africa's and Rhodesia's anti-black detention-without-trial laws. Although their presence poses an additional strain on Botswana's already fragile economy, "H.E." (as His Excellency is popularly known) regards his open-door policy toward blacks who flee from racist terror "an obligation we cannot shirk regardless of the consequences."

The most serious consequence so far has been the frequent incursion of refugee-pursuing Rhodesian troops into Botswana, accompanied by the burning of Botswana villages and the killing and kidnapping of Botswana citizens.

[14] Article by Hans J. Massaquoi, writer. *Ebony*. 34:124-8. D. '78. Reprinted by permission of *Ebony* Magazine, copyright 1978 by the Johnson Publishing Company, Inc.

To put a stop to this, Sir Seretse last year reluctantly scut-
tled his firmly established policy of running his country
without an army and ordered the formation of the Botswana
Defense Force, a fighting unit of undisclosed strength
trained in guerrilla tactics and conventional warfare. "We
have been forced by circumstances to abandon our long-
held belief that our weakness is our strength and our moderation and peaceful nature the impregnable safeguard for
our survival in this part of the world," explains H.E. with
characteristic eloquence.

Early this year, the president attended the funeral of 15
Defense Force soldiers who had been killed in ambush on
Botswana soil by Rhodesian troops. Undaunted, the President pledged his continued support of the liberation struggle, and vowed not to allow Botswana to be intimidated.
"We have not won our freedom and independence only to
give them away at the sound of a gunshot," he reminds both
friends and foes.

Coming from a virtually defenseless man who each night
sleeps almost within a grenade's throw from the border of
the greatest military power on the African continent (the
South African border is only 10 miles distant from Botswana's capital, Gaborone), such words of defiance smack
either of suicidal recklessness or of a confidence derived
from the conviction that the forces of destiny are on his
side. Anyone who knows President Khama is convinced
that the latter applies. For although some of his supporters
wish at times that H.E. were a bit more reticent about his
anti-*apartheid* sentiments, no one has ever accused him of
shooting from the hip.

Botswana's Dependence on South Africa

Even if viewed in the most optimistic light, Botswana's
strategic position is everything but enviable. Totally land-
locked and totally dependent on South Africa for the export of its copper, nickel and cattle (its economy's main
staples), it is also dependent on South Africa for the im-

portation of most of its food and manufactured goods. Add to this the fact that Botswana has no airport capable of handling large transcontinental jets and therefore can be reached from the "outside world" only via Johannesburg or Lusaka, Zambia, and its precarious position in the sharpening crisis in southern Africa comes into focus.

Such inauspicious circumstances notwithstanding, Sir Seretse has established an impressive record since his first election as president following independence from Britain 12 years ago. Not only has he built a politically independent and stable nation, a free, 800-student university and a capital city, all literally from scratch, he also did what many believed to be impossible—balance Botswana's budget and remove its name from the World Bank's list of the 25 poorest nations on earth. He accomplished this by running a tight, yet clean ship without finding it necessary to resort to dictatorial methods like so many of his African colleagues. US Ambassador Donald R. Norland gives H.E. high marks for building a nation characterized by democratic rule, non-racialism ("They don't count blacks and whites here; they only count people."), a completely independent judiciary, respect for human rights (and consequently an absence of political prisoners), virtually no corruption in high places, concern about equity in economic development, a military that is completely subordinate to civilian rule, and free enterprise and private entrepreneurship as the preferred ways of doing business.

Speaking of business, the brightest picture yet in Botswana's economy is that of . . . a veritable windfall in the form of diamonds, which are beginning to outstrip cattle and copper as the nation's best friend. First discovered in 1971, Botswana diamonds (both industrial and gem quality) are mined at a rate of five million carats per year—more than $100 million worth. President Khama concedes diamonds' "very significant contribution" to his country's development but cautions against too much reliance on this source of revenue lest the mines become depleted **or** the diamond market drops off. Instead, he is pushing for a diversified economy based on agriculture and other yet-to-be-developed industries.

President Khama Looks Forward

Standing in the eyes of hurricanes is no novel experience for President Khama. Thirty years ago almost to the day, he was the center of a raging international dispute when, as Prince Seretse, hereditary heir to the tribal throne of some 200,000 Bamangwatos in the British protectorate of Bech-uanaland (Botswana's pre-independence name), he married a White Englishwoman. Not since Britain's King Edward VIII gave up his crown in 1936 to marry American divorcée Wallis Simpson had a romance stirred up as much commotion as the marriage of Prince Seretse, then an Oxford University law student, to Ruth Williams, a London insurance firm clerk. Bamangwato elders, led by Seretse's regent uncle, threatened that the entire tribe would scatter rather than accept a white queen. Meanwhile, in London, the British Colonial Office, pressured by South African Prime Minister and apartheid architect Daniel Malan, banished the prince from his homeland. While forced to live in dismal exile in London he and his bride became targets of harassment and ridicule.

Not all Britons approved of their government's treatment of the African prince. Ousted wartime Prime Minister Winston Churchill, for one, called Seretse's forced exile "a disreputable transaction." Nevertheless, it was not until six years later, and only after he had renounced all hereditary rights to his throne, that Seretse was allowed to return to the land of his birth. Arriving as plain Mr. and Mrs. Khama, Seretse and Ruth received a tumultuous welcome from thousands of Bamangwatos, which left no doubt that, so far as the people were concerned, they were still their king and queen.

In the decade that followed, Seretse Khama, capitalizing on his popularity and legal training, forged the Bechuana-land (now Botswana) Democratic Party which at independence swept him into office as the new nation's first president. Now serving his third five-year term, and admitting that he intends to run for yet another term, President Khama looks with optimism to southern Africa's future despite dire prediction of a bloodbath of unprecedented magnitude as a result of white recalcitrance. "White people in Rhodesia are beginning to realize that majority rule is a tide that cannot be stopped," he says. "And in South Africa, too, a growing number of whites know deep down in their hearts that it is coming, that it is inevitable."

III. THE KEY:
SOUTH AFRICA'S ECONOMY

EDITOR'S INTRODUCTION

The combination of enormous mineral wealth and cheap labor might be thought to provide the ideal circumstances for prosperity and social stability, not only in the Republic of South Africa itself but in the entire surrounding region. Indeed, it is hard to imagine a white-ruled Rhodesia or Namibia without the buttress of neighboring South Africa's strongly developed industrial economy. However, as the first two articles in this section point out, the ideal circumstances do not seem (or perhaps no longer seem) to exist. In the first article, reprinted from the New York *Times,* Tom Wicker warns that a weakening economy and loss of foreign capital can have political consequences in South Africa. In the second article, an interview in *To The Point,* Jan Hupkes, professor of economics at University of South Africa, is more optimistic about South Africa's economy in spite of the present slump due to world economic conditions.

From the beginning, South Africa's natural wealth has attracted foreign investment. The growth of the country's economy has, in fact, depended to a large extent on capital from abroad, principally from Great Britain and the United States. This factor of foreign investment is important and controversial: in the United States some people believe that it is wrong for American corporations to support by their investments a regime founded on racial injustice; others, on the contrary, see the role of the American corporation as that of catalyst for social change within South Africa. One who holds the latter view is Herman Nickel, who writes in

Fortune that industrialization is a process that both dis-
courages apartheid and benefits the South African economy
as a whole, thereby helping the black majority. Both Nickel
and Roger Williams, author of an article from the *Saturday
Review,* are against American companies giving up their
operations and investments in the area. Williams nevertheless found, when he interviewed black workers in South
Africa, that they felt their cause would better be advanced
"if US corporations stopped investing in the country's
economy."

Another authoritative voice from South Africa itself
is that of Harry Oppenheimer, chairman of South Africa's
$7 billion Anglo American Corporation group, whose ad-
dress to the International Monetary Conference is reprinted
from *Business Week.* An outspoken critic of the government's ethnic policies, he equates poverty with apartheid
and predicts that worker violence would come with disinvestment. Writing in *Commonweal,* William Gould believes
that black labor unions could do the best job of safeguard-
ing individual black workers' rights and securing equality
in black and white pay scales.

The issue is plainly one of ethics as much as economics.
In the United States increasing pressure is being put on
colleges and universities to divest their often considerable
holdings of shares in companies who do business in South
Africa. This campaign is the subject of the final article by
Jack Magarel, writing in the *Chronicle of Higher Education.*

THE SOUTH AFRICAN ECONOMY[1]

South Africa's mineral wealth verges on the fabulous.
But that resource is not likely to be enough to avoid serious
political trouble stemming from a weakening economy.

[1] Article entitled "A Measure of Apartheid," by Tom Wicker, columnist.
New York *Times.* p A33. D. 22, '78. © 1978 by The New York Times Company.
Reprinted by permission.

The country has the world's largest reserves of chrome, from which the United States draws more than 50 percent of its supplies. South Africa's ample deposits of platinum, however, have lately escalated in value: the Soviet Union is holding its platinum off the market and the metal is in heavy demand for antipollution converters for American automobiles, as well as for Japanese jewelry.

The single biggest American import from South Africa is diamonds—although many actually come in from Europe and Israel, where they are processed. And South Africa produces 70 percent of the world's gold, at prices which have risen about $200 an ounce from a low of $103 in August, 1976.

Gold exports alone—adding 200 million rand (about $240 million) to South African exchange earnings with every $10 rise in the prices—have enabled the country to surmount its supposed "Achilles heel," a total lack of oil reserves in the age of OPEC. Even so, leftover gold reserves also have financed most of the nation's substantial recent military buildup.

But beyond these rosy statistics and beyond the modern skyscrapers rising above Johannesburg's "Gold Hills"—the piled-up tailings from the mines that surround the city—South Africa's economic problems are serious and fraught with political consequence. Capital, as the first example, has been flowing out since the Soweto riots of 1976 shook the country's reputation and (at least momentarily) its confidence.

Foreign debt, long- and short-term, has been substantially curtailed and Pretoria can no longer borrow long-term money except at exorbitant rates. Worried businessmen making illegal transfers of currency are believed to be costing the nation $600 million a year. "Disinvestment" by various means, such as foreign investors taking dividends out rather than ploughing them back into South Africa, has become substantial. American investment, although some continues, is believed by American officials here to be in a net decline.

The South African economy, moreover, is at best something of a contradiction—highly developed in part, but dragged down by the mere "subsistence economy"—not much more advanced than that of a bush country—allowed South Africa's 18.6 million blacks.

Partially as a consequence of this calculated waste of human resources, South Africa's gross national product is only one-fifth that of Canada. Then automobile producers turn out only 200,000 cars a year, for example, and even that production couldn't be sustained without cheap black labor. Paradoxically, the great reserves of such labor maintained by South Africa's apartheid system vastly reduce the potential consumers' market in this rich-white, poor-black nation.

South Africa's Recession

And for all its wealth, South Africa has been in a recession since 1976, when the consequence of the Portuguese revolution—notably, the independence of Angola and Mozambique—transformed the political situation throughout southern Africa. The days of white rule, everywhere it existed, suddenly seemed numbered.

South Africa had devoted its gold earnings to surviving the oil price crisis of the early 1970s and was heavily in debt to foreign countries for major infrastructural projects —harbor and power development and the like. Suddenly, it found its markets abroad diminished by recession in Europe and America.

In 1976, Soweto further undermined the world's confidence in South African stability. Foreign capital, which had been flowing in at $1 billion to $1.5 billion yearly, began to dry up almost overnight. All this forced South Africa to slow down economic growth in order to reduce imports and balance its current accounts.

As a result, a 1976 growth rate projected at 5.5 percent declined nearly to zero, and projections for 1978 and 1979 are only 2.7 percent and 3.7 percent. But in this country,

reduced growth bears the seeds of genuine political upheaval.

South Africa needs 5.5 percent growth annually just to
keep up with the yearly increase in the number of blacks
entering the labor market. At recent growth rates, the vola-
tile pool of black unemployed—already at about two million
—may be expanding every year by as many as 200,000 young
people, most already politicized by Soweto.

Here is the true measure of South Africa's claim that
"separate development"—apartheid—is designed to bring
blacks into the economic mainstream. For only about 33,000
white workers—less than one percent of the total—are unemployed in a country where 120,000 skilled jobs are unfilled,
almost all of them barred by law to black workers.

WHAT OF SOUTH AFRICA'S ECONOMY?[2]

South Africa enters 1979 with a combination of mild
optimism and acute anxiety. Recovery from two years of
recession is definitely under way. But without figures for
the final quarter of 1978, it is impossible to say whether it
is gathering momentum. Also, the array of problems now
threatening further growth, many of them well beyond
South Africa's control, make any kind of forecasting about
the year ahead hazardous at best. Professor Jan Hupkes of
the University of South Africa braves this peril to offer
his views about the prospects facing the economy in the
new year.

*Do you believe South Africa's economic recovery is
faltering, or do you see a sustained upswing to, say, the
middle of 1979? What rate of growth do you expect for 1979
as a whole?*

The latest preliminary statistics paint a somewhat con-

    [2] From "Accelerating Into the Unknown," an interview with Dr. Jan
Hupkes, professor of applied economics at the University of South Africa. George
Barrell, ed. *To the Point*. 8:38-9. Ja. 5, '79. © 1979 African International Pub-
lishing Company (Pty) Ltd., South Africa. Reprinted by permission.

fusing picture. A few amber lights have started to blink, but the indicators have been disturbed by a number of exogenous influences, and I think we should give these time to settle down before trying to be too definite. I am referring to such factors as:

—The wild gyrations on world currency markets of a dollar-tied rand.

—The hesitancy in the growth rates of our trading partners.

—The political situation in Rhodesia and South West Africa, with the concomitant threat of sanctions and boycotts.

—The unpredictable gold price, and our own "Information-gate."

I do not think the economy is faltering. At worst it is taking a breather, and for 1979 I see a growth rate of between three percent and four percent, indicating that the upswing will continue.

What main domestic and international economic factors are likely to determine the pace of South Africa's economy in 1979? What are likely to be the main constraints on growth?

Dominant among the domestic factors will be climatic conditions, the consumer mood and investment confidence. These last two are non-quantifiable, but are currently improving. In addition, there is the rate of increases in wages and salaries, and government expenditure. Monetary, fiscal and other government policies will also have a considerable effect.

Internationally we can look first at items on the current account of the balance of payments. Although merchandise exports should again show a healthy rise, the percentage increase will probably be lower than in 1978.

Imports will definitely rise faster as the growth rate improves, with the result that the substantial current account surplus of 1978 will decrease sharply. Although *net* capital inflows should be marginally favorable, it is clear that we cannot rely on the overall balance of payments to add substantially to our net reserves in 1979. I am afraid that the low level of these reserves will continue to act as a constraint, preventing us from going full-throttle for maximum growth. Other constraints will be the expected slow-down in world trade, persistent high inflation and the reappearance of skilled labor bottlenecks.

What Economic Growth Rate Is Needed?

It has been argued that South Africa needs a growth rate of at least five percent a year to meet growing demand for jobs and to improve real living standards. Is this realistic? How else can labor, employment and wage factors be balanced?

If we continue to grow along traditional lines—that is if we stick to the old pattern of growth inputs whereby capital and white entrepreneurship plus, somewhat as an afterthought, large numbers of blacks, are utilized in the production process—then we need an annual growth rate of at least five percent to absorb unemployment and increase real living standards. All indications are that this figure will not be achieved in 1979. In other words, we will have to get away from this pattern and move towards a situation where black entrepreneurial talents, as well as labor productivity, become important growth inputs in our economic structure.

Do you recommend any additional measures to stimulate the economy before the March budget, and if so what? What kind of budget would you like to see in March?

I hesitate to recommend any additional stimulatory measures at this stage, bearing in mind the constraints under which the economy is having to grow. For example, we have not been allowed to reap the fruits of the export boom of the past two years because large amounts of capital have escaped through the back door of the balance of payments. Also, it is only since 1975-76 that the authorities have started to get their own financial house in order by trying to balance the fiscal books. Only now are we in the private sector coming to realize how spoilt-dependent we had become on increasing government expenditure and the inevitable new money creation that went with it. By

overworking the stimulation pump now, we could undo a lot of the good work of the past two or three years. My ideal budget for 1979–80 would have to conform to the following:
—No excessive money creation. This by itself limits the scope for inflationary stimulation.
—Relatively more emphasis on government expenditure for education and training.
—Fiscal incentives for labor-intensive production processes.
—Equal tax for equal pay.
—If there is something left in the kitty, a reduction in the prohibitively high rates of personal income tax.

What do you think is likely to happen to the price of gold?

In 1973 I wrote an article entitled *Be Bold, Back Gold.* Today I am sorry I did not put my money where my mouth was. The same fundamentals still apply, although unfortunately at the moment Uncle Sam is rather trigger-happy with his supply of ammunition from Fort Knox. In the short run the price of gold depends very much on US Treasury sales—probably they will also act as a floor. My guess for 1979 is a floor price of $180 an ounce with an upward potential to $250.

What price and wage inflation do you expect in 1979? What will happen to wages and salaries, and to real purchasing power? How fast can black wages be improved without erasing the already minuscule annual improvement in the productivity of all workers, and especially blacks?

If we aim to measure price inflation by comparing the retail price index of one month with that of a year ago we will unfortunately have to wait until July 1979, when the distortions caused by the general sales tax have worked their way through the system. At that stage, the percentage rise should be in the vicinity of eight percent—that is below double figures. In 1979 I expect white real purchasing power to rise by one percent, the first increase in five years. The figure for blacks should be approximately two percent. Black productivity will only start to improve substantially when we begin to restructure the production process on the lines I have already indicated.

There are signs that South Africa's international borrowing prospects are improving. Do you think this trend will continue? To what extent should official economic policy remain dependent on foreign capital availability?

Our international borrowing prospects have improved owing to sound domestic, economic, financial, monetary and fiscal policies. If we continue on these conservative lines —that is provided we do not overwork the stimulation pump —our credit rating will continue to improve. For the foreseeable future, official policy should assume a neutral capital account for the balance of payments.

What broad changes in government economic management policies would you like to see in 1979? Do you favor a change in exchange rate policy?

Here I should like to plead the *sub judice* escape route. Until we have had the chance to study the De Kock Commission's findings, about all I can say is that I would welcome the introduction of some mechanism whereby the wild fluctuations on the capital account of the balance of payments need not have such a direct effect on the domestic economy. We must get away from this "tail wags the dog" situation. Maybe the solution lies in a two-tier market with a commercial and a capital rand. In any case, I would prefer market forces to do much of the work that exchange control is doing at present.

Would you like to see the beginning of any fundamental changes in the South African economy in 1979. For instance, the recognition of black trade unions, or a relaxation of the industrial decentralization policy?

I have already said that I would welcome changes. The fundamental point is that race discrimination—like religious or sex discrimination—is not compatible with the free enterprise system. This truth became clear to the authorities once it was realized the taxpayer was not able to finance the development of the homelands on a scale that would stem the drift of blacks to townships in white cities.

The consequences of the permanency of the urban black will have to be faced. I am not sure whether this implies categorically the recognition of black trade unions, but it sounds logical. As such the industrial decentralization policy is not a bad thing. But it should not overburden the taxpayer, nor should it stifle black entrepreneurship in black urban areas. In other words, what we need is the carrot, not the stick.

Do you see a recovery of industrial investment in 1979? How could the government best encourage an investment boom within the framework of its present policies?

Industrial investment usually follows an economic recovery. It does not lead it. The current revival in consumer demand can be looked upon as the self-starter of the latest expansionary phase. Its job was to get the engine going and the wheels turning. By mid-1979 the economy should be approaching capacity ceilings. This will be a crucial juncture. If, at this stage, private fixed investment outlays are not forthcoming, the boom will fizzle out. The authorities cannot make these investment decisions. But by clear statements of policy—on labor for example—they can reduce uncertainty and create the correct environment for investment.

I believe that a detached, cold, hard, calculating approach to the economic future of South Africa is all that is required to get the investment boom going, provided this future can be worked out within a non-discriminatory, free-enterprise system.

What of the US and Free World Economies?

How do you see the US economy developing in 1979? Do you think the dollar will stabilize and strengthen?

There is a saying that the business cycle has been replaced by the election cycle. According to this theory, US President Jimmy Carter will "allow" a mild recession in 1979, manipulate a "soft landing" towards the end of the year, then start pump-priming an economy purged of all inflationary evils.

My personal feeling is that Washington will over-react.

In the next six months or so we will see interest rates at historic highs and unemployment increasing. The dollar may strengthen. But once the president's men realize their actions could cost them votes, they will switch course. What I am really afraid of is the inevitable bout of stimulation that will precede the 1980 election. I do not think the international exchange markets will react favorably. Selling the dollar short may then prove too profitable an opportunity.

Where will the free-world economy be this time next year? Where will our economy be?

I would have preferred to skip the first half of this question, but my honest answer is—saddled with more controls. In the Western world the free enterprise system is being progressively overtaxed, both literally and figuratively. It is losing its locomotive function. The engine is so overburdened by subsidized passengers that the end result must be stagflation. However, South Africa is not in the same boat. All we need do is unleash the forces of growth.

THE CASE FOR DOING BUSINESS IN SOUTH AFRICA[3]

For some 350 American companies, doing business in South Africa has become much more than that. Whether they like it or not, they have become key actors in one of the more harrowing national dramas of our time.

At these companies, there is hardly a shareholders' meeting at which the chairman doesn't have to respond to cross-examination and criticism mainly from church and university groups, pressing them to explain why they are still in South Africa. Some harassed university trustees, confronted by the most vocal political-protest movement on American campuses since the Vietnam war, have begun selling off the shares of such companies, often with heavy losses.

[3]Article by Herman Nickel, editor. *Fortune.* 97:60-4+. Je. 19, '78. Reprinted by permission from Fortune Magazine; © 1978 Time Inc.

Other universities, led by Harvard, have taken the line that they will look at their portfolio case by case, to make sure the companies in which they own shares meet their exacting standards of corporate responsibility. Major American banks are being threatened with the withdrawal of accounts unless they stop lending to the South African government, and even to private South African firms.

The anti-South African campaign has also been making steady progress in Washington—particularly since the rioting in Soweto in 1976 and the explosion of worldwide outrage over the case of Steven Biko, the leader of the "Black Consciousness Movement" who failed to survive South African police "questioning" last September [1977]. In January, a staff report of the Foreign Relations subcommittee on Africa, chaired by Senator Dick Clark (Democrat-Iowa) charged that the "abysmal" record of American employers in South Africa threatened to undermine "the fundamental goals and objectives of US foreign policy." In the House of Representatives, a move to bar the Export-Import Bank from providing loan guarantees and insurance for transactions with South Africa has passed the Banking Committee. The Carter administration has not yet supported such extreme judgments or actions, but potential investors seeking advice are being warned about the labyrinth of problems they might be getting into.

In the public forum the critics of American companies charge flatly that whatever helps the South African economy also helps apartheid. So long as these companies go on conducting business as usual, so too will the South African government, with its politics of repression. For according to the indictment, this is a government so immune to persuasion that it can understand no language milder than an American economic withdrawal.

Frightened or fatigued by all such pressures, a few American companies—notably those for which South African business is only a marginal item anyway—have found it easier to wash their hands of the whole nettlesome affair. After all, business in South Africa is not nearly as profitable today as it used to be, with the once fabulous returns (a record 29.9 percent in 1973) sharply down to 8.5 percent in 1975. In these circumstances, the temptation can be strong to give withdrawal some moral gloss. When Polaroid recently announced its withdrawal, for example, it won applause from those who had been castigating the firm for supplying the government with the photographic equipment to make the hated passbooks that keep South African blacks from moving around freely in their own country. In fact, Polaroid conducted its South African business through a local distributor. Its products are still on sale. As for the passes, which existed well before Polaroid arrived on the scene, they are still issued as before.

This comparatively trivial instance merely hints at the massive difficulty besetting any grand design for American economic disengagement: the true nature and impact of any such withdrawal would bear little if any similarity to the avowed objective of its ardent advocates. And this essentially is why the vast majority of companies—after sober weighing of all risks and uncertainties—have chosen to stand their ground.

To be sure, one self-serving consideration plays its role in this decision. The fact is that any "heading for the exit" is not nearly as simple an exercise as some of its proponents seem to assume. For while South African foreign-exchange regulations allow the free repatriation of profits, this does not apply to capital. There is thus no way of packing up the plant and shipping it home. If an American corporation found a South African buyer, the proceeds would first have to be invested for at least seven years in low-yield South African government securities—a solution as unattractive politically as it is financially. The alternative of selling out to another foreign enterprise would merely give the buyer the competitive break of being able to pick up a plant at a knockdown price—and without any obvious gain for South Africa's blacks.

But going beyond these practical reasons, most American companies cast their decision to stay in South Africa in more positive terms. By their continued presence, they argue, they not only provide jobs for their 90,000 employees, including some 60,000 blacks; they also can serve as catalysts of peaceful social change. For them, the crucial question is: would US withdrawal bring the desired human, practical, and political rewards? And this is precisely where the case for withdrawal, flawed with many oversimplifications and half-truths, breaks down.

To begin with, one has to confront a truth that Americans often prefer to ignore in foreign relations: there is a clear limit to American power and leverage. While continued US investment, credit, and trade are important to South Africa, they are not a matter of survival. At least on this point, South Africa's Finance Minister Owen Horwood and US Ambassador to the United Nations Andrew Young are in perfect agreement. "South Africa will certainly not be forced to its knees by disinvestment of American capital, whatever that vague notion may mean and however it is supposed to be brought about," Harwood told me when I questioned him in his spacious Cape Town office. "South Africa is one of the most self-sufficient nations in the world," said Young in a recent interview. Even the staff report of Senator Clark's subcommittee on Africa, with its strong disengagement bias, concedes that US economic interests in South Africa "may not be decisive" after all.

In purely quantitative terms, the $1.6-billion (book value) US direct investment in South Africa represents 16 percent of total foreign investment there. This is dwarfed by the 57 percent stake of the European Community countries and amounts to only 4 percent of the total capital invested in the South African economy. It is true that in some sectors the American role is critical, probably the most important being computer technology, where US companies, led by I.B.M., control 70 percent of the market. But South Africa is by no means defenseless. Thanks to its near-monopoly in some critical metals (including 83 percent of the world's reserves of platinum and 74 percent of the chrome), it is quite capable of retaliating if the US

refused to deal in terms of quid pro quo. "Without South
African platinum for catalytic converters, the US government would have to call off the entire emission-control
program," a G.M. executive warns.

Since South Africa's economic relationship with Europe
is so much more important to both sides than its relationship with the US, a fully effective investment boycott would
need the support of the EEC. But precisely because the
European stake is so much greater, the chances for that
are very remote. Britain's Foreign Secretary David Owen
recently voiced concern that Britain's huge £5-billion portfolio and direct investment in South Africa, 10 percent of
all British investment abroad, makes his country "danger-
ously vulnerable" and urged that this exposure be reduced.
But successive Labor governments have been far too worried
about the 70,000 jobs allegedly dependent on British economic ties with South Africa to move decisively toward
economic disengagement.

A new and increasingly vital factor in this equation is
Western Europe's reliance on South Africa as a major supplier of processed uranium. The restrictive conditions that
have been put on the export of US and Canadian uranium
in effect increase this dependence. Though no official figures
are published, South African and Namibian uranium is
estimated to account for at least 50 percent of Western
Europe's supplies. As soon as ten years from now, top South
African officials expect uranium (even excluding Namibian
sources) to surpass gold in importance to the South African
economy.

Even South Africa's reliance on foreign credits, while
serious, has not made it vulnerable to an ultimatum from
the outside world. The fact that the South African government managed to turn a balance-of-payments deficit running at an annual rate of 2,592 million rand ($2,976 mil-
lion) early in 1976 into an annual surplus of 1,277 million
rand by mid-1977 shows that the government is prepared to
slow domestic expansion to make up for the reduced net
capital inflow (from 989 million rand in 1976 to 211 mil-

lion rand in 1977). Largely as the result of the mid-1970's recession, which hit South Africa about eighteen months late, the economy's real growth rate has nose-dived from 7 percent in 1974 to 0.5 percent in 1977.

Here one comes to the crux of the matter. Stopping the flow of foreign capital cannot bring South Africa "to its knees," in Finance Minister Horwood's phrase. But it does spell the difference between adequate and inadequate growth. The government acknowledges that South Africa's normal growth rate of about 6 percent would be halved if the flow of foreign capital came to a halt. Independently, academic analysts such as Professor Arnt Spandau of the University of Witwatersrand have come to the same conclusion. Of course this is a "worst case" assumption, but even a substantial decline in the capital inflow—and it reached 6 to 7 percent a year during the "golden Sixties"—could slow growth to below the level that is necessary to accommodate the 3 percent birth rate in the non-white population. South African blacks would thus face the prospect of growing unemployment, without the benefits of welfare checks and food stamps. That would be the harshly ironic result of a policy designed to help them.

The prospect worries most blacks deeply. In the blunt words of Freddy Sauls, a battle-seasoned organizer for colored and black workers in the Port Elizabeth auto industry: "It's all very well for people to urge disinvestment who sit in safe comfort in some nice office 8,000 miles away. But if the American auto plants here closed down, I'd have thousands of men looking for work and literally wondering where the next meal would come from." I found the same sense of realism echoed in scores of conversations I had with black workers. Whatever specific grievances they might have, the vast majority rejected any notion of foreign economic boycott of their country. And this simply confirmed the estimate of black leaders who told me that a poll of urban blacks would find 75 percent opposing any withdrawal by US companies.

In broad historical terms, there appears to be little logic

or reason in the idea that economic stagnation provides a better backdrop for the peaceful transformation of South Africa from institutionalized racism into a multiracial society. The notion would seem all the more bizarre when put forward by Americans, for the whole history of racial progress in the US points in the opposite direction. Practically every major step forward was linked with economic progress. Just as the hardheaded interests of Yankee businessmen helped to pave the way for the abolition of slavery, so the emergence of the "new South" and the opening up of equal opportunities for black Americans one hundred years later could have happened only against a background of growth, while they would have been unthinkable during the Depression. Economic growth did not strengthen the system of institutionalized racism in the US; it effectively destroyed it.

When Andrew Young first drew parallels between the role business eventually played in the civil-rights struggle in the American South and the role it might play in South Africa, his critics were quick to cite the essential differences: the reversed ratios between blacks and whites, the much wider cultural gaps, and the fact that South Africa has no US–type constitution in place. All these differences make the South African problem much more difficult—a fact some Americans should recall before unleasing their moralistic rhetoric. Nevertheless, this criticism should not obscure a central point in Young's thesis that applies to segregation and apartheid with equal force: institutionalized racism is plainly incompatible with the functional requirements of an expanding industrial society.

The same point is made in a different way by Harry Oppenheimer, chairman of the huge Anglo-American minerals empire and a persistent critic of the government. As the political philosophy of poor rural Afrikanerdom, he observes, apartheid could possibly have worked only in the context of a poor agricultural subsistence economy. Against the background of an industrial revolution that turned the Witwatersrand into the "only real industrial complex south of Milan" (*Fortune,* December, 1966), the contradictions of the system were bound to become ever more glaring, even to many of its Afrikaner supporters.

This is exactly what has been happening. The first consequence of industrial growth was the full enlistment of the country's limited supply of white labor for semiskilled and skilled jobs, and, accordingly, the necessity of proceeding to train nonwhite labor. Even though South Africa has yet to emerge from its deepest postwar recession, the unemployment rate among whites is less than one percent. The real burden of the recession has been carried by unskilled blacks. (Although, grotesquely, there still are no official statistics on black unemployment, the estimates run as high as 12 percent.)

The effect of this transformation has been to make an empty shell of the old system of "job reservation," conceived originally to shield poor whites from black competition. Last year the remaining twenty-five "reserved" job categories were reduced to a mere five, and even these are expected to be abolished soon. The only obstacle to this reform would be the fear of a prolonged depression, which could stir up opposition from some reactionary white unions. But if the South African economy could get back on its normal pre-recession growth path of almost 6 percent, it would require 3.8 million more skilled workers by 1980, of whom more than half would have to be nonwhite.

This structural transformation of the labor market has already had significant effects on the real earnings of black industrial workers. At least since 1970 their wages have been rising not just absolutely, but also in relation to those of whites. According to a survey by the Bureau of Market Research of the University of South Africa, average incomes of black households in the Johannesburg area rose 118 percent between 1970 and 1975, as compared with 58 percent for white households. Between 1975 and 1980, black per capita income is expected to rise 29.5 percent, as against only 7.3 percent for whites.

In contrast to what has happened in many independent

black African countries, the gap between black and white incomes has been narrowing steadily. Between 1970 and 1976, the gap in industry narrowed from 1:5.85 to 1:4.44; among employees in the central government, from 1:5.31 to 1:3.10; and in construction from 1:6.60 to 1:5.20. The most dramatic—and the most necessary—improvement occurred in the mining sector, where the gap shrank from 1:19.79 to 1:7.69. This is still by no means satisfactory, but it sharpens the point made by Economics Minister Chris Heunis when he observed that foreign critics can't reasonably demand, at one and the same time, an investment boycott and the narrowing of income disparities. In a new study, to be published later this year in the US, Professor Spandau documents a significant reallocation of racial incomes in South Africa since 1970. Between 1970 and 1977 the white share of total incomes declined steadily at a rate of one percentage point a year, from 70 to 63 percent. In another paper, economist Erich Leistner predicts that by the end of the century the black market will be twice the size of the total consumers' market in South Africa today. All these figures would seem to dispose of those baleful predictions that in a capitalist society like South Africa, growth can only make the rich whites richer and the poor blacks poorer.

The most important political consequence of these economic changes has undermined the central aim of apartheid, which was the effort to overcome the numerical disadvantage of the country's 4.3 million whites by decreeing the 18 million blacks to be citizens of ten fragmented, pseudo-independent tribal "homelands" (occupying just 13 percent of the land area of South Africa). The theory of apartheid regarded the urban townships as little more than dormitory towns for transient workers who—rather like Turks in Germany—were not supposed to stay forever and would have political rights only in their "homelands." Hence the reluctance to improve the townships to a point where people might want to stay for good and others would be attracted to move in from the impoverished homelands.

Hence also the resistance to giving blacks in the townships property rights, as well as the insistence that no one be allowed to move to the urban areas without a passbook. But the gravitational pull of the urban industrial centers has proved too strong for all such barriers. The huge, sprawling township of Soweto outside Johannesburg—home for as many as one million people, including 300,000 to 400,000 unauthorized "squatters"—became the dramatic symbol of apartheid's failure to face up to the reality of the urban black.

When Soweto erupted into violence in 1976, this failure could no longer be masked, and there is now a virtual consensus that the status quo will no longer do. Moreover, this failure is no longer discussed just in private. Among *verligte* (enlightened) Afrikaners, the reliance on repression to cope with the system's contradictions is perceived as not only ruinous to South Africa's desire to be recognized as a member of the Western world: it would also be blindly defiant to the real needs of the economic future. The ferment of this "agonizing reappraisal" contrasts with the outside world's popular perception of the Afrikaners as one monolithic and immutable bloc.

It is not surprising that Afrikaner businessmen, themselves a fairly recent product of economic growth, should be playing a prominent part in this reappraisal. It is, after all, in business's own interest that the status of the ten million urban blacks be improved and given full recognition, for they are the indispensable workers. There is little point in spending time and money on training migrants, as distinct from a stable work force living with their families under decent conditions. It was simple recognition of this that led in 1976 to the forming of the Urban Foundation, an effort by businessmen to mobilize the resources and influence of private enterprise to improve the quality of life in the townships. Having raised 14 million rand, even in the midst of a recession—including a million each from Barclays and Standard banks, half a million from

Ford, and a quarter million from Mobil—the foundation is now embarked on a variety of projects to improve housing in the townships and set up community centers, kindergartens, early-learning centers, and recreational facilities.

The success of this enterprise still hangs in the balance. As the foundation's executive director, Justice Jan Steyn, concedes, its biggest problem is to overcome suspicion and hostility among urban blacks toward still another white-sponsored effort to improve their lot within the political straitjacket of the apartheid system. He acknowledges that "without securing their involvement, the changes we seek will be beyond our reach." Steyn hopes that the foundation's credibility was enhanced by its role in prodding the government to drop the fiction of the "transient" urban blacks, at least to the extent where they can now acquire permanent leaseholds on which they can borrow money and which they can sell and bequeath. On the employment front, the foundation has gained the endorsement of more than 700 South African employers for a code of practices that commits them to abolish job discrimination, train their black employees, and give them equal pay for equal work. Whatever its limitations, the Urban Foundation symbolizes the emergence of the Afrikaner businessman as a force for change. Andrew Young has aptly noted that South Africa is one country where the business community stands to the left of the government.

As the politicians of the ruling National party try to dodge the new realities—with contorted schemes to recognize the economic role of the urban black without letting him share in political power—they have succeeded only in disenchanting the intellectuals at Afrikaner universities, such as Stellenbosch, who used to serve as the party's brain trusters. The ranks of the estranged include even the current head of the legendary Broederbond, the secretive fraternal society that is the watchdog over 300 years of Afrikaner heritage. Professor Gerrit Viljoen is now quietly prodding the government to face the facts by accepting urban blacks as permanent residents and to move on from separate development toward a multiracial federation, with even eventual political integration not ruled out. Coming from the head of the Broederbond, this is a quantum leap forward.

Unfortunately, this kind of *verligte* thinking continues to come up against the *verkrampte* (uptight) hardliners in the National party. The result of their inertial resistance is to slow the evolutionary process to a pace that is not nearly brisk enough for the outside world—and what is much more critical—for a new generation of politicized blacks in South Africa itself. Inadequate reforms, grudgingly made, help to create the tensions that Alexis de Tocqueville described in his classic account of the end of the Ancien Régime in France: "Patiently endured so long as it seemed beyond redress, a grievance becomes intolerable once the possibility for removing it crosses men's minds." Such is the situation in Soweto today. The most militant talk comes not from the downtrodden poor but from members of an intellectual and professional elite who have already achieved their economic takeoff and are now insisting on the political rights to go with it.

Yet there is little doubt that, however erratic and confused, an evolutionary process is at work. The striking mark of this process is that the forces for change in the political sector receive their strongest thrust from progress in the economic sector. In the light of this fact, it hardly seems sensible to argue that political redemption can be accelerated by a full-scale American retreat from the economic arena. The constructive question is what role American companies have been playing in the past—and what they should be doing in the future—to speed profounder change.

If the prospects can now be viewed more positively than in 1972 when *Fortune* first examined them (July, 1972), much credit is due to the Reverend Dr. Leon Sullivan, the civil-rights activist who is minister of Philadelphia's big Zion Baptist Church and a member of the board of General

Motors. It is an ironic fact that the Reverend Dr. Sullivan
has never erased his own reservations about the presence of
US companies in South Africa. But a brief visit there in
1975 quickly persuaded him that, so long as the companies
were doing business, they should at least pioneer principles
of fair-employment practices and equal opportunity, rather
than simply blend into the apartheid scenery, as many had
been doing with embarrassing ease. In March, 1977, Sullivan's meetings with the top level of major US companies
produced a carefully drafted code of conduct based on six
principles:

—Nonsegregation of races in all eating, comfort, and
work facilities

—Equal and fair employment practices

—Equal pay for comparable work

—Training programs to prepare blacks and other nonwhites for supervisory, administrative, clerical, and technical jobs in substantial numbers

—More blacks and other nonwhites in management and
supervisory positions

—Improving employees' lives outside the work environment in such areas as housing, transportation, schooling,
recreation, and health

Today the number of signatories to this code has risen
from the original twelve companies to ninety-eight, and
task forces—one for each point—are meeting regularly to
compare notes and develop new approaches. The code, to
be sure, is hardly revolutionary; and with the sole reservation that it should not apply just in South Africa, the South
African government has even given it approval—a fact that,
in the view of some militants, automatically renders it suspect or meaningless.

It is no such thing. The code has provided both a forum
for discussion and a criterion for judgment where none before existed. Fully aware that the Reverend Dr. Sullivan has
ready access to the top levels of US corporate management
—and that failure to perform can lead to damaging publicity and nasty scenes at shareholders' meetings—the local

managers of American companies in South Africa now have to address themselves seriously to each of the six principles, report back to the home office what they have been doing, and spell out concrete objectives for the future. The result has been to inspire a new kind of corporate competition. The fact that Ford has now established itself as a leader in implementing the Sullivan principles may well be as painful to G.M.'s ears as the fact that Ford is No. 1 and G.M. No. 5 in South African car sales.

The reputation of American companies is now much better than it used to be—and deservedly so. Freddy Sauls, who organizes nonwhite auto workers in Port Elizabeth and is not given to easy flattery of any bosses, grants that "most of the American firms now are pretty good, certainly a hell of a lot better than the British firms." Henry Chipeya, a young black union organizer in Johannesburg, pays the US companies a backhanded compliment by complaining that many of them try to keep black unions out by providing above-average wages and benefits. In 1972, twelve out of fifteen companies examined by *Fortune* turned out to be paying starting wages below the minimum subsistence level of the government's Poverty Datum Line. All the firms visited this time paid starting wages above the higher standards of the Household Subsistence Level, as set by economists of the University of Port Elizabeth, with average wages usually 50 percent and more above that level. In Port Elizabeth, the coastal city with the biggest concentration of American factories, the average monthly cash income of black workers at Ford this March was 216.02 rand, compared with a Household Subsistence Level of 132.84 rand. Even the lowest unskilled starting wage encountered this time—.80 rand an hour at Firestone—worked out to 105 percent of H.S.L.

Since the principle of equal pay for equal work means nothing so long as there is no equal work, a training program is as crucial to blacks as their pay scale. Most major American companies recognize this now and are either supporting industrial-training centers like Chamdor in the

Transvaal . . . or running their own programs. For example, Ford is spending $1.1 million on job training this year, an increase of 70 percent over 1977, despite the fact that it lost $8 million in its South African operations last year. This is one of the advantages of a large multinational that smaller South African companies envy.

The programs offered by the companies range all the way from courses for tool-setter and foreman positions to literacy and language training. For many blacks these company courses represent a major part of their entire education. More concretely, the blacks are gradually making inroads into skilled and supervisory positions that used to be all-white monopolies. One major limitation remains—an anachronistic law that still prohibits blacks from becoming apprentices (except in the homelands). But companies like Ford have got around this by providing the essential training under a disguised name.

Compared with the importance of training for a good job, the better pay to go with it, and the opportunity for advancement, the right to use the same lavatory and to sit in the same cafeteria with the white supervisor ranks rather low on the list of priorities of the average black worker. By itself, says one black leader, "it doesn't mean a damn thing." But it does mean a great deal to whites. Perhaps this is why white management devotes enormous care to implementing the Sullivan code in ways that will prevent a "white backlash" incident. But this sometimes produces nervous exercises in gradualism that trigger a black backlash against mere tokenism.

A prime example of this, ironically, comes from the company on whose board the Reverend Dr. Sullivan sits—G.M. In line with the Sullivan code, G.M. duly removed the offending written signs from the lavatory doors in its Port Elizabeth plant, only to replace them with color-keyed doors: blue for whites and Chinese (the latter considered honorary whites for lavatory purposes), orange for blacks and coloreds. Far from "lessening the insult," as one G.M.

official in Detroit tried to explain to *Fortune,* it infuriated a number of black trade unionists, for it seemed to confirm their worst suspicions that G.M. was using the code as mere window dressing. "Who do they think we are?" fumed one black shop steward. The fact that black hourly workers at G.M. eat in a segregated cafeteria, while white hourly workers are allowed to use the cafeteria for salaried employees (pending the planned construction of a new, integrated facility), has built up further resentment, which threatens to obscure G.M.'s good record in training and upgrading black employees.

The episode illustrates the gap in perception and communication that plagues South Africa generally and its paternalistic industrial relations in particular. Ford has found that its channels of communication were much improved by establishing a good working relationship with the black United Automobile Workers Union. This is something that G.M. has not managed to achieve so far.

The white-backlash problem is by no means entirely a figment of a timid management's imagination. Earlier this year, when Borg-Warner began to integrate its white cafeteria, a recent emigrant from Yorkshire stirred up a boycott, backed by the white union, to force re-segregation. The South African government reacted not by sternly enforcing the law requiring separate facilities, but by quietly dispatching an aide to the Minister of Labor to calm the scene. Taking the Yorkshireman aside, the official expressed puzzlement about why he was making such a fuss when he should have been used to sharing facilities with colored immigrants in Britain. "Why did you think I came here in the first place?" came the reply. The problem is now straightened out, but the incident throws light on the government's awareness that if it wants American companies to stay, it is in its own interests to see the Sullivan code put into effect—a clear hint of the bargaining position of American firms in nudging the government toward change.

As a rule of thumb, the Borg-Warner kind of trouble tends to disappear the higher up one goes on the educational and social ladder. Integration of facilities poses few problems, if any, at banks, white-collar operations, and in companies like I.B.M. and 3M, and others that deal with more sophisticated technologies. The task is much harder in auto plants and such hot, dirty, and dangerous operations as the Firestone and Goodyear tire plants, where fewer and fewer whites are prepared to take jobs as production workers. For the same reason, the opening of South Africa's top hotels to the tiny number of blacks who can afford to patronize them poses no problems, while the down-market establishments remain strictly limited to "whites only."

What can American companies collectively contribute to progress in a political environment so strange and snarled? In the view of moderate black leaders, it is possible—and necessary—for American business to deliver, in effect, a message to the South African government. This message would not be a hostile threat, but simply a statement of the facts of life. Beneficial as continued foreign investment may be for peaceful change, such investment will simply not happen to any adequate degree so long as the prospect for long-term political stability does not improve. But this improvement can only be achieved by reform and not by repression. Already new US investment has slowed to a trickle, and most American companies now in South Africa are essentially in a holding pattern. Another Soweto, another Biko case, would not only further inhibit investment but also would greatly strengthen the pressures for sanctions and the withdrawal of American firms. If US companies are to stay, they need tangible evidence that their presence does indeed contribute to change. This means more than formal abandoning of the more obnoxious remainders of "petty apartheid" (some of which, like the Immorality Act making sex between the races a crime, are no longer being strictly enforced anyway). It means above all facing up to the necessity of starting a dialogue between the races. What formula for sharing power this dialogue should devise is not up to the outside world, but for black and white South Africans to work out among themselves.

It may well be that the South African government will ignore this message, as it has other messages in the past, for the forces of fear and inertia within the ruling Nationalist party are still all too strong. But at least the chance of American business getting a hearing will be better than that of foreign polemicists from afar, including those of the Carter administration. After all, as Professor Willie Esterhuyse of Stellenbosch University puts it, "You rather take advice from a friend than from an enemy." Unfortunately, all the Carter administration has managed to achieve with its rhetoric so far has been to stiffen the will of the forces of resistance and complicate the task of black leaders struggling for reform.

An outstanding figure among these leaders is forty-year-old Percy Qoboza, South Africa's foremost black journalist. An articulate and dedicated believer in the principles of non-violence, he has long been recognized as one of his country's most courageous black foes of apartheid. During five months of detention, which ended only last March, he agonizingly reviewed the dilemmas besetting South Africa and his own convictions. Qoboza has found himself confirmed in his belief that the American—and other foreign —companies have at least the potential of becoming "one of the most vital links in bringing about peaceful change." But today he attaches important conditions. The foreign companies must, he says, "put their money where their mouth is" and do those things that give blacks a sense of dignity. This means the training to be productive workers earning the wage they deserve; equal opportunity for work and in the process, the liberation from pride-killing, paternalist charity.

An essential part of the process, he insists, is to let black workers deal through their own unions. In a country full of institutions created by whites for blacks, black unions have a very special role to play, he argues. In the present South

African context, multiracial unions are unions dominated by whites. Concerned that the educational efforts of American companies tend to be concentrated either at the doctoral or the literacy training ends of the spectrum, Qoboza urges multinationals to stress the middle level—"the production manager who can keep the factory running while the boss is away." And if this kind of training cannot be carried out in South Africa, he asks, "Why not do it in America or somewhere else abroad?"

In the office of his new paper, the Johannesburg *Post,* Qoboza sits at his work under a picture of Martin Luther King and a framed certificate of his Nieman Fellowship at Harvard in 1975–76. Here he talks darkly about the lengthening shadows that are falling on his naturally beautiful, richly endowed, and politcally imperiled country. "Today people like myself can still say 'cool'—but how much longer?" he asks. Persecuted as a radical by the government, under mounting attack from young militants who detest his moderation and dedication to nonviolence, he briefly considered moving himself and his family to safety in the US after his release. It was his fourteen-year-old daughter who dissuaded him, telling him that by staying he might be able to save more lives than just his family's.

While Qoboza's great inspiration, Martin Luther King, had a dream, Qoboza today has a nightmare. It first came to him in detention, and it is the vision of his children standing over his grave and demanding angrily, "Why didn't you do more to stop the holocaust?" Qoboza knows that a racial war would be the ultimate South African tragedy—staggering in its human suffering, with incalculable international ramifications—and in the end inconclusive. Just as Arabs cannot push Israelis into the sea, so the white Afrikaner tribe would still be there when the killing stopped, and Afrikaners and blacks would have to face up to the same test they are facing now: the historic task of living together and sharing power in their common country.

These are events that American business cannot, of course, control. But it can influence them. This is why the searing question in Percy Qoboza's nightmare is addressed to them, too.

US BUSINESSES SHOULD STAY IN SOUTH AFRICA[4]

Almost a decade after the height of the Vietnam War, American campuses are again alive with political protest. This time the target is the American corporation and its investments in South Africa. While no one yet imagines the protests reaching a Vietnam-like crescendo, the corporations and universities involved are frustrated, embarrassed, and worried. Several large universities have announced their intention of selling the portfolio shares they hold in corporations and banks doing business in that country. Business firms have made changes—substantive or cosmetic —in their South African operations to relieve what is becoming a corporate headache.

The issue reaches far beyond the campuses and boardrooms. It has become a nagging concern for the members of the Carter administration and Congress who are wrestling with the questions of whether and how to force American corporations to be aggressive advocates of progress in South Africa or to get out of the country altogether. Several bills that would cut off tax credits and deny government-guaranteed loans to US firms operating in South Africa are already before Congress. And pressure is being exerted on the administration to sever trade relations— despite the fact that South Africa provides the West with strategic minerals.

All this is being played out against an unusual background of public emotion. To American liberals and many moderates, South Africa's government ranks as the world's most offensive regime, symbol and substance of blatant

[4] Article entitled "American Business Should Stay in South Africa," by Roger M. Williams, senior editor. *Saturday Review.* 5:14-21. S. 30, '78. © Saturday Review, 1978. All rights reserved.

racism and outmoded white colonialism that have no place in the framework of nations. Although conservatives seldom say so straight out, they see the same government as fighting for the survival of white nation-builders against the demands of blacks who have neither the right nor the ability to rule the country; the specter of Communist domination, about which conservatives do talk straight out, adds to their reluctance to apply pressure for fundamental change in South Africa.

Two weeks in South Africa, talking with whites and blacks, Americans and South Africans and others, lead me to this conclusion: American business is not supporting apartheid, either deliberately or in effect, but is helping swell the rivulets of change that may one day join to radically alter South African society and that, in the meantime, will at least mitigate the shocking conditions under which black people live there.

Some 350 American firms, with book-value holdings of approximately $1.7 billion, now operate in South Africa. The United States ranks as South Africa's leading partner in trade, its second largest overseas investor (after Great Britain), and the supplier of roughly one-third of its foreign credit. More than half of *Fortune*'s top 100 companies have subsidiaries in South Africa, and among them are many of the biggest names in American (and multinational) business. American firms control outsized shares of some highly important markets: 23 percent of the automobile market, 43 percent of petroleum, and 70 percent of computers, according to a report issued late last year by the Washington-based Investor Responsibility Research Center. US banks have extended loans and credits totaling about $2 billion to South African companies and governmental entities. Our federal government has a deep involvement, too, through insurance and loan guarantees provided by the Export-Import Bank, credits granted to US corporations for taxes paid abroad, and the power to embargo items of trade.

American business, therefore, touches many elements of

South African life. It has an important bearing on questions that are central to the country's future: Can the white regime be expected ever to bring the black majority into full participation in South African society? Even if the regime permits change to evolve, is sufficient evolution possible, or is violent revolution inevitable? Do foreign corporations have any legitimate and valuable role in an evolutionary process?

Talking with South Africans

South African scenes: May Machaba, 35, slender, bearded, and black, stands in the bright autumn sunshine before his house in the Steelpoort Valley, 175 miles northeast of Johannesburg. Machaba is a shift supervisor at the Tubatse Ferrochrome smelter, which is half-owned and wholly managed by Union Carbide. His house, seven road miles from the smelter, is also owned and managed by Union Carbide. May Machaba says it is the finest house he's ever lived in—"something I never dreamt of"—and one can easily see why. Constructed of concrete block with a corrugated roof and small yards fore and aft, this house and others around it are sturdy and well maintained. The rooms seem uncomfortably small and drab. But compared to the large urban townships and to the primitive conditions in most of South Africa's basic metals industry, these houses are first-class. Along the road from the smelter, in fact, we pass more typical worker facilities, built a decade or more ago and still used by a local South African-run mining concern: little thatched huts called *kraals,* circular or rectangular, most with a single window and with floors made of a dirt and manure mixture.

The black housing area also contains a recreation center, with swimming pool and locker rooms, and an attractive, green-and-cream-colored primary school. A man whose children attend the school tells me it is one of the best schools for blacks in the entire republic; a large claim, but given the dreadful state of black South African schooling, not difficult to believe.

A few miles across the valley sits Tubatse's white housing area. The dwellings and plots are larger, the appoint-
ments nicer, and there are tennis courts and paved streets.
Racism at work? Yes and no. Whites have higher-paying
jobs at Tubatse, as everywhere else, so they can afford
higher rents. They have tennis courts because they play
tennis; the blacks play soccer, and their recreation area includes a soccer field (May Machaba is goalie on the company team). In any case, living in those smaller houses represents a much bigger step up for Tubatse's blacks than
living in the larger ones represents for its whites.

Tubatse Ferrochrome employs about 400 blacks. American companies in South Africa generally pay their lowest-
level workers well above the government-determined "minimum living level." In Union Carbide's case, it is 25 percent
above; that means an income of about $160 a month
plus a month's bonus at the end of the year. Seventeen
categories higher, the pay averages about $740 a month.
There are no longer wage differentials between blacks and
whites, and although it is true that few blacks currently
hold jobs in the highest categories, they are being trained
for and gradually moved into them.

In the South African workplace, responsibility is as significant a measure of progress as wages, and here the Tubatse record looks very impressive. The smelter has four
computerized operations, and all four are manned by
blacks. In addition, they work in the quality-control lab,
manipulate cranes and other heavy equipment, and direct
the crews that "tap" the blazing furnaces to remove the
chrome and slag. "We tap these furnaces an average of
seven times a shift," Don Legg, general manager of the
smelter, tells me. "No place else in the world does it that
often." Tubatse also has an excellent safety record, despite
groundless warnings that black workers would not wear
safety glasses because of tribal superstition. Union Carbide
is so pleased with the performance at Tubatse that it plans
to make the smelter an essentially black-run facility.

There is one jarring bump on Tubatse's road to racial

progress: segregated locker rooms for the workers. Legg explains that the Mines and Works Act "requires" segregation. But I know, and Legg knows, that American firms ignore such requirements all the time. This is one of many examples of management's giving in to pressures—real or fancied—from the white work force. The give-ins are often rationalized as being necessary to avoid friction, even violence, in the plants, and at times perhaps they are. In any case, the results can be almost funny. Taking "whites only" and "blacks only" signs off rest-room doors, some companies have substituted doll-like figures in colors that get the same point across. General Motors has become famous for putting a blue figure on a rest room intended for Orientals; G.M., like the government, doesn't quite know how to classify Orientals. Other companies have made an elaborate process of taking down the partitions that traditionally have separated black, white, and colored dining areas. (An assortment of South Africans of mixed racial ancestry are designated "colored." Among them are descendants of seventeenth- and eighteenth-century unions between Dutch settlers and indigenous Hottentots. The 2.4 million coloreds have been granted higher social and political status than blacks; for example, they are permitted to own property and they are allowed to live in some otherwise all-white areas.) At the Ford Motor Company, the process has been unfolding in carefully timed stages, like the explosion of a nuclear device; during one stage, a soft-drink dispenser was "casually" placed in the no-man's-land between the separate dining areas so that everybody would have to refresh himself on common ground.

Three Black "Radicals"

In a back room at the American Cultural Center in Johannesburg, I talk[ed] with three black "radicals." In light of the endless "detentions" of persons who advocate black rights, even the most moderate of advocates must exercise great care these days. The Cultural Center (formerly the USIS) is safe ground. The three blacks—two journal-

ists and a businessman/writer—tell me I may use their
names, but I decide not to. To advocate disinvestment by
foreign corporations is to risk prosecution under the rightly
feared Terrorism Act. There is no point in subjecting these
three people to that, especially since they are so coopera-
tive in speaking with me.

All three say emphatically that the cause of South African blacks will be best served if US corporations stop investing in the country's economy. "If American business
gets out and stays out," says the writer, "at least one arm
will have been cut off from a very sick body. The fact that
American plants give us jobs is not a good reason for being
here. The best jobs go to whites and the chances of that
changing are very slim. What does American business do
here except help strengthen the existing regime?"

That rhetorical question poses the major argument
made by advocates of disinvestment, in the United States as
well as in South Africa, and the first journalist emphasizes
it: "All foreign investment simply serves to prop up the
regime. They make some improvements for their workers,
but the improvements are solely intended to justify their
companies' presence in South Africa and are of no benefit
to the black community as a whole." The second journalist
adds: "These companies were taking advantage of cheap
labor and a ready market. That's why they came here. And
whether they stay or leave, they're not helping us." The
first journalist again: "People talk about 'creating a black
middle class.' I don't mind that, but I don't want a middle
class created at the expense of the black masses."

Revolution per se is not mentioned, but the business-
man/writer declares: "Moving to the point of bloodshed is
inevitable. The hurt that we're getting now—the ridiculous thing of pushing us into so-called homelands—will
drive us to that."

South Africa's Detroit

Port Elizabeth, on the southeastern coast. "South Africa's Detroit." Windswept beach, dingy little airport, Ford

and General Motors and assorted other giants of the automotive industry. A tough town where street crime is common, blacks are outspoken, and the agents of BOSS, the ruthlessly efficient security police, are said to be even more vigilant than elsewhere. (The late Steven Biko was mortally abused here.) Shortly before I arrived, the *Christian Science Monitor* reported that Port Elizabeth BOSS agents were demanding of foreign companies that they fire politically troublesome blacks and stop contributing to organizations that promote black interests; executives with whom I spoke disclaimed knowledge of such demands.

Ford has a good reputation for black personnel relations, and the reputation is confirmed by two local labor leaders, one of whom heads the company's "liaison committee," or black union. Ford gets high marks for paying blacks decently, promoting them to better jobs, and recognizing their right to organize. The committee head, John Mke, tells me a fine story about how the company conspired with black unionists to secure the dues check-off (automatic company deduction), a vital organizing tool forbidden to blacks under South African law. The only legal deduction from a black man's paycheck is for burial insurance. So the company arranged with the insurance fund serving Ford workers to deduct dues along with premiums and to rebate the dues to the committee.

"We assume the government is aware of the arrangement," says a company official blandly, "and we understand that it's expressed some reservations." Veefook Ah Shene, an officer of the colored motor assembly union, says: "Ford simply wanted to be certain that 50 percent of the black workers wanted a union. Once we showed 50 percent, they were with us."

Ford has attacked the black personnel situation with corporate gusto, drawing up a detailed ten-year plan that involves quarterly progress reports to stateside headquarters. To spur progress, it has assigned as full-time "coordinator" a white Briton named Ian Hayhoe, who is cheerfully Messianic in approach. Hayhoe will tell visitors more

than they want to hear about how Ford is adhering to the
so-called Sullivan plan, a set of principles for dealing with
black personnel to which more than 100 American firms
operating in South Africa now subscribe. [See "Case for
Doing Business in South Africa" in this section.]

In fact, Ford is in numerous respects going beyond the
guidelines—and in some cases South African law—to train
blacks for artisan positions, to place them in jobs where
they supervise whites, and to carry on a beyond-the-plant
program that is almost dazzlingly paternalistic. Under the
ten-year plan, increasing numbers of blacks and coloreds
will be trained for a broad range of desirable jobs, from
skilled technician to foreman to secretary to junior member of management. Secretarial training is now exclusively
for nonwhites, and the graduates are being assigned to
white executives, whether the executives like that or not.
The salaried staff now includes 106 nonwhites, up from 62
a year ago. A high official of Ford says a black will be at the
managerial level "within a year, and he won't be a 'show
nigger,' a guy whose picture we can put in magazines back
in the States. He'll be somebody who can and will do his
job."

Ian Hayhoe can't wait to drive me around Kwaford, the
black township in which the company has recently taken a
zealous interest (the name in Zulu means "of Ford").
Housing is Hayhoe's special pride. Some 50 units of boxy,
prefab housing have already been occupied, and 250 more
are on the way. They will include a number of "prestige"
houses—larger, more expensively built units that Ford will
offer to its expanding force of higher-paid blacks and coloreds. Ford also has a plan, awaiting government approval,
for raising mortgage money for black workers who want to
buy their houses; that is important psychologically in a
country where blacks own little, not even—by law—a piece
of land.

The emphasis on housing seems sound. With income
levels constantly rising among nonwhites in Port Elizabeth's large factories, the ability to pay for a decent house

has outstripped the ability to find one. The rest of the ex-
tracurricular efforts, including scholarships, social clubs,
and a garden club competition, have about them a paternalistic sense, as if industrial barons were trying to atone
for decades of social guilt with an instant re-creation of
American suburbia. But the blacks will tell you that they
want those suburban trappings, and who can blame them?
As a sign in a black grocery put it, "things go better with
big, big Coke."

An Afrikaner's Approach

Across town from Ford, at Firestone Tire & Rubber,
sits G. Peter Morum, a crusty Afrikaner [Dutch ruling
group] who has been with Firestone South Africa for 33
years and managing director for the past seven. Morum has
a reputation as being outspokenly against application of
the Sullivan principles to South Africa, and after a dose of
Ian Hayhoe, he seems refreshingly, if antiquatedly, sour on
the whole notion of American corporations deliberately
aiding black progress.

"Yes, I was a holdout against signing the Sullivan plan,"
Morum says, "for two reasons. First, signing is almost an
admission that you've been acting badly all these years. Second, the principles should be applied all over the world,
to the Communist countries, for instance, not just to South
Africa—and we signed with that proviso." Morum makes
clear that he gave in, last February, only after heavy pressures from the United States.

Referring to a handwritten list, Morum perfunctorily
answers my questions about Firestone's record of upgrading black wages and working conditions. It is a poor record compared to Ford's, but Morum neither apologizes for
it nor tries to make it look impressive. Asked about putting
blacks into management positions, he replies, "We have
plans, yes, but on an individual basis. My job is to make
some money for the shareholders, and all these peripheral
concerns don't help." Unlike many other top executives,
he does not give even lip service to the idea of preferential

treatment for blacks: "We'll make a conscientious effort to move them along—because of necessity. We need them in those jobs."

A Black Junior Executive

In Johannesburg, a black junior executive and I, thrown together by chance, talk for 15 minutes. Several minutes are spent feeling each other out, the rest in a rush of urgent conversation that brought home to me, as nothing else did, the emasculated half-world of the black who labors in the low echelons of US South African subsidiaries.

Now around 40, the man was the company's first salaried nonwhite. In five years with the company, he has been through a succession of training courses, but he has not been promoted and at this point doesn't expect to be. As he talks, his bitterness spills out: "I'll take my chances on merit, not preference because I'm black. But how long am I going to be held in this position? When will I be moved up, the way the whites are?"

With the lack of advancement goes lack of authority: "I am able to make so few decisions on my own, even in my area of responsibility. Often I'm not called to meetings involving our department or informed in advance about changes that affect me and my work. Even if I know that something, some way of doing things, is wrong, I must go to a white man to change it."

He talks briefly about how the white workers continue to maintain "their" toilets, despite official pronouncements to the contrary, and how the black side of the still-segregated cafeteria is "most unhygienic." But he adds quickly that these matters are trivial compared to promotion and pay scales: "I don't mind where I eat, because I know with whom I want to associate. I'm much more interested in the security of my job and my chances for advancement. You know," he says, returning to the problem of on-the-job impotence, "I don't think that's bad just for me. You feel the company is not using you for its own profit."

Then he excuses himself and leaves, and it is some time

before I remember that he called me "sir" throughout our conversation.

US Business: How Important to South Africa?

How important to South Africa is the American business presence? More important, psychologically and symbolically, than absolute numbers make it appear. American companies employ roughly 100,000 South Africans (70 percent of them black), a mere one percent of the total work force; $1.7 billion, while an impressive figure, is a similarly small portion of the total value of South African business holdings. US companies account for only 17 percent of the foreign investment in South Africa. The significance of that figure becomes clear when one considers the estimate by Arndt Spandau, a respected South African economist, that a 50 percent cut in foreign investment would produce only 90,000 unemployed and a 1.3 percent reduction in the nation's disposable income.

Drying up loans to South Africa would have a greater effect, although it would be hard to measure. Several dozen American banks, including many of the largest, have made loans to the South African government and South African industrial concerns. Some of these strengthen the nation's infrastructure and, by extension, perhaps its defensive capabilities.

A total trade embargo, as distinct from the military material sanctions now in effect, would have by far the greatest effect. According to Professor Spandau, "In 1976, a 50 percent trade boycott would have reduced South Africa's exports by nearly $5 billion. . . . More than 1.1 million people would have become unemployed." But because of domestic political pressures and US imports of vital minerals from South Africa, a total embargo is highly unlikely. As a Carter administration expert on southern Africa told me privately, "Nobody has wanted to fool with trade."

Spandau's calculations regarding withdrawal of industry are critical to a realistic assessment of American political leverage. Some zealous proponents of disinvestment have the idea that withdrawal would leave gaping holes in the South African economy. In fact, the holes would close quickly, and the biggest losers would be the Americans themselves.

Zac De Beer, a business executive and member of South Africa's liberal opposition, explains the process: "It would obviously be a buyer's market, what the Australians call 'buying back the farm.' The rest of the business community—South African firms and other multinationals—would move in looking for bargains, and the bargains would certainly be there. Normally a company sells for five to six times earnings, but in this forced-sale siuation, it might go for three or four times." Even those reduced proceeds, De Beer added, would not necessarily be bankable in the United States: "The South African government, exercising exchange control powers, would determine the degree to which General Motors, say, could move the assets recovered from the sale. The government might say, 'We'll give you your money, but it'll take you ten years to get it out.' "

South Africa's modern, sophisticated economy already has demonstrated an ability to plug holes left by faltering foreigners. Between April and July of this year, South African corporations bought controlling interests in six British firms, at a total price approaching $200 million. With the possible exception of a few high-technology industries, which do not make up a large part of the American business presence, the South Africans and other foreign companies would experience no major difficulties in absorbing abandoned plants.

This explains why Spandau's projections on unemployment are so low. Because few divested companies would close permanently, few jobs—for blacks or for whites—would be lost. The workers involved, however, would be left to the often less-tender mercies of European, Japanese, and South African top managements.

The problem of equipment that aids repression would seem a poor reason for forcing out the companies that sell it—as well as other products that are wholly apolitical.

South Africa surely can obtain computers for its secret police from companies other than IBM. The American part of the problem can be solved by adding selected items to the lists embargoed under the US Export Control Act or United Nations policy. In addition, through public pressures on stateside headquarters, corporations can be made to appreciate the social costs inherent in the sale of certain products. Polaroid terminated its South African franchise arrangements in 1977 after learning that the franchisee was selling the government film used to photograph blacks for their police passes. The same kind of public pressure, perhaps coupled with federal government sanctions, could be used to influence industrial site selection. Those arguing for disinvestment claim that some American companies at least unwittingly support the nefarious homeland scheme by locating plants in or at the edge of homeland areas.

Disinvestment and South African Blacks

Although arguments for and against disinvestment are frequently based on the alleged sentiments of South Africa's blacks, the fact is that black opinion is sharply divided. Pro-disinvestment sentiment is hard to fathom these days, because people are fearful of expressing it; but no impartial observer doubts that it exists in strength, particularly among the young and the better educated. Not surprisingly, blacks with a decent job or the prospect of one tend to value the economic opportunities that American companies represent. And some of them see well beyond pure self-interest. "If it [disinvestment] would change the government quickly, I'd say 'go ahead,'" Ford's John Mke told me. "But change will take years. In the meantime, how will we live? This is a white-dominated society, and breaking down its ways of thinking is going to take a long time."

Aside from the illogic of forcing American companies out of South Africa, is there reason to be satisfied with what they are doing there? I think the answer is yes—provided we don't misconstrue the nature or overestimate the importance of their involvement. Especially in an alien society, private enterprise is not, and cannot be made to be, an aggressive, steadfast agent for social change. A corporation is formed not to effect change but to sell goods. It can be pressured into treating its employees more equitably. But it can't be expected to openly challenge the laws and, as some would demand, the precepts of current South African society. Those who insist otherwise are trying to get a businessman to do a diplomat's—or a soldier's—job.

So, too, with the importance of American business involvement. The fact that the South African regime itself has endorsed the Sullivan principles should demonstrate conclusively that it fears little from social change in the workplace. The regime has its own, internal political strategies to spin out, and one of them calls for relaxing the strictures of so-called petty apartheid while keeping the right wing of the Nationalist party—even *more* right-wing than the ruling faction—reasonably content. If black workers care little about integrating plant cafeterias and toilets, the regime cares little more. Those who do care are reactionary white workers and their unions, and the latter exercise considerable influence in the Nationalist party. The same unions resist promotions and job training for blacks.

The regime does care, and deeply, about black trade unions and their possible use as bases for political activity. It is significant, therefore, that American companies have made the least headway in this area. Indeed, until last summer, the Sullivan principles did not even include recognition of black union rights, although full-fledged unions would themselves be able to bargain for many of the improvements that Sullivan and his cohorts want to see enacted. (Under South African law, black unions are barred from taking part in the normal industrial process.)

Even if the steps undertaken by American companies are not so daring as they might seem, they are nonetheless significant for the future of South African blacks. As America's own civil-rights advocates well understood, it is important to have the *right* to eat and go to the bathroom in common facilities, whether or not one chooses to do so. It is also important, for the long-term adjustment of the races to each other, to have blacks supervising whites, working as secretaries to white executives, and selling products to white customers. At the 3M plant, a longtime low-level black employee has been made manager of fleet operations, meaning that white salesmen who want to sell automobiles to 3M have to deal with—and please—a black man. Imagine the beneficial effect of such a position, multiplied many times over several years, on the attitudes of white middle-class South Africa.

Some of the companies' out-of-plant programs may well be as important as those within the plant. Housing is one, if only to help instill in blacks a sense of dignity and thereby raise their aspirations and expectations. Schooling is more vital still, and a good many American companies are helping to upgrade it for their black workers and the workers' children. Even Peter Morum, at Firestone, speaks warmly of his company's plan for underwriting the education of black engineering students. Less obviously self-interested is the program by which Colgate-Palmolive's South African subsidiary pays all school fees for the children of its black employees—an expense that the average employee has difficulty meeting. Colgate has "adopted" a particularly run-down school in the neighboring black township and has installed the lighting, heating, books, and even window panes that the government has not managed to provide. (Per capita expenditure for blacks in South Africa is one-sixteenth that for whites.)

Corporate efforts in behalf of working-class blacks have thus far been a good deal more laudable than those in behalf of blacks with management potential. The latter are still regarded as boys placed in a man's position—with a pat on the head and a nice notation on the charts that are sent back to stateside headquarters. But if blacks are ever to be effective participants in South African society, they must have a trained, sophisticated managerial class. Where better for that class to develop than in the ranks of American companies? With scant exception, however, the companies show no understanding of their role in developing managers. And they show an appalling blindness to the devastating effect that the give-'em-the-title-but-no-power policy has on the few black employees they do elevate.

Some blacks with whom I spoke are convinced that this corporate attitude is deliberate. But a large part of the problem, various sources told me, is that Afrikaners predominate in middle management in American corporations. Typically, a firm will have an Afrikaner personnel officer and a black assistant who is wholly dependent on him. Without the cooperation of his boss, and of the white colleagues with whom he must work, the black cannot hope to discharge the full responsibilities of his job and move up the ladder.

What US Corporations Can Do

Helen Suzman, liberal leader in Parliament and for two decades a strong voice of conscience in South Africa, admits to having vacillated over the issue of American disinvestment. Not long ago she sat in the study of her sunny, spacious Johannesburg house and mused, "It depends on what you Americans want to achieve here—reform or punishment. Disinvestment, I'm afraid, will only punish, and so will revolution. Maybe I'm too old and out of touch, but I'm not for revolution. That's not a happy end, nor, probably, is it even possible."

Indeed, in the quiet, orderly streets of Johannesburg and even in the dusty, wretched Soweto, revolution seems light-years away. White liberals abroad talk, almost wistfully, about the onset of black urban terror, but that would hardly dent a regime as powerful as South Africa's. "We're really afraid of only one thing," an articulate white salesman told me in an airport coffee shop. "That's a Russian invasion. Anything else we can handle."

Militarily, yes. But the white South Africans' fear of Russia is matched by their desperate desire for American approval (they insist that they're part of the "free world").

So the United States can exercise great influence over South African events if it hits the right pressure points in the right way and if it takes advantage of concessions the regime is willing to make. While the forced withdrawal of US corporations would be a futile gesture, the corporations should nonetheless be continually pressured to improve the lot of their black employees—in pay, in training, in job promotion, in community life, in the respect and responsibility that are due any person who does his job honestly and capably.

Pressure from the government and from private groups has produced notable results, and there is no reason to believe it won't continue to do so. It should be applied with particular firmness where a corporation's actions clearly benefit the South African regime or work to the detriment of nonwhites: making a loan to a company that produces instruments of repression, for example, or siting a new plant, without compelling reason, in a location that will foster the homelands policy.

Executives of several South African firms told me candidly that foreign companies can go a good deal farther in violating apartheid's laws of the workplace without bringing down the wrath of the regime. "A lot of us," says John McLean, former managing director of Colgate-Palmolive's subsidiary, "feel the government is quite willing to let us break down the barriers and then come along after." Break them down to a point, of course—a point whose limits are only generally discernible from the outside. Certainly the regime will balk at changes that threaten the white man's domination.

A government commission is about to recommend changes in national labor practices, and the best guesses have the commission calling for some relaxation of restrictions on black-worker organizing. Through selective, quietly applied pressures, especially from the US government and American trade unions, these boundaries can be further expanded. One might think that American corporations would be little help in this enterprise, since many of them were attracted to South Africa by its low level of effective unionization. In fact, however, a substantial number of the larger firms seem perfectly willing to recognize and deal with "real" black unions.

If that development occurs, it could prove very important to the future of South African blacks—much more important than integrated toilets or cafeterias or the elevation of an educated few into management positions. Massive amounts of black labor are essential to the South African economy, and an organized, increasingly demanding labor force can provide the foundation for political action that South African blacks have never had. It can do more. It can, as a thoughtful reader wrote the *Economist* in May, "[make] irresistible the power of the African workers to wreck the apparently monolithic grip of Afrikanerdom over the South African polity. . . ."

In the meantime, students, dissident stockholders, and other Americans with a genuine desire for change in South Africa should keep them cards and letters comin' in to the US business establishment—and to universities of their choice. Corporations in this country are increasingly vulnerable to pressure in areas of social responsibility; and, as the record in South Africa shows, the pressure produces significant changes. American business can be used as a weapon against apartheid. That is not a role businessmen relish, but they can and should be made to play it.

INVESTMENT NOT VIOLENCE[5]

Those who seek to bring about change in South Africa's racial attitudes and policies by cutting us off from the capital markets of the world should understand clearly that in practice, if not intent, they are aiming at change by violence.

[5] Article by Harry Oppenheimer, chairman of South Africa's Anglo American Corporation. *Business Week*. p 27-8. O. 9, '78. Reprinted from Business Week by special permission. © 1978 by McGraw-Hill Inc.

It would be naive in the extreme to suppose that by iso-
lating South Africa economically it would be possible to
bring about a change in mind or heart in our governing
party. Even if it did, could anything be more absurd than
to expect that a rapid changeover to majority rule, based
on one-man-one-vote, which is apparently what many of our
liberal critics aim at, would be likely to boost the confidence of foreign investors? That confidence may be at low
ebb, but it is certainly far higher than in many of the black-
ruled countries of Africa.

More than 40 percent of South Africa's population is
less than 14 years of age. This percentage is even higher
than in India or Brazil, and it is about one-third higher
than in the United States. The total population is now 26.2
million, and the most widely accepted projection into the
future suggests that the population will double between
1975 and the year 2000.

To absorb the new entrants into the labor market,
South Africa will have to create about 1,400 jobs every
working day from 1980 to 1990, and about 1,700 jobs per
working day from 1990 to the year 2000. Is it going to be
possible to create jobs on this scale, and at the same time
maintain, or as we may hope increase, the real per capita
income of the people?

According to the official Economic Development Program, the gross domestic product must grow at a rate in
excess of 5.1 percent a year to absorb the increase in the
economically-active population. This is well in excess of
the present growth rate of under three percent, and certainly cannot be attained in the near future without substantial injections of capital from abroad.

Even on the basis of a growth rate of 4.8 percent to five
percent, if the personal diaposable income per capita of the
whites were to remain unchanged in real terms or even fall
slightly, the average income per black family in real terms
would still remain below the so-called minimum living
level. Most progressive companies, including the major
American companies, who have accepted the code of em-

ployment practices drawn up by the Reverend Leon Sullivan, have undertaken to accept this living level as a guide in determining the level of minimum wages they should pay in South Africa.

What of the Sullivan Code?

What, then, are we to make of the Sullivan Code and the similar codes which have been drawn up in Europe and in South Africa itself, and which have been accepted by most progressive companies? I doubt whether in calling for the immediate establishment of minimum wages above this minimum living level, much real regard was given to the historical background of our situation, or to what the country at the present stage can afford.

Nevertheless, it is my belief that these codes do have a real value, even if it is plain from the figures that the possibility of improving the living standards of the black people to an acceptable level depends not so much on a different distribution of the national income, as on a much more rapid economic growth that can in present circumstances be envisaged.

It is surely not enough for a few large companies to soothe their consciences by using standards for their operations which cannot possibly, in the present circumstances, be of general application. They need also to accept as a conscious aim the need to do everything possible to improve the overall environment in which they work.

It would be irresponsible, even if it were possible, to insist on the universal acceptance of standards which in many industries would not at present be economic and which would result in the closing of established enterprises and further increases in the already large number of unemployed. It is better, surely, to live below the so-called minimum living level than to starve with no work or income at all.

In South Africa, as in many other developing countries, there is a dual economy. On the one hand, there is a simple subsistence sector and on the other a modern, capital-intensive sector.

Usually the apartheid policy is presented in political terms and I am sure that most of its protagonists think of it mainly in connection with the balance of political power. The system is based on the belief that it is not possible to accommodate different races and cultures within one nation or for different races to share one patriotism. There is, unfortunately, a good deal of evidence to be found around the world in support of this contention.

It follows, or so our government argues, that blacks can be allowed no share in the central government of a united South Africa but should be offered instead autonomy on a tribal basis with the right, if they wish, to secede from South Africa as fully independent states. But, if this is the political basis to the government's racial policy, there is also an economic side.

Toward a Broad Based South Africanism

The policy of separate development or apartheid implies not only a political separation between black and white, but also an economic separation. The blacks are to be denied any significant further share in the shaping of the modern, capital-intensive sector of the economy which has grown up and, with minor exceptions, undoubtedly must remain outside the tribal areas.

So long as the advanced sector of the economy is growing, it is bound to draw more and more blacks away from the rural areas to live in or near the large white cities where the major industrial development is taking place. The faster the modern sector of the economy grows, therefore, the greater the proportion of the black population that will live and work outside the homelands.

The apartheid policy really only becomes plausible to the extent that a shortage of investment capital makes it impossible to provide jobs in the advanced sector for the numbers who would wish to enter it. Thus, a high level of investment in the advanced sector, not a low level, is best calculated to end racial separation and discrimination.

Since there is no real possibility of reverting to a simpler, more labor-intensive system in the advanced sector of the economy, the main effect of a shortage of investment capital will not perpetuate the dual nature of the economy. Also, on account of the absence of sufficient job opportunities in the advanced sector, the effect will be to increase the size of the primitive subsistence sector.

The only economic situation which is compatible with apartheid is one of stagnation in which development of the modern sector of the economy is limited to a level at which the majority of the skilled work can be handled by whites and black participation is kept to a minimum.

To my mind, our only hope is to work towards a broad-based South Africanism in which tribal interests, black and white, would be merged. There is at least one major factor which works powerfully in the direction of unity and that is the growth of a strong free-enterprise economy in which black and white would, for the reasons I have touched on, necessarily have to share.

Changing South Africa's Economy

Leading companies—American, European and South African—are paying civilized wages and are undertaking to eliminate racial discrimination in employment. So far as it goes, I believe this to be a valuable contribution not only in relation to the immediate moral problem, but in helping to change the structure of the South African economy in a manner likely to promote a broad-based national unity.

The process will not go far, however, unless capital investment is available both for the public and private sectors on a scale which will enable us to provide work and higher standards in the modern sector for all who have the will and ability to enter it.

To call for higher wage rates and the end of racial discrimination in industry, while at the same time seeking to deny South Africa the capital inflow which is necessary in order to offer these conditions to the majority of the people, involves muddled thinking, if not intellectual dishonesty.

Let us be quite clear that in South Africa, poverty and apartheid belong together. The requirements of a growing modern economy call for a united effort by all South Africans, black and white. This effort cannot be reconciled with the tribal outlook, tribal fears and tribal prejudices which are at the root of the politics of apartheid.

The policy of the international banking community may be decisive in this situation. The application to South African problems of a sound business judgment is likely to do much more for the welfare and freedom of black South Africans than anything likely to be achieved by the incongruous alliance of church groups and communist-armed freedom fighters, who are so widely accepted in the world today as the leaders of opinion and formulators of policy in our sensitive and highly complicated area.

ARE BLACK UNIONS THE KEY?[6]

It is a brave man who dares write a scenario for South Africa. Yet one point which seems reasonably self-evident is that while it may be desirable for the West to exert economic pressure through such measures as, for instance, discouragement or prohibition of bank loans to South African industry, the notion that business pressure on the Vorster government will induce it to change in the foreseeable future seems fanciful. When business speaks up against government policy, the response is likely to be an unyielding one. Said Prime Minister Vorster to the Association of Chambers of Commerce a year ago: "Giving in to unreasonable requests from business organizations would be adulterating the whole political process."

Equally significant in assessing the impact of outside

[6] Article by William B. Gould, law professor at Stanford Law School, who spent several months in South Africa in 1977. *Commonweal.* 105:718-20. N. 10, '78. Copyright © 1978 Commonweal Publishing Co., Inc. Reprinted by permission.

pressure on South Africa is the improbability of involving Britain (she has 60 percent of the foreign investment there) in severe economic sanctions because of the UK's shaky economic position. This means that American pressure—to take the extreme example, withdrawal or a refusal to make future investments—can only have a long-range impact. At some point in the future, lack of access to foreign technology will make South Africa's goods less competitive. This gradual decline will inevitably affect white living standards—although the bite is likely to be felt only in conjunction with two other pressures, i.e., (1) guerrilla-type military incursions from increasingly aggressive black countries on South Africa's borders; (2) the post-Soweto exodus of professional whites—in 1977 for the first time in memory there was an outflow of whites from the country: 1,329 as opposed to an increase of 25,190 in 1976.

In the meantime, calls for American action against apartheid are likely to continue—both from countries like Nigeria (America's second largest oil supplier) and the "front line" [Angola, Mozambique, Botswana, Tanzania, Zambia] states in central and southern Africa.

My judgment is that one of the best hopes for change in South Africa is through a viable and ultimately strong labor movement, and that both the Carter administration and American unions can play an important role in shaping this process.

South Africa's black unions have a history which reaches back until about 1918. In the late-1920s the major black union had a membership of more than 100,000. After World War II the African Mineworkers Union conducted a lengthy strike which was ruthlessly crushed by the government. And in the 1950s, as well as the post-Sharpville '60s the multiracial South African Congress of Trade Unions (SACTU) was banned, most of its leadership jailed or in exile.

Today, South African labor law excludes blacks from its coverage and thus denies black unions the negotiating machinery available to white and colored (mixed blood) unions. Instead, the Bantu Labor Regulation Act of 1973 establishes plant-level works and liaison committees for blacks. These committees do not bargain about wages but rather are consulted by management on relatively unimportant matters.

But black unions are lawful—employers may enter into negotiations with them even though the law never requires them to do so. (White unions are registered and may bargain industry-wide; black unions are unregistered, unprotected by law, and may bargain company-wide.) There are 28 black unions in South Africa today with approximately 50,000 paid-up members. Their principal strength is in Johannesburg and Durban.

The Case for Black Unions

What is the case for black unions? In the first place, black unions would permit blacks to directly shape their own employment conditions—in contrast to the existing system where whites will often bargain for blacks without the latter's involvement. Although South Africa's major labor federation, the Trade Union Council of South Africa (TUSCA), admits black unions (it has flip-flopped on the issue in the past and is regarded with suspicion by many black unions as a result) its black union affiliates are "parallel" organizations, i.e., organized in industries where there are white organizations already in existence. The administration of affairs of such parallel black unions is generally handled for them by their white counterparts. This is one reason why the Johannesburg and Durban-based black unions do not desire affiliation with TUSCA.

If black unions are less subservient, they are in a position to protest against the reservation of job categories to whites by white unions. If all races have access to collective bargaining procedures the influence of numerically dwarfed white unions is likely to be diminished substantially.

Second, black unions can do much of the same in dealing with the infamous wage gap—a black-white differential, sometimes exceeding a ratio of 10:1—far more inegalitarian than anything known in this country or Western Europe.

Third, black unions will always be more effectively equipped than any outsider ever can be to assess objectively the extent to which any phasing out of discriminatory policies is satisfactory, as well as to monitor the implementation of changes.

Fourth, after the October 19 bannings, black unions are about all that is left of any representative black institution in the big cities. With some 60 individuals, 18 organizations, and three newspapers affected by the government's crackdown, there are few if any alternatives.

Finally, of course, black unions may commend themselves to anyone interested in peaceful change as an institution which would support such through nonviolent means.

The unanswered question, of course, is whether the triumphant Nationalists now possessing an unprecedented majority will crush the black unions before they can get moving. Even short of that, the problems facing black unions are formidable.

The government does all that it can to informally discourage black trade union organization. The South African Security Branch has visited plants to interrogate management officials about seminars held on plant premises in conjunction with black unions. The government can bring pressure to bear through delay or refusal to provide necessary business permits—and it is generally thought that the failure of British multinational Smith and Nephew to renew its important and innovative collective bargaining agreement with the black Textile Workers' Union was attributable to discouragement from official sources.

Moreover, detentions as well as bannings instituted against black union leaders in 1974 and 1976 have had a chilling effect on labor organization. For one thing, those who are banned not only cannot converse with more than one person at a time or be quoted or named in the press, but they are also required to give up their union work. To the extent that black unions are recognized by law, an attempt may be made by the government to subordinate them to the existing white trade union structure. If integration of union structures takes place—something which would be advertised to the West as the phasing out of segregation—some form of effective black union power and thus black majority rule would be properly required. The practical reality is that South Africa's racial history coupled with the current distrust of TUSCA means that black unions which have a voice at all levels of union-employer relationships are the best vehicle for the expression of majority rule in the unions.

Organizers' Troubles

There are yet other obstacles beyond overt government harassment. Unless unions are able to organize workers at plant facilities, they must gain access to them at their homes in the black townships. Unless the organizers are residents they must obtain permits to enter the township—permits which are unlikely to be forthcoming for trade unionists. And where the union organizers are white (a number of whites have worked with black unions) by definition, under the Group Areas Act, which requires that each racial group must live in its own area, such organizers cannot lawfully enter the township without authorization. (In Soweto, race rather than residency determines whether one must gain permission to enter.)

Equally troublesome for black unions is the requirement that an unregistered union under law cannot negotiate check-off provisions which permit employees to authorize the deduction of union dues from their paycheck. This means that union representatives must spend valuable time collecting this money on their own initiative and thus the inability to provide a steady income flow to the union treasury—and this in turn makes it difficult to provide services which are the *sine qua non* for gaining new members.

Penultimately, although black workers not employed in

essential services have had the legal right to strike since 1973, the hard reality is that this is not a right which exists in practice. Before striking, blacks must wait for the expiration of a 30-day cooling off period. Since most black strikes are spontaneous and without any kind of formal union authorization, this means that most do not even meet the cooling off period requirement. But even after the cooling off period, the government can delay the strike indefinitely. When a strike is unlawful, the workers are quickly imprisoned and bail is often denied.

Even in the unlikely event that all of the problems set forth above were dealt with adequately through reform, it is doubtful whether black labor unions will ever gain real strength until the migratory labor system is altered. Under the laws which support it, no black worker may be in "white" South Africa more than 72 hours unless: (1) he was born there; (2) has lived there for 15 consecutive years or been employed by one employer for 10 consecutive years; (3) obtained special permission from government authorities. At least half of the existing black work force falls into category (3) —and this coupled with an embargo on black women in white areas means that such blacks are employed on a contract labor basis and are therefore temporary sojourners.

In such circumstances, if a black worker displeases an employer—or worse yet strikes—he can be immediately "endorsed out" of the white area and sent to the tribal "homeland" in rural South Africa. But there is no work in the homelands. The power held by management means that blacks will always be uncertain and insecure—and thus reluctant to protest employment conditions in any manner.

Meanwhile, black unions must tread a narrow path between the apolitical stance they currently adopt for obvious reasons and growing militancy.

Black trade unionists have been militant enough to disassociate themselves from white trade union opposition to the boycott of South African goods. At the same time they do not promote or support general boycotts on the ground that their members will be the first to be hurt. But a new tide of radicalism amongst black South Africans—engendered in large part by government policies—could easily push them aside as defenders of the system. If, on the other hand, such trade unionists stress their unwillingness to temporize with apartheid they may find themselves behind bars. But even if this happens, active encouragement of black unions will have been worth the effort because the experience and skills gained will be critical to the construction of a new South Africa (or Azania, as black nationalists call it) when union leaders emerge from prison.

What of the Long Run?

Obviously, speculation about the role of black unions must look to the long-run. Yet in the short-run the fact that several progressive and far-sighted employers seem willing to deal with black unions because of some managements' preference for industrial peace and a rational dialogue provide some basis for optimism. (Between 1971 and 1975 there were nearly 600 unlawful strikes by black workers.) Harry Oppenheimer's Anglo-American Corporation conglomerate—it has more of an impact on the South African economy than does any company in the US on our own economy—has announced a policy in support of bargaining with black labor organizations. Both Ford Motor Company and the Swedish multinational SKF have agreed to a modified form of "check-off" with the black Auto and Rubber Workers' Union—though not fullfledged collective bargaining itself. South African business organizations like the Johannesburg Urban Foundation, established in the wake of the Soweto riots, have recently developed codes on their own and called for collective bargaining with the black unions. And finally, Mr. Oppenheimer has facilitated the establishment of an Institute of Industrial Relations which brings black and moderate white union leaders together with management.

There are other encouraging signs. Discussions are proceeding with a view toward establishing a South African

Black Federation—because of the unacceptability of the Trade Union Council of South Africa or the South African Confederation of Labor.

In any case, the demand for black unions will not go away easily—before or after the new detentions. The work force becomes more exclusively black with each passing day. Black strikes continue, even though they are generally unlawful, and it is quite possible that labor is a field in which the government may give some ground grudgingly, albeit not much, on the theory that political rights and the vote are not at stake, but rather the dictates of economic reality—and that if black union leaders become interested in politics they can always be locked up in due course.

Outside pressure effectively applied could help to tip the scales toward the black worker. Financial assistance of church groups and international trade union secretariats based in Europe has thus far permitted independence from TUSCA and allowed these unions to seek bargaining for themselves as autonomous organizations as a first order of business. Last year, the European Economic Community announced the formulation of a Code which, while without force of law, requires its multinationals in South Africa to recognize representative black unions and to facilitate their organizational efforts. This Code, promoted by British Foreign Secretary David Owen, could serve as a model for a Carter administration willing and able to match its words with action.

The Carter administration could follow suit and live up to its own rhetoric by fashioning a code of conduct which requires American multinationals to both eliminate discriminatory practices and to recognize representative black unions as a condition of doing business in South Africa. Already, approximately 50 American companies with promotion facilities in the Republic have agreed to a private code of sorts developed by the Reverend Leon Sullivan. The difficulty is that the Sullivan principles are so amorphous that virtually any company will assert that it is now and has been complying with them. Moreover, until late this summer, the "principles" did not even address the specific issue of employer recognition of black trade unions.

As previously noted, Ford and SKF have accepted a modified check-off which allows for a percentage of monies deducted to be remitted to the black union, the remainder going to a benefit insurance scheme. The Carter administration should require American multinationals to take this tentative first step toward full-blown collective bargaining.

What of American Labor's Help?

The American labor movement could assist South Africa's black unions through a number of measures. In the first place, both the AFL-CIO and unions which are not affiliated with it, like the influential United Auto Workers, can provide much needed organizational and negotiating skills through courses, and seminars which can be held in southern Africa, if not South Africa itself. Direct financial assistance—European unions have already given some—can be provided. The AFL-CIO, which until late 1977 kept itself at arm's length from the black unions, announced its willingness to consider "selective" product boycotts of South African goods at its Los Angeles Convention. Black trade unionists from that country were fraternal delegates at the convention.

The same frustrations and hopes that are felt with regard to the total South African picture have relevance to the struggle by black labor in that country. With weapons and technology in the hands of the ruling whites, blacks have faith only in themselves and in their numbers—a faith which is based in substantial part upon what they have seen transpire in Angola and Mozambique. So long as whites have collective bargaining rights and blacks do not, the dualistic system will engender bitterness. So long as so many black pay-packages remain below the South African poverty line, the same grievances which produced the '73 Durban strikes will continue to fester. For the lesson of the South African black protest is that despite periodic silencing, the revolt against racial injustices can never be fully quelled. With or without attendant violence—and the smart betting is that violence of some kind must take place before South Africa will change—black unions provide a positive feature on an otherwise dreary horizon.

US COLLEGES AND SOUTH AFRICA INVESTMENTS[7]

Efforts are under way to organize a national coalition to press colleges and universities to withdraw their investments from corporations operating in racially segregated South Africa.

Intensified action seeking divestiture of such investments will be on the agenda at regional meetings this month at the University of Michigan and New York University.

Plans are being discussed for a "national week of action" on the South African issue. It is tentatively scheduled next March.

In other recent developments:

—Representatives of 18 colleges and universities met in New York to exchange information on how and whether they should sponsor shareholder resolutions on South African issues.

—Vassar College trustees voted unanimously to drop their institution's investments in five banks that had made loans to South Africa.

—Michigan State University trustees who had voted for divestiture received a legal opinion from university counsel indicating that they might be held personally liable for reduced investment earnings.

—Several hundred students rallied, marched, and held

[7] Article entitled "Colleges Face Greater Pressure to Bar South Africa Investments," by Jack Magarell, senior editor. *Chronicle of Higher Education.* 17:9-10. N. 6, '78. Copyright © 1978 by Editorial Projects for Education, Inc. Reprinted by permission.

a candlelight vigil during the October meeting of Cornell University's trustees, opposing investments involving South Africa.

Vietnam Issue of the Late 70s

Investment of college and university funds in American corporations doing business in South Africa has been the focal point of increasing student protests against the apartheid policies of the South African government.

The issue has become the most prominent of the few areas of campus activism remaining in the post-Vietnam era.

"The divestiture movement is developing into the Vietnam issue of the late 1970s," said a Midwestern leader of the movement, Dennis Brutus.

Mr. Brutus, an exiled black South African who is now a professor of English at Northwestern University, said last week that "the movement is growing with increasing rapidity." He said he expected the campaign against South African investments to intensify in the year ahead.

A similar, though more guarded, assessment is found in a report just completed by the Investor Responsibility Research Center in Washington. The center, a non-profit research organization, was established in 1972 with support from foundations, universities, and other institutions to provide impartial reports on social and public-policy issues that they face as investors.

More Colleges Consider Divestiture

In the center's report, David M. Liff, an IRRC policy analyst, concludes that there is a growing willingness among colleges and universities and other investors to consider divestiture, at least on a selective basis and usually as a last resort in cases where a corporation fails to demonstrate good intentions in its South African operations.

"Few schools seem eager, however, to sell any of their South-Africa-related holdings at this point," Mr. Liff says, "because the financial ramifications of such a policy appear ominous in the absence of proven alternative investment programs."

Mr. Liff says most campus groups pressuring institutions to drop their investments in corporations operating in South Africa believe US corporations should withdraw from South Africa to put pressure on the white government to adopt reforms to aid the country's black majority.

Although only a few institutions have advocated the withdrawal of American corporations from South Africa, the number taking that position has grown in the past year and could increase further, the IRRC report says.

"By endorsing either complete or partial withdrawal of US investment, these schools have provided a certain respectability to a point of view that most parties concerned with South Africa considered to be extreme and unsupportable several years ago," the IRRC report says.

About 25 colleges and universities and about 15 trade unions were represented at a meeting at Northwestern University last month on South African investments, Mr. Brutus reported.

Jailed in Olympic-Team Dispute

Those at the meeting called for intensified action on the issue of divestiture, endorsed the idea of a "national week of action" in March, and urged the building of a national group to coordinate efforts of campus, community, church, and labor organizations.

Mr. Brutus was chosen at the October meeting to convene a meeting in Ann Arbor on November 12 [1978]. An attempt will be made, he said, to set up a continuing steering committee with more than 100 members to plan future divestiture campaigns.

South African authorities jailed Mr. Brutus in 1963 for organizing a protest against South Africa's all-white team's participation in the Olympic games. After two years in prison and one year under house arrest, he was allowed to leave the country under the threat of being sent to prison again if he should ever return. He has been on the Northwestern faculty the past six years.

Mr. Brutus said the Midwest committee would seek to establish links with similar groups on the West Coast and with the already organized Northeast Coalition for the Liberation of Southern Africa.

The latter group held its first meeting in April and now includes divestiture groups from about 48 campuses, a spokesman said.

The coalition has scheduled a meeting on November 17–19 at New York University. Eric Perkins, an organizer of NYU's divestiture organization, said about 1,500 people were expected to attend the regional meeting.

Sponsoring Shareholder Resolutions

Representatives from 18 institutions met last month at New York's Union Theological Seminary to consider the effectiveness and appropriateness of sponsoring shareholder resolutions on the South African issue.

Although resolutions sponsored by shareholders usually receive little support at corporations' annual meetings and have little or no direct impact on management, such resolutions have served to draw attention to social and public-policy issues.

Traditionally, colleges and universities automatically voted with management, but in recent years an increasing number, usually at the urging of campus pressure groups, have voted their shares in favor of shareholder resolutions that were opposed by corporate management.

Last year, for the first time, a few colleges and universities went beyond the support of shareholder resolutions and themselves sponsored or co-sponsored resolutions.

The meeting at Union Theological Seminary was sponsored by Bryn Mawr and Haverford Colleges to provide an exchange of information among institutions that might consider sponsoring shareholder resolutions.

Joseph S. Johnston, assistant to the president at Bryn

Mawr, said there had been no attempt at the meeting to form a coalition or to plan concerted action. The purpose, he said, was to give interested institutions information they might need in making their own decisions.

The trustees of Michigan State University, at their regular meeting next week, will face the problem of how to carry out the divestiture policy they adopted last spring.

The trustees announced in March that in December they would begin a program of "prudent divestment" of stock in firms doing business in South Africa unless they demonstrated that they were planning to withdraw from that country.

When asked if they would withdraw from South Africa, all of the corporations contacted by Michigan State said, more or less emphatically, No.

The trustees last summer asked their lawyers for an opinion on whether they could divest themselves of stock related to South Africa and still meet the legal requirement that they manage university funds in a prudent manner.

In September, the legal opinion came back: The trustees' fiduciary duty was to protect the principal and maximize the return of university funds. To place social or political considerations ahead of financial interests might be construed as a breach of their public trust, the opinion said.

If divestiture were so considered, the opinion added, the trustees might then be held personally and collectively liable for any damages incurred.

Lower Yield Predicted

At the lawyers' suggestion, the trustees then asked their investment advisers whether they could divest and still manage the investment portfolio prudently.

At their October meeting, the trustees were told by the advisers that prudence in investment is a legal question. Financially, they said, it could be estimated that the elimination of investments in corporations operating in South Africa would reduce the university's long-term yield on investments by about 1.1 percent.

At that point, the trustees asked the university administration to explore the possibilities of putting university funds into federal securities or some other form of investment as an alternative to common stocks.

Vassar College's trustees announced at their October meeting that they were withdrawing investments in bonds of five banks because it appeared after investigation that they had made loans to South Africa's government or government agencies and intended to continue doing so.

A Vassar official said the bank bonds to be sold had a market value of about $2.25 million.

The trustees, in announcing their unanimous decision, said that although ordinarily "only economic reasons will be the basis for investment of Vassar funds," rare instances may occur in which overriding social concerns will lead to a moral consensus of such intensity in the Vassar community that treatment of investments must take into account that concern in addition to economic return."

No Wholesale Divestiture

"The trustees believe," they continued, "that wholesale divestment represents a simplistic response to the plight of the black South African and ignores the range of available alternative strategies, including voting shareholder resolutions and associating with others to initiate shareholder resolutions.

A policy of highly selective divestment after careful study and interaction with the corporations may be effective in encouraging change in South Africa. We also believe only individual actions based on detailed analysis would satisfy the prudence required by our legal responsibilities as managers of the funds left in our trust.

The banks whose bonds Vassar decided to sell were identified as BankAmerica, Export-Import Bank, First National Bank of Chicago, Charter New York Corp., and Manufacturers Hanover Trust Corp.

Cornell University trustees are not expected to adopt a formal policy on investments related to South Africa until early next year after getting a report from their advisory committee, but their regular October meeting on campus touched off student demonstrations.

A university spokesman said about 300 students advocating divestiture had participated in rallies and demonstrations outside buildings in which the trustees met.

IV. SOUTHERN AFRICA'S RELATIONS WITH THE WORLD

EDITOR'S INTRODUCTION

Aware of world opinion on the matter of *apartheid*, the government of South Africa under President John Vorster has sought to counteract its image through a series of extraordinary steps that included the bribing of key foreign figures to influence world opinion and the secret financing of a newspaper to influence opinion at home. Despite the scandal raised by the revelations of these activities and Vorster's resignation on June 4, 1979, the South African government, with P. W. Botha as president, seems firm in its present course, even as it casts a wary eye on developments in Rhodesia and Namibia. South Africa is not yet ready to accept basic reform in her social system, in at least some aspects of *apartheid*, such as the hated pass laws. The country's attitude toward its neighbors is discussed in the first selection by J. E. Spence, writing in *World Today*, and how Britain is handling this recalcitrance is examined next by Colin Legum, writing in *New Society*.

As far as the United States is concerned, its policy toward South Africa has been influenced by political, economic, and strategic forces. In this section's third article, Richard Bissell, in *Current History*, describes how a change in administration in this country has brought about a renewal of commitment to human rights and a new demand for reform in South Africa. However, as Stephen Zunes then points out in the *Progressive*, our economic considerations tend to close the eyes of many to the evils of apartheid. In addition, by facilitating South Africa's acquisition of the atom bomb, as revealed by Robert Manning and Stephen Talbot in their article in *Inquiry,* we have strengthened not only white South Africa's security, but also its racial intransigence as well. For economic reasons, too, the Congress passed the Byrd Amendment in 1971 to circumvent the embargo of Rhodesia and to allow the importation of Rhodesian chromium despite the economic sanctions imposed by the United Nations after Rhodesia's unilateral declaration of independence from Great Britain in 1965. A possible shift in our position on Rhodesia is the subject of the next two excerpts, interviews with Senators Hayakawa and McGovern, in *U.S. News & World Report.*

At present, American policy toward the nations of southern Africa seems to be preoccupied with the Communist influence, particularly in the light of Communist incursions in Angola and Mozambique. In the last two articles in this section, both Sol Sanders and Richard Payne, in *Newsweek* and *Africa Today,* indicate that our policy has been and continues to be dictated by Soviet and Cuban initiative. Our strategy involves renewing our human rights pledge and accommodating guerrilla demands in order to avoid greater armed conflict that would be an invitation to Communist intervention.

SOUTH AFRICA'S FOREIGN POLICY[1]

The selection of a new prime minister by the Nationalist party caucus provides an opportunity to review current South African perceptions of events in Africa during the last two years, and—in a more general sense—analyze the changing position of the Republic in the wider spectrum of international politics.

To put the issues involved in some historical perspective, it is worth remarking that Mr. P. W. Botha comes to

[1] Article entitled "South African Foreign Policy: Changing Perspectives," by J. E. Spence, chairman, department of politics at Leicester University, England. *World Today.* 34:417-25. N. '78. © Royal Institute of International Affairs 1978. Reprinted by permission.

power in circumstances very different from those attending his predecessor's election to office in 1966. Twelve years ago the Republic had clearly recovered from the economic dislocation induced by the post-Sharpeville crisis [demonstration against pass laws by Pan-African Congress]; indeed, the country's growth rate was often favorably compared with the phenomenal success of Germany and Japan in staging economic revival. Internal security seemed assured with the collapse of the underground remnants of the African National Congress and the Pan African Congress, while in the realm of foreign policy the government had begun its first tentative steps towards dipomatic and political accommodation with its black counterparts to the north. Mr. Vorster, despite an image as the "Iron Man" of South African politics, seemed a more pragmatic figure than his predecessor, Dr. Verwoerd, and the white electorate appeared confident that the effects of continued economic development, coupled with the inability of the outside world to undermine white supremacy, would produce long-term political solutions in keeping with the Republic's traditional attitudes to race relations.

Mr. Vorster, however, passes on a legacy much less comforting to his successor: the economy has not sustained the high promise of the late 1960s and early 1970s and like that of virtually every other Western state has fallen victim to the twin evils of inflation and unemployment. It is true that there are few outside observers willing to predict the collapse of the apartheid state through internal revolution, external pressures or a combination of both in the short term, but the shock administered to the political system by the Soweto disturbances in 1976, together with recent developments in Rhodesia and Namibia, have meant that there is far less confidence abroad about the Republic's capacity to survive unscathed over the long term (say, five to ten years) —a time-scale which may well shorten as events in southern Africa gather momentum.

With regard to foreign policy, the détente initiative so

confidently launched by Mr. Vorster in 1974, with all the promise of a corresponding relaxation of internal rigidity, floundered in the ill-conceived Angolan intervention and none of the original parties involved among the "front line" states has made any serious attempt to revive it. Worse still, Mr. Botha inherits a breakdown in negotiations with the United Nations over the pace and scope of de-colonization in Namibia, and the possibility that sanctions may be imposed to compel the Republic to conform to the requirements put forward in the Secretary-General's report to the Security Council. There is, too, the added complication presented by events in Rhodesia; these threaten to overwhelm the best efforts of those—whether in Pretoria, Washington or London—to halt the war, which, if allowed to escalate uncontrollably, raises the spectre of Cuban intervention and a South African counter-response.

What may we expect of Mr. Botha in these circumstances? In domestic terms, it is hard to see any major shift in government policy. Twenty years ago, the choice as Prime Minister of the leader of the party in the Cape Province might have suggested a swing to the more *verligte* (enlightened) wing of the Nationalist party. On this occasion some commentators have suggested that, despite his tough stance on external affairs, Mr. Botha shares the *verligte* assumptions about domestic policy characteristic of his Cabinet colleagues, Dr. Piet Koornhof, the Minister for Sport, and Mr. Pik Botha, the Foreign Minister. Yet while there is some evidence that Mr. Botha has always regarded the aspirations of the Colored community with a degree of sympathy (hence the role assigned to him as one of the chief architects of the new two-tier constitutional structure to take effect in 1981), his commitment to the homelands policy is absolute and he is not on record as displaying any pronounced sympathy for the plight of the urban African. Indeed, the rejection by the party caucus of the claims of his two rivals in the contest for the leadership—Dr. Connie Mulder and Mr. Pik Botha—both of whom have demonstrated *verligte* tendencies in the past, suggests that the party as a whole wanted a leader who would take a stern, uncompromising stand on relations with the outside world, and by definition resist external pressures to make significant internal reforms.

The Namibian Issue

In the external arena, the most immediate problem is that of Namibia. At first sight, Mr. Botha might seem to have little room for maneuvre, given the blunt rejection by his predecessor (on 20 September 1978) of the Secretary-General's report, and in particular the latter's insistence that the size of the United Nations force be increased to 7,500, that a 360-strong police component be introduced and, finally, that the election date be deferred well into 1979. On the other hand, given Mr. Botha's standing in the Cabinet and his crucial role as a "hawkish" Minister of Defense, it is reasonable to conclude that Mr. Vorster's rejection of the Report had his full backing—if indeed he was not the main opponent of any further concessions to the United Nations. With South Africa's traditional distrust of the United Nations, and its scepticism about the latter's ability to act impartially in the delicate period leading to the goal of independence, it is hardly surprising that Pretoria should view a 7,500-strong UN contingent as an "operational peace-keeping force, or an occupational force."

What the government fears is that a UN presence of this size would in effect be strong enough to legitimate any and every action taken by the South-West Africa People's Organization (SWAPO) to extend its influence throughout the territory by whatever means. In other words, the South African government, which has an obvious interest in electoral victory for the non-SWAPO parties, regards the establishment of a large UN presence as clear evidence of a United Nations intention to reduce Pretoria's role to a minimum in the transfer of power to an independent Namibia. This is evident from Mr. Vorster's allegation that the Secretary-General's Special Representative was guilty of "lack of consultation with the Administrator-General of

the territory" during his visit in August to lay the ground-
work for UN participation. Thus Pretoria drew the in-
ference that its administrative structure in the territory
would have little, if any, share in the decision-making
process in the period before and after the pre-independence
elections. In these circumstances, the government concluded, only SWAPO could benefit.

The Security Council's endorsement in late September
of the Secretary-General's Report and the implicit threat
of sanctions if South African compliance was not forthcoming present the new Prime Minister with his first major test in foreign policy. Both Mr. Vorster in his valedic-
tory statement of 20 September and the terms of the
Security Council's Resolution of 29 September 1978 left
open the possibility of further negotiations between the Republic and the so-called "contact" group of the five Western
powers. Whether Mr. Botha, whose appeal to the Nationalist party was largely based on his past record of intransigence in dealing with South Africa's external difficulties, is
capable of flexibility on the Namibian issue can only be a
matter of speculation at this stage. What is clear is that
many in the ruling elite are convinced that, in the last
analysis, no amount of concessions on specific issues such as
Namibia to the demands of their critics abroad will favorably affect their long-term position in the sense that such
concessions will be interpreted as evidence of weakness and
only accelerate ultimate confrontation on the fundamental
issue of apartheid itself.

It could, of course, be argued that Mr. Vorster's willingness to agree to a United Nations-sponsored transfer of
power in April 1978 was in itself a major concession, a first
major step in the ultimate transformation of southern
Africa in the direction of black majority rule. But this
thesis requires qualification on a number of grounds: (1)
agreement in principle to de-colonize Namibia would not,
in Pretoria's view, indicate a weakening of commitment to
maintain white supremacy in the Republic; (2) an "independent" Namibia under the rule of, for example, the

Democratic Turnhalle Alliance would presumably be sympathetic to "co-existence" with South Africa and, more important, maintain the existing economic linkages; (3) in strategic terms, it would be more sensible to regard the Republic's defensive perimeter as coterminous with traditional state boundaries rather than face a commitment of troops to a counter-insurgency campaign, which would not only complicate relations with neighboring states such as Angola and Zambia but also has the added and more profound disadvantage of weakening South Africa's efforts to maintain a relationship with the West, free of precisely the diplomatic and military tensions that have arisen over the Namibian issue in the more recent past.

Some observers have claimed that South Africa's willingness to accept the Western plan for Namibian independence was simply a confidence trick, designed to impress upon the five-power contact group its good faith, but in reality a gamble on the assumption that SWAPO would ultimately find the proposals unacceptable and leave South Africa in a position to pose as the morally aggrieved party. The evidence of the South African attack on the SWAPO base at Kassinga in Angola (in which 600 people were killed) is cited in support of this view. The truth in matters of this kind can rarely be established with any degree of authority; it may simply be that Pretoria wanted to impress upon SWAPO the strength of its commitment to prevent a military "revolutionary" solution should SWAPO elect to pursue this option rather than one involving a negotiated transfer of power. (In this context, the bombing of North Vietnam by the Nixon administration during the Paris peace negotiations is an analogy that readily comes to mind.)

Yet, whatever interpretation is placed on South Africa's motives for initially accepting the Western proposals and then ultimately rejecting them, there remains the strong possibility that Mr. Botha will be willing to risk the threat of sanctions on the ground that the Western powers will draw back from a strategy, the political and economic consequences of which are at best uncertain and at worst damaging to the existing pattern of trade, investments and, more important, to continued access to vital strategic raw materials of which South Africa is a major repository. Even selective sanctions (on oil, for example) present difficulties: the Republic has long been aware of this particular threat and has taken measures to stockpile oil to support its indigenous production from coal.

Furthermore, any decision to impose sanctions will not make its impact in the short term and in itself reflects the dilemma facing the outside world in trying to find refined and appropriate external instruments for inducing a change of policy in a state, the history and political culture of which have long inured it to survival in a hostile environment. Indeed, Mr. Botha's determination to resist the clamor for concessions on the Namibian issue (and any others that may arise during his Premiership) may be strengthened by the conviction that it is better to face the worst now rather than give way in the knowledge that "appeasement" of the United Nations over Namibia can only be a prelude to greater pressures in due course on the more crucial and fundamental issue of apartheid.

The Rhodesian Issue

Since the collapse of the Geneva Conference nearly two years ago, the South African government appears to have played a relatively passive role in such private negotiations as have continued to promote a settlement between the Patriotic Front and the Interim government in Salisbury. The increase in the scope of the guerrilla war, the stalemate on the political front (despite the efforts of John Grahame, the British Foreign Office Representative, and the United States Ambassador, Stephen Low), together with the perception of Robert Mugabe, the Zanu leader, as a Marxist revolutionary, bent on the violent destruction of Rhodesia's economic and political structures, have induced a mood of disillusion in Pretoria about the likelihood of a negotiated transfer of power from white to black. Mr. Botha was, after all, a witness to Mr. Vorster's efforts to bring the warring parties to the conference table, and the failure of the resulting talks hardly provides him with an incentive to renew the offer to use South Africa's good offices in helping to achieve a settlement. Indeed, there is some evidence that Mr. Vorster welcomed the establishment of the Interim government, but its lack of success in establishing a cease-fire and winning international credibility has contributed to the Republic's withdrawal from an active diplomatic role.

South Africa's policy-makers find themselves in a dilemma over Rhodesia. Even if they were willing—at the behest of the United States and the United Kingdom—to cut off economic support for the Smith regime, there would be no guarantee that a successor government—the product of negotiation, but dominated by the Patriotic Front—would be one which Pretoria felt it could live with, especially if the changeover was accompanied or followed by a prolonged period of civil strife in which the lives and property of the white minority came to be at risk. Pressure on Mr. Botha to intervene would mount from the *verkrampte* (hardline) elements of the white electorate on the grounds that a decisive defeat of South Africa's "enemies" abroad would be more sensible than to wait passively for the inevitable incursion of freedom fighters from the sanctuary of a newly liberated Marxist-dominated Zimbabwe. But a strategy of this kind would conceivably call forth a Cuban counter-response and a widening of the conflict beyond limits which South Africa, despite its large and sophisticated military capability, would regard as tolerable. On the other hand, if events are passively allowed to take their course and the Rhodesian issue is settled by the gun rather than at the conference table, the incentive to intervene remains the same, as conceivably do the consequences resulting from such a course of action.

In other words, the time has passed when South Africa could confidently bank on a policy of active support for Western pressure on the Smith regime producing a society in which the values of political order, economic development and co-existence with the Republic would inevitably prevail over those making for disorder and hostility to the Republic, which it now—correctly or incorrectly—perceives to be the likely outcome if the current trend of violence maintains its momentum.

South Africa and the Carter Administration

In any case, the international climate in which the Vorster-Kissinger strategy was formulated in 1976 has altered radically since the Carter administration came to power: the southern African policy of the Ford administration was compatible with South African interests in the sense that Kissinger's brief encounter with southern African realities explicitly demonstrated the conservatism that has underpinned traditional Western strategies in this area. Believing that there are no final solutions to the problems that beset the statesmen in international politics, that all that can be done is to "patch up" holes in the fabric of international society in the certain knowledge that such partial solutions will inevitably generate new crises in due course, it is hardly surprising that Dr. Kissinger saw the three problem areas of southern Africa (Rhodesia, Namibia and the Republic) as compartmentalized into distinct and to a large degree separate issues.

Pragmatism demanded that Rhodesia be dealt with first in the hope that a settlment there would encourage one in Namibia; South African help was required if these objectives were to be achieved—hence a willingness on Kissinger's part to place the South African problems on the "back-burner," a policy which suited Mr. Vorster's government in so far as it appeared to give the latter the status of an influential and detached protagonist working closely in cooperation with the Western powers and to a degree compensating for the collapse of detente and the debacle of the Angolian intervention. Indeed there is some evidence that Mr. Vorster expected (and was probably promised) a variety of quid pro quos for his assistance: ultimate recognition of the Transkei, more sympathetic treatment on the issues of arms sales and a more pronounced willingness to defend the Republic's policies at the United Nations.

By contrast, the Carter administration (and Dr. David Owen) have recognized that the conflict between black and white in southern Africa cannot be broken into neat, discrete elements; that it has a dangerous potential to spill across national boundaries; that "solutions" in Rhodesia and Namibia—whether the product of negotiation or successful drawn-out revolutionary violence—will hardly confine their effects to the territories in question, but will have an immense psychological impact on the large, dispossessed black majority in South Africa. In practice, no doubt, US and UK policy will operate pragmatically, but it is noteworthy that events have forced both governments to proceed simultaneously with attempts to (1) persuade SWAPO to adopt the Western plan for decolonization of that territory and (2) to bring the rival groupings in Rhodesia together before the guerrilla war gets completely out of hand.

South African assistance, it is true, is still required if both ventures are to succeed, but Mr. Vorster and presumably his successor (judging from outbursts over the last year directed at the Carter administration) know very well that the Republic cannot expect to escape unscathed following any such fundamental changes in the status and political structure of the two territories on its northern borders. And the greater urgency in forming Washington's policy towards southern Africa (in contrast to the relative passivity of earlier administrations) is made all the more disturbing for Pretoria by the knowledge that it is dealing with an American government which is trying to reassert a genuine concern for human rights wherever these are in jeopardy—i.e. a concern to revive a liberal tradition of American foreign policy that can be traced back to Woodrow Wilson. The more cynical would point to President Carter's electoral dependence on a large domestic black constituency as the prime explanation for the shift in policy from that of his Nixonite predecessors; but whatever the motivation behind this policy, there can be no doubting

that southern Africa has assumed the status and the proportions of a major foreign policy priority for the United
States government.

Perspectives on Communist Penetration

South Africa's reactions to the spectacle of Soviet gains
in Ethiopia and the anti-government rebellion in Zaire
have been predictably hostile and it is significant that it was
Mr. Botha (then Minister of Defense) who led the attack
on the pusillanimity of the Western powers in the face of
Communist expansion. In May 1978, he made it abundantly clear that his government regarded both these developments as clear evidence of a "global Communist strategy to conquer the whole of southern Africa, seize its wealth
and control the Cape sea route." Later in the month, he
claimed that unless the free world stopped inexorable en-
slavement of Africa by Marxism, the continent would become totally exploited by "the games of the super-powers."

It should be remembered that it was Mr. Botha who in
the period 1968–70 engaged in a bitter debate with Mr.
Dennis Healey, the Labor government Minister of Defense,
about the "correct" interpretation of the Simonstown
Agreement [giving Britain naval base at tip of Africa]. He
has been in the forefront of these who claim that the Republic is a vital bastion of Western security in the southern
oceans. Throughout the late 1960s and early 1970s, Pretoria
continually stressed the value of the Simonstown base, the
Republic's well-equipped ports and harbors, and the value
of its extensive military capability to the Western Alliance.
This, of course, was part of a wider political strategy to
promote a greater degree of integration with the West on
the assumption that an ever-increasing network of economic and military linkages would actively inhibit any attempt by Western governments to disassociate themselves
from South Africa. In the military field, the argument made
little impression on Western policy-makers, and until the
evidence of growing Soviet influence in the Horn and else-

where presented itself, the Republic appeared to have let the argument about its value go by default in the hope that ultimately its predictions about Communist subversion would come true and lead to a transformation of Western attitudes.

Yet the growth of a Soviet presence in Africa has coincided with the emergence of an American administration that—for a variety of reasons—declines to counter Russian moves in kind. Thus a renewal of South African claims to be taken seriously by the West as an ally in the struggle against an expanding Communism (and this has been the burden of recent speeches by Mr. Botha and his senior military advisers) is not likely to impress an American audience which believes that the appropriate response to a Soviet build-up in Africa should be diplomatic and economic rather than military in scope. It is this profound difference in principle between Washington and Pretoria which—if it persists—is likely to lead the new Prime Minister into a determined effort to make a virtue out of South Africa's growing isolation; we can expect an increasing preoccupation with the needs of military security, and, in particular, a determination to gird South Africa's defenses to deal with the threat of guerrilla incursions from neighboring independent states.

In circumstances of growing isolation, the garrison state option will look increasingly attractive with all that it implies negatively for any prospect of internal change of a reformist kind. Finally, it is conceivable that the constraints against an open declaration of nuclear weapon status will weaken as policy-makers in Pretoria search for any means available to strengthen their image of impregnability. The new Prime Minister, after all, spent twelve years as Minister of Defense; it would hardly be surprising if "the worst case analysis" in a military sense had more appeal than the intangible and uncertain benefits to be derived from following a more flexible diplomacy abroad and a *verligte* strategy of reform at home.

WHAT BRITISH POLICY ON RHODESIA?[2]

The publication, this week, of the well-perceived Bingham report on the operation of the oil embargo against Rhodesia has coincided with a sharpened public awareness that the British government cannot much longer postpone taking some difficult decisions to avert a final disaster in its rebellious colony. Not only has Ian Smith now admitted that Rhodesia has entered the worst period of its crisis, but that he has no further ideas about what to do about the situation—except to hang on. The measure of his desperation is shown by his willingness to accept, at long last, that it might be worth considering a "return to legality"—that is, to hand back to Britain the responsibility for getting Rhodesia out of the terrible mess created by his policies.

It is important that the desperate new crisis over Rhodesia should not be allowed to overshadow the importance of the considerable scandal disclosed by the Bingham report (*Report on the Supply of Petroleum and Petroleum Products to Rhodesia*, T. H. Bingham, QC, and S. M. Gray, FCA, available from the Foreign Office, unpriced). It clearly establishes a prima-facie case for legal action against some prominent oil executives, and perhaps others.

The Bingham report, however, does not deal with the political aspects of the evasion of oil sanctions. The defense offered by the oil companies is that their activities had been disclosed to successive Labour and Conservative administrations and that any wrongdoings, of which they now stand accused, were not only known to, but assented to, by the governments of the day.

It is clearly important that the truth should be established by a further inquiry—preferably under the Tribu-

² From article entitled "Rhodesia in Turmoil," by Colin Legum, editor. *New Society.* 45:610. S. 21, '78. This first appeared in New Society, London, the weekly review of the social sciences. Copyright © New Society 1978. Reprinted by permission.

nals of Inquiry Act of 1921, as has been proposed by the Liberal leader, David Steel. This further inquiry should be completed before the DPP [Director of Public Prosecutions] finally makes up his mind about whether to issue summonses against any of the oil executives. Considerable difficulties would arise if the case became *sub judice*. It is, in fact, hard to see how the courts could act properly before clarification of the contentious issue of who was ultimately responsible for the decision to evade sanctions.

Meanwhile, the British government is going to have to face up to the fact that it is no longer realistic to hope for a negotiated political settlement in Rhodesia. The country's security has already reached the stage where Smith has had to tell the Melsetter community—which has suffered the highest casualty rate through guerrilla activity—that the Rhodesian forces are now so thinly stretched that it is impossible to draft any more forces into that area.

With the collapse of the Smith regime now surely in sight, the pressing need is to ensure that Rhodesia will not simply subside into chaos and civil war among the rival black forces, which would trigger off a massive exodus among the 200,000 white Rhodesians. There is no alternative leadership inside the country capable of filling the growing political vacuum. And it is hard to see how the Patriotic Front can take power other than by grinding the country into submission through its guerrillas. Even then, there is the further danger that the rival forces of Joshua Nkomo and Robert Mugabe might turn against each other in a final struggle for power.

Should the British Take Over?

As a way to avoiding this tragedy, could the British themselves fill the vacuum in Rhodesia during the difficult transition period to independence? This alternative was being put forward by, for example, Colin Legum in the *Observer* last Sunday.

The argument is that if Smith did now agree to return to legality, it might still be possible to get the "frontline"

African states and the Patriotic Front to accept the temporary presence of Field-Marshal Lord Carver as the Resi-
dent Commissioner-General in charge of both the administration and the security forces. They have said that once
Smith has been "toppled," they would be ready for a cease-
fire, and would be prepared to negotiate over how to carry
out the Anglo-American proposals for free elections before
independence.

However, there are several problems in this suggestion.
The major one is that no dealings with Ian Smith leave
anyone reliant on his word. Is what he says about a return
to legality any more reliable?

What, then, would be the realistic choices for the British
government? It could, of course, stay on the sidelines while
the country collapses into chaos and Britain licks its own
moral wounds, as re-opened by Bingham. Another tactic
would be an ultimatum—backed by the Americans and, possibly, the South Africans, who have a strong interest in
avoiding chaos in Rhodesia—to Ian Smith to make way for
some kind of British presence, probably with other nation-
alities included.

White Rhodesians are getting increasingly desperate
and might well listen to this—though the siren voices of
those further right than Smith have also been singing their
song. But all this would require a show of British determination at a time when we have a Prime Minister who
has just had his decision to postpone an election hailed as
his boldest stroke ever.

One MP, Malcolm Rifkind, a Tory, last week called for
the use of British troops. This might point to the possibility of a national consensus over a belated British willingness to assume its international responsibility for its rebellious colony. On the other hand, another MP, John
Pardoe, the Liberal, almost simultaneously called for Britain to pull the troops out of Ulster. The country seems
quietist, rather than activist. Anyway, we'd better start getting ready beds for white Rhodesian refugees. Will that

provoke the same headlines as the Gatwick hotel for East
African Asians?

US POLICY IN AFRICA[3]

One of United States President Jimmy Carter's first ap-
pointees, in January 1977, was an Ambassador to the
United Nations: former Congressman Andrew Young
(D-Ga.), who was active in the American civil rights movement and dedicated to bringing a new look to American
foreign policy toward Africa and toward the third world in
general. Early in 1977, the new administration made many
public statements about its innovative foreign policy: "in-
stilling an American sense of justice in foreign policy,"
"making foreign policy an open process," and "putting human rights at the top of the agenda in African policy and
elsewhere."

The highly publicized African policy of the new administration raised a number of questions. Were Ambassador Young and President Carter talking about a *radically*
different policy? When they tried to implement it, what
was the reaction in Africa and in the United States? What
have they accomplished? To answer such questions, traditional United States policy must be remembered.

The last ten months of the administration of President
Gerald Ford and the reign of Secretary of State Henry Kissinger witnessed the first revolution in United States diplomacy toward Africa. The United States failure to block
Soviet/Cuban influence and revolution in Angola shook
the foreign policy establishment in the United States. The
implicit threat to all United States interests in Africa, economic, trade, investment, strategic, and political, was clear.

[3] Article by Richard E. Bissell, managing editor of *Orbis* Magazine and
visiting professor of political science, Temple University. *Current History.*
73:193-5+ D. '77. Copyright © 1977, by Current History, Inc. Reprinted by
permission.

The influence of Communist states in Africa had never before been so strong; it was previously limited to a few minor military facilities (in Guinea and Somalia). The advent of the Cubans and Russians in Angola and Mozambique marked a new era. In response to that situation, many Americans considered it time to abandon a traditional axiom of United States-African policy, i.e., that Europeans should take the lead in setting Western policy toward Africa.

The principal effect of changing American perceptions of the quality of European leadership in Africa, which involved establishing American leadership, was the personal involvement of Secretary of State Henry Kissinger. His penchant for shuttle diplomacy, so well applied in the Middle East, was lavished on the problems of southern Africa in mid-1976 without positive result.

Kissinger and Our African Policy

Kissinger's effectiveness was limited to a large degree by the existence of National Security Study Memorandum (NSSM) 39, and the "historic tilt" toward South Africa. Any African leader who had read the text of NSSM 39 and knew that it reflected Kissinger's personal views realized that Kissinger did not regard Africa as valuable in itself. Indeed, he had no desire to become involved in African problems; Africa was only one aspect of *global* problems and a fairly minor one at that, until the Soviet Union intervened in Angola on a massive scale.

In many small ways, Henry Kissinger viewed Africa from the same perspective as early Portuguese mariners, seeing it as a large obstacle to be circumnavigated on the way to a larger goal—for the early explorers, Asia, and for Kissinger, global understanding with the Soviet Union. When Kissinger chose to favor the South Africans, he was permanently suspect in African eyes.

A second problem Kissinger faced was the African leaders' need to conduct diplomacy openly. There are few countries in Africa where the control of the government is

strong enough to enable the government to conduct negotiations secretly and to enforce the resulting decisions. In
dealing with the liberation movements of southern Africa,
in particular, the control of political leaders over military
guerrilla groups is far too weak to give the political leaders the power to negotiate with an "honest broker" like
Kissinger. Thus Kissinger found it difficult to negotiate
with the leaders of the "Front Line States," Tanzania,
Zambia, Mozambique, and Angola, since they could not impose their decisions on the liberation movements. And he
found it equally difficult to negotiate with the leaders of
the liberation movements, since they did not always control the guerrilla bands. Out of frustration, therefore, he
found that Prime Minister John Vorster of South Africa
was his most congenial negotiating partner.

Because of his good working relationship with Vorster
and his own approach to diplomacy, Kissinger believed in
step-by-step solutions that entailed linked compromises.
Kissinger maintained that the interested parties, whether
American, European, or African, could not simultaneously
tackle all the sources of instability in southern Africa. Instead, he approached the most prominent issue, then Rhodesia, and asked all parties to help in defusing that issue.
His approach made it necessary for black African leaders
to work with the United States and with South African
leaders to negotiate a controlled, evolutionary answer in
Rhodesia. The result of his diplomacy was the agreement
of September 21, 1976, whereby Prime Minister Ian Smith
of Rhodesia agreed to a joint proposal made by Kissinger
and Vorster to transfer power to a multiracial government
over a period of two years. This agreement was concluded
in a manner that expressed the Kissinger approach:

(1) Vorster was a guarantor of the agreement and was
also recognized to be a prime force in persuading Smith to
accept the proposal, given South Africa's control over the
sanctions-busting transit routes for Rhodesian goods;

(2) Kissinger thought that the black Front Line leaders had also agreed to the proposal, in the hope that they

could enforce it on the liberation movements. Only later did the Front Line leaders disavow the agreement.

(3) Kissinger suggested to Vorster that the United States would not raise the issue of change in South Africa or Namibia until the Rhodesian issue was settled—thereby giving Vorster time to undertake the types of change he desired in South Africa without United States pressure. Vorster thus felt he was getting something in return for putting pressure on Smith.

Underlying the Kissinger approach was a willingness to recognize the need for change, coupled with a determined belief that change should be controlled and nonviolent—a delicate, political balance that is not easy in the most sophisticated policy environment.

Kissinger left office with his Rhodesian agreement unfulfilled and with instability in southern Africa causing even greater concern than in the past. But his personal involvement did, at least, stimulate debate in the United States about the goals and processes of United States foreign policy in Africa. And in initiating that debate, Kissinger freed United States policy from some shackles of the past. The United States no longer deferred to European opinion on African problems and it recognized that an ostrich-like policy was no longer viable. African conflicts would involve United States interests, and the new administration would have to find a way to defend those interests.

The Carter-Young Initiatives

The most important step undertaken by the incoming President in January 1977 was offering the post of United Nations Ambassador to Andrew Young, who accepted the post and claimed responsibility for United States policy in Africa as well. The new administration thus took a major new tack, in style if not in substance, in formulating a new foreign policy in Africa.

The symbolism in appointing Young was clear: the United States had a black man in charge of its policy in Africa. He would deal not only with the black regimes in

Africa but with the white-dominated governments of South Africa and Rhodesia. Diplomatic negotiations would no longer be conducted to please the South Africans. Discussions would be laid on the press table. Events in 1977 demonstrated the discomfort these moves caused the South Africans.

The second step undertaken by the administration would be largely symbolic: the repeal of the Byrd Amendment. The original measure, sponsored by Democratic Senator Harry Byrd, Jr., of Virginia in 1971, had allowed for exceptional imports of chrome from Rhodesia into the United States, thereby contravening the sanctions voted by the United Nations. Although dozens of nations carried on a lively, if surreptitious, trade with Rhodesia after 1965, the United States suffered the embarrassment of doing legally what other nations did covertly. Even when the Byrd Amendment was in force, various American importers discovered that the chrome they imported from Japan, South Africa, or the Soviet Union was on occasion re-exported Rhodesian chrome. As a symbolic gesture to the black Africans, however, President Carter strongly backed the repeal of the Byrd Amendment, which was accomplished in the summer of 1977.

Finally, the new administration established an agenda of foreign policy goals in Africa that consisted of one item only: the implementation of human rights. Such a priority was first perceived to be a revolution in United States diplomacy, a throwback to the priorities of President Woodrow Wilson, particularly when the doctrine was applied to a region like Africa, where respect for human rights has played little part in recorded African history. The human rights policy was interpreted immediately as a slap at the white governments of southern Africa—in effect, a message from President Carter that his first priority would be the installation of black governments throughout southern Africa. This impression was encouraged by both Young and President Carter. And analysis of the new policy included all possible motives: the need to repay the American black community for its support during the 1976 election campaign, a sincere Christian view of African-American relations, or possibly, a desire to re-enact the United States civil rights struggle on foreign soil.

How Effective Is Young?

Given the priority ascribed to human rights, however, what actually happend to American policy in succeeding months? Was it possible to effect a revolution in American diplomacy? The record shows, by and large, that Young in practice was not so different from Kissinger in practice.

Ambassador Young spent much of 1977 in Africa. He needed to reassure the leaders of black Africa about President Carter's intentions, and to obtain their support of his initiatives in southern Africa. The principal topic of Young's conversations was Rhodesia: the scene of the most violent conflict in southern Africa, and the country where the decisions of the independent black leaders of Africa might have the greatest impact. The major African leaders, Young discovered, were President Julius Nyerere of Tanzania, and General Olusegun Obasanjo of Nigeria. What these leaders had in common was a certain skepticism about United States goals in Africa. Was the United States merely interested in arresting Soviet influence, or was there a stronger commitment to justice and development in the region? Beyond these concerns, however, the two leaders presented very different challenges to Young's diplomacy.

Julius Nyerere of Tanzania

Nyerere was one of the fathers of African independence. In his public image, he also expressed the African desire to stand apart from superpower disputes and to be free of "neo-colonial" bondage. Most important, Nyerere controls the Liberation Committee of the Organization of African Unity (OAU), and thus has major influence over the flow of money and arms to the guerrilla movements of Rhodesia and southern Africa. He does not have sole control, needless to say; if he attempted to thwart the efforts of the guerrilla movements in the Liberation Committee, the arms flow would be routed instead through Mozambique or Angola, or elsewhere. But through the OAU he is influential in determining the political direction of the liberation movements. Young thus needed Nyerere's cooperation in case a negotiated settlement could be reached with the white government in Rhodesia. And in the meantime, Nyerere could exercise a great deal of influence in determining the extent of Cuban and Soviet participation in the Rhodesian struggle.

Olusegun Obasanjo of Nigeria

Obasanjo occupied a rather different role. The leader of Africa's richest and largest state, in the last few years Obasanjo has indicated a willingness to alter Nigeria's traditional introspection. The future of Africa as a whole now interests Obasanjo and Nigeria's military leadership. And perhaps most important, Nigeria possesses an army large enough to have an impact on Africa's military future. In addition, Nigeria is now the second largest exporter of petroleum to the United States. Even though the United States could obtain its petroleum elsewhere, the United States hopes that Nigeria will not begin playing politics with her oil, like the Middle East nations.

Andrew Young thus perceived the Nigerian-United States relationship as important economically and politically, because Nigeria's wealth can be translated into political power in Africa and abroad. Young thus appeared anxious to keep Obasanjo informed and in tune with United States policy objectives and—always unstated—to keep Nigerian armed forces from intervening on the side of the Rhodesian guerrillas.

Thus Ambassador Young was careful to offer Nigeria some form of participation in the Rhodesian settlement. Most often, Young mentioned that Nigerian troops might serve as a "peace-keeping force" during the transitional period between white rule and majority government. This proposal was made informally. Nonetheless, no Rhodesian settlement was achieved. But Young clearly believed that Nigeria should play an important role in the "balance of power" in Africa—a Kissingerian concept that could be readily understood in terms of Nigeria's economic and military power. Whether Nigeria can act in such a role is not yet proved, but Young will certainly encourage this development.

As United States views of the Rhodesian settlement emerged during 1977, key elements sounded far more traditional than revolutionary: (1) the need for human rights and majority rule, to be achieved without violence; (2) the need for reducing white resistance to change by guaranteeing compensation to whites for property rights; (3) the confidence that the economies of southern Africa would continue to be closely tied to the United States and West Europe, whoever ruled the area; and (4) the recognition of the African quest for stability, law and order. Overall, no combination of these views appeared to be acceptable to both black and white Africans.

The Campaign For Human Rights

The campaign for human rights ran into trouble when various observers demanded its application in black and white Africa. The black nations preferred to interpret human rights as a doctrine of majority rule; the whites in southern Africa then accused the United States of a double standard: why not press for human rights against Idi Amin of Uganda and Emperor Bokassa I of the Central African Empire? Indeed, the African presidents might well have been embarrassed by the issue of human rights when it was revealed that they had imprisoned more than 1,000 members of the Namibian liberation movement, the South-West Africa People's Organization (SWAPO), on the orders of SWAPO president Sam Nujoma, simply because the dissident members were asking for free elections.

The forthright Young approach toward property rights and compensation did not particularly interest the black governments. They regarded the offer of compensation as a means of buying cooperation from the white residents in Rhodesia and possibly in Namibia. With this realistic approach, Young found a reasonably congenial negotiating environment in Rhodesia, with Premier Ian Smith. Indeed, where Kissinger had found it hard to work with Smith, and easy to work with Vorster, Young generally had the opposite experience. Most negotiations about a Rhodesian settlement involved Young, Smith, and British Foreign Minister David Owen. Smith and Owen harbored great bitterness toward one another; thus Young took the ironic position of honest broker in their talks.

Young often expressed his belief that the economies of southern Africa would always be linked to the United States. To a degree, he was expressing one of the most overlooked lessons of the Angolan civil war: if a country can continue to earn currency of universal value for its exports, it will do so. The Angolan government's need for hard currency meant that Gulf Oil was never ejected from its Cabindan oil concession. This is a fundamental weakness of the Soviet/Cuban position in Africa. Young stated explicitly that the United States would continue to play an economic role in southern Africa, whatever the ideological complexion of the governments coming into power.

Young on Southern Africa

Finally, Young attracted a great deal of criticism in the United States when he indicated that Cuban troops served as a source of stability in southern Africa. Such a *realpolitik* statement generated a significant backlash, in view of the Cuban role in the liberation movements of Rhodesia and Namibia. In making his statement, however, Young tapped an important segment of African opinion, to whom the greatest challenge in the world is the creation of viable, stable regimes. In Angola, after all, the government controls only Maputo, the capital, and the major towns of the country. The threat of insurrection or invasion faces nearly all African countries intermittently. In his statement on Cuban troops in Angola, Young took an objective view of their role—Angola's government was so weak that it needed Cuban troops in order to remain in power.

The Young initiatives in Africa thus reflected a curious mixture of liberal and conservative, revolutionary and reformist views. Young was blessed, too, by the existence of conservative outside forces that could defend United States interests without forcing the United States to take action. At the time of the invasion (rebellion) in the Shaba province of Zaire, in the summer of 1977, the United States could afford not to act, because the French were willing to fly in Moroccan paratroopers and supply weapons to Zaire's government. In terms of an Angolan policy, too, the South African government's willingness to supply and train the forces of UNITA (National Union for Total Independence of Angola), opposing the Angolan government in southern Angola, allowed the Americans to stand by without taking a position on the future of Angola.

Reversing Kissinger's Policy

In its policy toward South Africa, however, the new administration has reversed Kissinger's policy direction and its entire African policy has reflected the shift. No longer would the United States mollify Prime Minister Vorster by avoiding pressure for change in South Africa. Vorster's gradual alienation from the United States government, from the talks between Vorster and United States Vice President Walter Mondale in Vienna in May 1977 to the fracas over South Africa's reported nuclear test in August, was reflected in Vorster's unwillingness to put pressure on Rhodesia's Premier Ian Smith for a settlement. The United States shift was deliberate. Particularly in the light of the Soweto riots of 1976, which continued into 1977, apartheid could not be overlooked. Young tried to identify and communicate with other potential leaders in South African politics (Harry Oppenheimer among others), but the overall effect of his attitude was further to alienate the general public of South Africa. The Vorster government, so close to falling in the summer of 1976, used the criticism voiced by Young and Mondale to rally public opinion behind the "do-little" policies of the Nationalist government.

Experimenting with new approaches to Africa, the Carter administration has undertaken a difficult task. The first year showed the inevitable mix of failure and success. Because Africa is apparently the least stable area of the world, an unorthodox foreign policy may be necessary, a foreign policy characterized by open diplomacy and an emphasis on shared moral values like human rights.

FRIENDS OF APARTHEID[4]

That black majority rule will come eventually to the Republic of South Africa is beyond doubt. Less certain is how this transition will be accomplished and what role the United States will play in such a cataclysmic upheaval.

The rhetoric of the Carter administration is a notable improvement over that of its predecessors, but the substantive emphasis continues to be on maintaining "stability," regardless of the consequences to the non-white majority. Through NASA [National Aeronautics and Space Administration] tracking stations located in South Africa, vetoes of United Nations resolutions of censure, and subtle shifts in gold policy, the US government continues actively to support the white minority regime at the expense of 80 percent of the nation's inhabitants. Unless the United States withdraws such support, the result may be a bloody race war of horrifying proportions.

The United States is now South Africa's largest supplier of imported goods and is second only to Great Britain in overall investments. South African trade in 1977 exceeded $2 billion, including $1.35 billion in imports from the United States. Direct US corporate investment has tripled

[4] Article by Stephen Zunes, senior at Oberlin College and editorial intern. *Progressive.* 43:42-4. F. '79. Reprinted by permission from *The Progressive,* 408 West Gorham Street, Madison, Wisconsin 53703. Copyright © 1979, The Progressive, Inc.

in the past 12 years to more than $1.7 billion, and by 1980 should constitute the largest block of investments from any one country.

American investments have been a major factor in the rapid technological modernization of the South African economy, whose postwar rate of growth is surpassed only by Japan's. Senator Dick Clark of Iowa, in a report of his subcommittee on African affairs, stated, "The net effect of American investment has been to strengthen the economic and military self-sufficiency of South Africa's *apartheid* regime."

US corporations, echoed by the Carter administration, defend their presence in South Africa by claiming that economic growth and increased industrialization generate pressures that will force the whites to accept greater black participation in society. The claim is contradicted by the last thirty years of South African history: As the economy has expanded dramatically, repression has increased and *apartheid* has intensified.

The South African Economy

A strong South African economy makes it possible for the ruling white population to tolerate the inefficiencies and duplications necessary for *apartheid* to function. And it is unrealistic to expect, as corporate propaganda suggests, that South Africa would be willing to assimilate skilled and educated Africans. This same thirty-year period has witnessed the disenfranchisement and further segregation of the 2.4 million coloreds, whose culture is virtually the same as that of the whites.

Despite the substantial growth of the economy, the wage gap between black and white workers is rising, as is black unemployment. Because of the capital-intensive nature of foreign investment, South Africa has been able to maintain rapid economic growth while enlarging its reservoir of unemployed and untrained black labor. For this reason, less than one half of one percent of the black labor force is employed by US corporations—hardly enough to cause the massive repercussions that the corporations predict would result from their withdrawal from South Africa's economy.

Though an embargo would undoubtedly decrease the blacks' already marginal standard of living to some extent, it would be felt much more severely by the whites, whose lifestyle depends on imported consumer goods. As a Soweto shopkeeper told J. Regen Kerney of the Washington *Post,* "Some 40 percent of my goods are American. Take them away and who do you hurt? The African? We can live on mush and water."

Black political leaders and their organizations have been virtually unanimous in their demand for a total embargo on trade and a withdrawal of foreign investments. Oliver Tambo, president-general of the African National Congress, observed, "Companies are not motivated by the desire to bring employment to the African people or to improve economic conditions of the African workers [but] . . . largely by considerations of profit, their share of the market, and the sources of raw material supplies they require."

UN Ambassador Andrew Young publicly denies that most South African blacks favor an embargo, but a confidential State Department cable obtained by the Southern Africa Committee reveals US Ambassador to South Africa William G. Bowdler admitting, "[It] must be expected that the role of American firms here will become increasingly controversial and rationale for [their] continued presence will seem less and less persuasive to growing numbers of blacks."

What Role for Corporations?

Corporations claim they can play the role of an "equal opportunity employer" through integrating factory cafeterias, providing equal pay for equal work, and placing blacks in supervisory positions. Through their example, they argue, they will undermine the *apartheid* system. What they fail to mention is that South Africa's complex web of *apartheid* legislation specifically prohibits many of these proposed reforms from being implemented. Moreover, the very presence of the corporations supports a system explicitly designed to prevent equal opportunities for blacks. Meanwhile, the intimidated, low-paid labor force which the system provides offers little incentive for the corporations to seek the kinds of change which would only reduce their profits.

Such moral questions have never troubled multinational corporations, of course, and there are many reasons for their desire to maintain close economic relations with South Africa. The unique combination of an affluent consumer society with a large, cheap, exploitable labor pool is inviting. The average return on investment has run as high as 20 percent annually during the past two decades—about twice the world average and among the highest anywhere.

Only two or three American corporations were directly affected by the UN embargo of Rhodesia, yet they were able to force Congress to violate these sanctions through the Byrd Amendment. Since as many as 350 US corporations would be affected should similar sanctions be imposed on South Africa, it is difficult to imagine that they would allow Congress to approve such action. Though the Executive has the power to enforce sanctions unilaterally, the present administration is not at all likely to take such a course.

Corporate investment is not the only means by which the United States supports the South Africa regime. As much as one third of South Africa's borrowed foreign capital—a total of $2.2 billion in outstanding loans and credits—comes from American banks. The US government itself has lent billions of dollars to South Africa in the past three decades, chiefly through the US Export-Import Bank and the International Monetary Fund.

What Policy for the US?

Because of world reaction to its racial policies, South Africa cannot fulfill former Secretary of State Dean Acheson's plan for making it the bulwark of US imperialism in the region. Ideally, the US government would like to see a black moderate regime that would maintain the economic status quo. In the meantime, US policy seems to rely on propping up the white minority government until a suitable alternative can be found. This approach rests on twin fallacies: that the fanatically racist white minority would eventually be willing voluntarily to surrender its absolute political control, and that the non-white majority would accept token political leadership without a major redistribution of wealth.

The tragic irony of this policy is that the temporary stability the American presence provides increases the likelihood of a full-scale racial war. Polarization of blacks and whites is widening as the South African government becomes increasingly repressive and intransigent and the non-white majority grows more and more militant. This trend is likely to continue as long as the South African government is assured of US economic support and non-violent liberation movements are denied American assistance.

Though there is little indication of imminent change in US policy, other industrialized nations are already re-examining their relationship with South Africa. The Canadian government recently announced it is phasing out its consulates and ending its support of commercial relations. West Germany and the Netherlands have acted to restrict export credits. Last November, British Chancellor Denis Healey announced that his government intends to discourage investment in South Africa by prohibiting bank loans, eliminating trade missions, strictly curbing exchange control legislation, and withdrawing investments by nationalized industry.

Such actions have not been strictly enforced, nor have they proved to be as effective as hoped, but they do indicate a shift toward more cautious relations with South Africa. Pressures on these governments from students, labor unions, religious organizations, and leftist political groups have been mounting.

South Africa's Recession

The withdrawal of US corporations may come about, however, not as a result of such pressures or US government action, but as a consequence of the fact that South Africa is no longer the attractive investment opportunity it has been in recent years. The country entered an economic slump in 1974, and has not recovered.

Blacks have suffered most from the recession. There are more than one million unemployed in a labor force of about six million, creating what one government official calls "an economic time bomb." As a result, South Africa is becoming an increasingly insecure investment. A recent survey by the University of Delaware placed South Africa second highest in the "moderate risk" category of nations, with only Indonesia above it. Within three years, South Africa is predicted to be a "prohibitive risk" and within seven years it should be the "highest prohibitive risk of all countries." Already, South Africa is paying an extremely high premium on foreign loans.

For American corporations, profits from South African operations dropped to 10.5 percent in 1975 and 1976, while the world average remained constant. US firms used to reinvest 60 percent of their South African earnings, but now they repatriate all but 35 percent. In 1976, total US investment grew only 5.5 percent, a dramatic decline from the 24 percent average growth in the previous three years.

It would not be a hardship for the United States to place an embargo on trade, since South Africa is far more dependent on American technology and industrial goods than the United States is on South African raw materials. South Africa has no minerals which the United States could not find readily elsewhere, except for chromium and platinum—and even these can be obtained from secondary sources, recycling, and conservation programs.

US withdrawal and embargo are not only becoming increasingly feasible, they may soon be obligatory. A major uprising would cause far too much instability for US corporations to risk attempting to stay in South Africa. In addition, several black African countries have threatened economic retaliation to nations investing in South Africa; if they follow through, they could place serious pressure on American corporations to pull out. Not only does 38 percent of America's crude petroleum come from Africa, but the potential domestic markets of the rest of the continent dwarf South Africa. Secretary of State Cyrus Vance recently stated, "Our trade with Nigeria alone is double the value of that with South Africa."

What Support for Liberation Groups?

Change in US policy toward South Africa, then, may come in spite of corporate and government intentions. The region offers an opportunity to abandon Washington's traditional Cold War orientation and to make way for a more flexible regional approach. One can still hear dire predictions that a Communist-controlled South Africa would threaten oil tanker shipping lanes—ignoring the fact that there are more than 3,000 miles of navigable waters south of the Cape of Good Hope. Still, the State Department is beginning to pay attention to the "Africanists," and the shift in rhetoric from the Kissinger days could signify an important turn in direction.

Even those policymakers who adhere to a bipolar perspective are beginning to recognize that liberation is inevitable. The experience in Angola and Mozambique has produced the realization that it would be more pragmatic to give support to liberation movements early, even if their ideology deviates from American economic interests. Otherwise, South Africa may become another case where a nationalist movement is forced into the Soviet camp because of US hostility; it is too important a country to "lose."

An embargo and withdrawal from South Africa would be a major victory, even if it came for the wrong reasons. Yet there are still powerful interests that would have much

to lose should such sanctions be imposed. The United States
has rarely taken a progressive foreign policy stance without
widespread public advocacy. Grass-roots activism may be
the only real hope of preventing a bloodbath in South
Africa.

CARTER'S NUCLEAR DEAL WITH SOUTH AFRICA[5]

In the summer of 1977, a Soviet spy satellite photographed what to the untrained eye appeared to be some
innocent-looking sheds and a tower located in the barren
Kalahari desert, 400 miles west of Johannesburg, South
Africa. But to Soviet experts, these photos were a sign that
the apartheid regime of South Africa was preparing to set
off an atomic explosion. On August 6, Soviet Premier Leo-
nid Brezhnev alerted the United States to this discovery,
and, in the following weeks, the Carter administration
entered into an intense round of secret diplomacy aimed
at forestalling the suspected South African nuclear test.
Finally, on August 23, President Carter was able to an-
nounce that "in response to our own direct inquiry and
that of other nations, South Africa has informed us that
they do not intend to develop nuclear devices for any purpose, either peaceful or as a weapon . . . and that no nuclear explosive test will be taken in South Africa now or
in the future."

Now, more than a year later, Carter is preparing to
strike what may be a Faustian nuclear bargain with South
Africa in order to get it to put that pledge in writing. Ever
since photos from Big Bird 56A, a US Air Force reconnais-
sance satellite, provided enough evidence to convince the

[5] Article by Robert A. Manning and Stephen Talbot. Mr. Manning writes
about Africa for such publications as Le Monde Diplomatique and New Africa;
and Mr. Manning, African correspondent for International Bulletin, writes frequently for Inquiry. Inquiry. 1:7-10. O. 30, '78. Copyright 1978 by Cato Institute, 1700 Montgomery St., San Francisco, CA 94111. Reprinted by permission.

Carter administration of the accuracy of the Soviet warning, the United States has been involved in top-level, be-
hind-the-scenes negotiations to convince South Africa to
sign the Nuclear Nonproliferation Treaty and open all its
nuclear facilities to international inspection. This effort has
apparently met with success. But the price the South African regime is exacting for its acquiescence is that the
United States guarantee to supply the enriched uranium
and the nuclear technology and equipment that South Africa
needs to fulfill its ambitious plan to become a "nuclear
OPEC" in the 1980s.

The pending nuclear deal has been one of the better-
kept secrets in both Washington and Pretoria. During top-
level, highly secretive talks in Pretoria last June 25 to 29,
American and South African negotiators worked out a complex, step-by-step process and timetable that would lead to
South Africa signing the nonproliferation treaty in exchange for US supplies of enriched fuel and nuclear technology. The US delegation was led by Carter's top nuclear
negotiator, Ambassador-at-Large Gerard Smith.

The Ball Is in South Africa's Court

According to sources at the Arms Control and Disarma-
ment Agency (ACDA) in Washington, the scenario that
has been worked out begins with the South African prime
minister swallowing his pride and announcing his intention
to sign the nonproliferation treaty. Then Pretoria would
invite the International Atomic Energy Agency (IAEA)
to begin discussing the inspection of South Africa's nuclear
plants. Sometime after an IAEA team visited South Africa,
the white-minority regime would actually sign the nonproliferation treaty. This would be followed by the implementation of the treaty's safeguards system, which would
take some 18 to 24 months. Finally, if all went according to
plan, an agreement with IAEA on actual inspection procedures would be worked out.

ACDA sources say that "the ball is now in South Africa's court," and that they expect Pretoria to "respond af-

firmatively" and set the complex process in motion. Although these sources predict that South Africa might respond in a few weeks, State Department African specialists say it will probably take much longer. They argue that Pretoria's immediate priority is negotiating a settlement with the West on the future of Namibia, now illegally occupied by South Africa, and that it might be several months before South African leaders could sell the nonproliferation treaty to their suspicious, hard-line domestic constituency.

US-South African Cooperation

The Carter administration believes that South Africa's acceptance of the nonproliferation treaty would be a major victory in its campaign to halt the spread of nuclear weapons. South Africa, on the other hand, is primarily interested in a public display of cooperation with the United States, and in securing US nuclear material. (Carter has been withholding 57 pounds of enriched uranium for Pretoria's American-built reactor, SAFARI I.) On top of that, South Africa wants enriched uranium for its two nuclear reactors at Koeburg, currently under construction by a French consortium, FRAMATOME. Finally, the South Africans want a pledge from Washington that US technology and equipment will be forthcoming for its top-secret uranium enrichment plant at Valindaba, outside Pretoria.

Although South Africa has temporarily shelved a $1.5 billion plan for a large commercial uranium enrichment plan because of difficulty in obtaining Western financing, its state-owned nuclear industry is viewed as a major trump card to safeguard the white-minority regime's political and economic future. Not only does South Africa possess between ten and 20 percent of the world's uranium reserves, it has also developed sophisticated uranium enrichment techniques held by only six other nations. South Africa is already the world's leading producer of uranium and hopes to become the top exporter of enriched "yellowcake" (uranium oxide) to the expanding market for nuclear-reactor fuel in the West and the Third World. Pretoria's dream is to become a "nuclear **OPEC.**" Albert Louw, vice-president of South Africa's Atomic Energy Board, has said, "We now have the bargaining power equal to an Arab country with a lot of oil."

Ironically, South Africa's nuclear prowess is largely a product of more than 20 years of close cooperation with the United States and, more recently, with West Germany. A newly published book, *The Nuclear Axis,* by Barbara Rogers and Zdenek Cervanka, describes this Western collaboration and explains, "The US gave South Africa the possibility of setting up its nuclear research development in the first place, by developing a uranium mining and processing industry for the American post-war nuclear arms race." In testimony last year before Representative Charles Diggs's House International Relations Subcommittee on Africa, the architect of Carter's nuclear policy, Deputy Undersecretary of State Joseph Nye, Jr., said that

South Africa became an important supplier of uranium to the United States beginning in 1953. These shipments continued until the early 1960s. . . . We entered into an agreement for nuclear cooperation with South Africa on July 8, 1957. . . . The initial type of cooperation was in the area of research, but eventual cooperation in nuclear power was envisioned from the beginning.

Under the 1957 pact, which has been extended to the year 2007, an American firm, Allis-Chalmers, built what is still South Africa's only operating reactor, and the United States has provided this SAFARI I reactor with 231 pounds of enriched uranium—enough to make ten medium-sized nuclear bombs. More than 155 US nuclear experts have participated in South Africa's nuclear development program, and 90 nuclear scientists from South Africa have received training in the United States. The United States has also provided an IBM 360/40 computer for the Pelindaba SAFARI I research facility. Perhaps most controversial are the two computers provided by the Foxboro Corporation of Massachusetts for South Africa's experimental enrichment plant at Valindaba. (Valindaba is a Zulu expression meaning "the talking is over.") Unlike SAFARI I, this plant is off-limits to any international inspection. It is at this facility that some experts believe Pretoria may already have diverted spent uranium to be reprocessed into weapons fuel.

Dr. Roux, the South African Atomic Energy Board president, underlined the US role in South Africa's nuclear development by telling a group of visiting Americans in 1976, "We ascribe our degree of advancement today, in large measure, to the training and assistance so willingly provided by the USA during the early years of our nuclear program, when several of the Western world's nuclear nations cooperated in initiating our scientists and engineers into nuclear science."

America's Tasks Ahead

If the United States and South Africa do conclude a nuclear pact, the Carter administration may still have a difficult time convincing some countries, especially in Africa and elsewhere in the Third World, that the South Africans have really forsaken development of nuclear weapons. Last year, Information Minister Connie Mulder told the Washington *Post,* "Let me say that if we are attacked, no rules apply at all if it comes to a question of our existence. We will use all means at our disposal, whatever they may be." He then specifically referred to South Africa's nuclear facilities and uranium resources. Prime Minister John Vorster also told *Newsweek:* "[South Africa] can enrich uranium and we have the capability of mounting a nuclear defense." Even if South Africa signs the nonproliferation treaty, some experts believe that South Africa has already diverted enough nuclear fuel to create a bomb. Others argue that nuclear safeguards provided under the treaty may not be sufficient to prevent South Africa in the future from diverting nuclear material from its enrichment plant for weapons production. In fact, an entirely new inspection system would have to be devised to monitor Pretoria's secret enrichment process.

African countries and other critics of apartheid also fear that even if Carter can restrain the South Africans from developing and using nuclear weapons, a US–South African nuclear pact could be more of a triumph for Pretoria and yet another indication of the West's commitment to the regime there.

Undersecretary Joseph Nye, Jr., has said that one tactic Washington has adopted for encouraging nations to sign the nonproliferation treaty is to offer the protection of the US nuclear "umbrella" as a substitute for the development of their own atomic weapons. South Africa has been angling for a formal military relationship with the United States and NATO for years. Although a distant possibility, a US–South African mutual security agreement may be in the back of the minds of South African strategists as they seek to gain the most they can in return for signing away their nuclear weapons development.

What Economic Implications?

The economic implications of a US–South African nuclear pact are at least as ominous as the military consequences. If the United States agrees to supply the enriched uranium South Africa needs to develop its own uranium-enriching industry, Pretoria—with its vast reserves of uranium—could corner the uranium enrichment market in the 1980s. Documents leaked last year uncovered a secret uranium cartel in which South Africa played a key role, along with Australia, Canada, and Gulf Oil Corporation. The cartel, which first met in Johannesburg, successfully conspired to drive the price of uranium from $6 a pound to $41 —an increase that dwarf's OPEC's best efforts.

A US commitment to continue aiding in the development of South Africa's nuclear industry would also help South Africa in an area where it is potentially vulnerable —energy. Although South Africa has major coal reserves, oil is one of the few strategic resources it lacks. By developing nuclear power, Pretoria will become that much more self-sufficient in energy and less susceptible to an oil embargo, which a recent UN study said could bring down the apartheid regime in two years.

The South Africans are already suggesting that a major nuclear pact with the United States would indicate improved political ties between Washington and Pretoria. As a Johannesburg daily, *Die Vaderland,* pointed out, "A nuclear agreement between South Africa and the US could be made only between two governments which cooperate and which do not seek each other's downfall." And the *Christian Science Monitor* warned, "A US–South Africa agreement would show the West is supportive of the current government." The administration is aware of these implications. When questioned about the ramifications of a nonproliferation agreement with South Africa, an ACDA official admitted that the nuclear deal "might cause us some problems in Africa," where the bargain could appear part of a larger pattern of US cooperation with South Africa.

US Silence on Apartheid

The Carter administration, which has made human rights a keynote of its foreign-policy rhetoric and which has projected the image of being strongly opposed to the South African regime, has been conspicuously silent about apartheid in the last year. In fact, during congressional hearings last August on US investments in South Africa, Assistant Secretary of State for African Affairs Richard Moose echoed Henry Kissinger's old policy of not pressuring South Africa in hopes of winning South African cooperation for negotiated settlements in Namibia and Rhodesia. Since Vice President Walter Mondale told Vorster in May 1977 that the United States favored "one man, one vote," the administration has taken only one significant action against South Africa—voting in favor of a mandatory UN Security Council arms embargo. But that was largely symbolic, since it is generally recognized that the West, including the United States, had already built up South Africa's huge arsenal of

modern weapons—and the embargo was too little, too late.
In his last major policy address on Africa, delivered in June
in Atlantic City, Secretary of State Cyrus Vance scarcely
mentioned South Africa, saying only that the country's
"failure to begin to make genuine progress toward an end
to racial discrimination and full political participation for
all South African citizens can only have an increasingly
adverse impact on our relations." As if those brief words
might appear too harsh, Vance hastened to add, "We do
not seek to impose either a timetable or a blueprint for
this progress."

But the Carter administration's toned-down criticism
of Pretoria does not correspond to any improvement in the
human-rights situation in South Africa. There has been
no let-up in the repression of black political rights and no
substantive move away from apartheid. The few changes
have been token. The ministry of "bantu" (black) affairs
is now called "plural development." In a continuing crackdown on dissent, the white-minority regime has begun a
series of so-called "terrorism trials" that the police say will
involve some 300 political detainees in 67 separate cases.
Lungile Tabalaza, a 20-year-old black detainee, "fell" five
floors to his death in July, another "suicide," according to
the South African police. His death occurred during inter-
rogation in the same Port Elizabeth jail where black leader
Steve Biko was kept chained and naked before his death
in detention last year. Amnesty International reported
earlier this year that police torture in South Africa is almost
routine and concluded that "no reforms in the present structure will be sufficiently far-reaching to remove the causes
of political imprisonment unless the whole system of apartheid is dismantled."

Nuclear Weapons and Diplomacy

The South African government is keenly aware of its
international isolation, its dependence on foreign capital,
and the threat it faces from a black majority whose politi-

cal, human, and economic rights have long been denied. The apartheid regime is particularly worried about the various campaigns in the United States and Western Europe to cut off or even withdraw investments. Under these circumstances, South African leaders are not about to give up the "ultimate weapon"—the atomic bomb, or at least the capacity to make one—unless they believe they can secure sufficient guarantees from the United States to justify such a psychologically potent concession.

In fact, nuclear weapons are of more diplomatic than military use to South Africa. The apartheid regime can't very well drop the bomb on Soweto, only a few miles from "white" Johannesburg. The atomic bomb cannot solve the apartheid regime's internal problems. South Africa could use the bomb to threaten the capitals of the "front line states" that support the guerrillas who are now beginning to infiltrate across the border; the British long ago provided the 20 Canberra and Buccaneer light bombers that could be used to deliver nuclear weapons. But such an eventuality is unlikely. The United States would almost certainly intervene to prevent such an attack, and the Soviet Union would probably threaten retaliation. So all that South Africa really gains in developing a bomb is a desperate doomsday weapon. It may prove satisfying to the Afrikaner's "fortress mentality," but it will not provide much security.

That is why—in return for strong US commitments—Pretoria is prepared to consider signing away South Africa's development of nuclear weapons. In offering these commitments to Pretoria, the Carter administration seems more interested in scoring at least a symbolic victory in its nonproliferation campaign than in opposing apartheid. And African nations are likely to see the nuclear pact as a sign of continuing US–South African cooperation at a time when Nigeria and other important African states are calling for a policy of complete ostracism as the only effective way of dismantling the apartheid system.

YES: US SHOULD SHIFT POLICY ON RHODESIA[6]

Q. Senator Hayakawa, now that Rhodesia has a multi-racial government, should the US change its policy on Rhodesia by lifting the economic embargo?

A. I have believed this all along. By so doing, we would stop taking sides.

We promised to lift the embargo if they formed a government in Rhodesia that would head toward majority rule. And that's precisely what they have done. It seems to me that we ought to give them that chance.

Q. Do you also favor a change in American policy toward the guerrillas of the Patriotic Front?

A. Well, I've been very disappointed when, for example, the guerrillas under Robert Mugabe recently slaughtered a whole group of missionaries and small children, and when the guerrillas under Joshua Nkomo shot down a civilian airplane.

I can't imagine why it didn't occur to anybody in our State Department to denounce such barbaric behavior. Certainly if the Rhodesian government had done this, we would have raised all hell about it.

This is what gives many people the feeling that our government is taking sides with the so-called Patriotic Front against the transitional government under Prime Minister Ian Smith.

By joining with other senators to get Smith and the Reverend Ndabaningi Sithole to this country, I wanted to demonstrate that we are capable of being fair, that we're capable of listening to the other side, too.

Q. Are you saying the Carter Administration is biased in favor of the Patriotic Front, rather than being neutral as it claims?

[6] From article entitled "Shift US Policy on Rhodesia?" by S. I. Hayakawa, Republican Senator from California. *U.S. News & World Report.* 85:31-2. O. 30, '78. Copyright © 1978, U. S. News and World Report, Inc. Reprinted by permission.

A. That's the way it seems—that's the implication everybody gets. The administration claims vigorously that it's being neutral; but, insofar as we impose economic sanctions on Rhodesia while we pour so-called humanitarian help and World Bank loans into Zambia—which in turn helps the ZAPU forces, the Zimbabwe African People's Union—I'm not sure that we're being at all neutral.

Q. What about the administration's insistence that there can be no settlement of the Rhodesian conflict without the participation of the Patriotic Front? In your opinion, should that position be discarded, too?

A. It depends on the conditions that the Patriotic Front require. For example, one of the conditions that both the British and the Patriotic Front have insisted on at one time or another is that the Rhodesian Army be disbanded or made to turn in their arms before such a coalition be negotiated. Well, this is asking the interim government of Rhodesia to publicly commit hara-kiri of their own will, and you can't expect them to do that.

The transitional government has repeatedly invited Nkomo to sit in the executive council and to appoint his own ministers on equal terms with the others, but Nkomo doesn't want to come in on those terms and stand for election like the rest of them.

Q. What do you say to the administration argument that violence cannot be ended in Rhodesia without the participation of the Patriotic Front in a settlement?

A. I have never been able to see any sense in that argument, because the Patriotic Front is responsible for all the violence that is going on there now. That is, they are trying to win, by force of arms, what they cannot win at the ballot box.

Actually, I think what would happen if they won would be, first of all, considerable slaughter of Rhodesians—black and white—on a far greater scale than is going on now.

On top of that, there's likely to be the slaughter of ZANU—the Zimbabwe African National Union—forces by

ZAPU forces, and vice versa. That is, there would be a nice little civil war between the two conquering armies. I think that would be inevitable.

Q. Do you believe the US would jeopardize its relations with all of black Africa by doing business with the present Rhodesian government?

A. Not one bit. It seems to me the administration continues to frighten itself with bogymen. They say, "What will the front-line states say?" Well, it's not what they're going to say that matters; it's what they're going to do that matters.

Just in the past few weeks, Zambia opened up its borders to Rhodesia because they're just having such a terrible economic crisis there. Zambia, Botswana, Malawi, Mozambique —all depend enormously either on South Africa or Rhodesia or both.

And so, front-line states can make all the angry noises they like, but they're still dependent upon the advanced nations like Rhodesia and South Africa.

Q. What role should the US now play in the Rhodesian conflict?

A. We are trying to keep out of it. I think that's a great, great mistake. The United States is a multiracial nation. In its own Constitution and its own behavior, especially for the last 20 years, it has shown that it is determined to have interracial harmony, interracial justice. Granted we have a long way to go; we have set an inspiring example to the rest of the world.

The US has deeply affected whites as well as blacks in South Africa, in Rhodesia and elsewhere. I think we would have an influence if we tell the people in Rhodesia that we will back them if they, like ourselves, try to create an interracial government with visible steps toward real racial equality in the future.

As it is, the United States is so frightened of the disapproval of the so-called front-line states—those miserably weak, economically fragile front-line states which put on a big front, backed up by Russian weaponry, but have no inner strength—that we don't dare do anything. And we're peculiarly paralyzed by our own fears.

I am very much ashamed at the present time that the United States is frightened of Russia. Damn it, Russia should be frightened of us.

But every move we take we say, "What will the Russians say? What will the Russians say?" The hell with what they say. They should be asking about every move they make, "What will the Americans say?"

NO: US SHOULD NOT SHIFT POLICY ON RHODESIA[7]

Q. Senator McGovern, why shouldn't the US change its policy and support Ian Smith's multiracial transitional government in Rhodesia?

A. What the US is trying to bring about in Rhodesia is a peaceful, orderly transition to majority rule. Supporting one side or the other would not contribute to that effort.

Supporting the internal settlement—which created the multiracial government—would make it extremely difficult, if not impossible, for the US to play a role as mediator; once we did so, we would become a party to the conflict. That's a course of action I don't think most Americans, on reflection, would support.

Q. Given Smith's acceptance of American demands for "one man, one vote," does the Carter administration have a moral, if not legal, obligation to back this Rhodesian government?

A. Our obligation toward Rhodesia is to promote a settlement which can bring peace to that nation, and thereby give its people a chance to select their leadership in free

[7] From article entitled "Shift US Policy on Rhodesia?" by George Mc-Govern, Democratic Senator from South Dakota. *U.S. News & World Report.* 85:31-2. O. 30, '78. Copyright © 1978, U. S. News & World Report, Inc. Reprinted by permission.

and fair elections open to all parties. The settlement reached in Salisbury does not offer that.

The internal settlement's ability to deliver a genuine and irreversible transfer of power to the majority is open to the most serious questioning. This is true not only because it has failed to deliver the cease-fire it promised, but also because it will permit continued white-minority dominance in many areas, including the judiciary and public service.

Q. Does it serve America's interest to support Patriotic Front guerrillas who are armed and financed by Russians, and some of whom are Marxists?

A. Your premise is wrong: The US is not supporting the Patriotic Front. We are not supporting either side. I understand that the US has rejected proposals from the Patriotic Front which would give to them a dominant role in a settlement, a position we would not have taken if we supported them.

What we have said is that we believe they are entitled to participate on an equitable basis in any settlement. And without their participation there isn't, as a practical matter, going to *be* a settlement.

Q. Why is the US continuing to support an economic boycott, now that the principle of black-majority rule has been accepted?

A. The US continues to enforce economic sanctions on Rhodesia because, as a member of the international community, we are obliged to adhere to sanctions until the conditions which would call for the lifting of those sanctions have been met—namely, an internationally recognizable settlement resulting in a genuine transfer of power to the majority. Moreover, lifting sanctions now would constitute support for one party to the conflict. This would not be helpful in the search for a peaceful solution.

Q. Why is it necessary for Nkomo and Mugabe to continue their guerrilla war? Are they fighting to get power they could not win through the ballot box? Why are they unwilling to participate in elections that the transitional government proposes?

A. The Patriotic Front leaders—Messrs. Nkomo and Mugabe—have agreed to accept the results of free and fair elections to choose Rhodesia's first majority government. But they do not believe that truly fair and impartial elections can be conducted under the auspices of the present regime. Given recent Rhodesian history, I think there is real reason for them to be skeptical on this score.

Q. Isn't America accepting dictation through terrorism by insisting that there can be no settlement without the guerrillas?

A. I don't believe it's a matter of letting violence dictate our policy. I think that we're simply recognizing facts. There is a war going on, there is violence on both sides, and each side firmly believes in the merits of its case. Our object is to try to get them together so that they can build on areas of common agreement and resolve their differences through negotiations.

Q. In your view, can the present regime in Rhodesia restore order to the country?

A. No. It has certainly failed to do so. Since the agreement of March 3, the fighting has escalated. The Salisbury government has steadily lost ground in the countryside. Schools have closed. Many governmental services in the rural areas have ceased, and the number of deaths—on both sides—has mounted. Without broader agreement among the parties, it is difficult to see how order can be restored.

Q. Isn't the transitional government offering the black Africans an end to racial discrimination and all they could want in the way of political freedom?

A. I would certainly not want to say that there are not some positive features about the internal settlement. The ending of racial discrimination—even though this has not been implemented—is to be welcomed.

However, the fact is that under the Salisbury agreement, for at least ten years, one third of Rhodesia's parliamentary seats will be reserved for that 1/20 of the population which is white. Many blacks find this unacceptable.

It is not for us, however, to decide this question. It is for the people of Rhodesia to decide. Our aim is to help give them a chance to do so in free and fair elections, held in peaceful circumstances.

Q. Is there any prospect, as you see it, of finding a settlement in Rhodesia without a civil war between blacks?

A. I believe so, if arrangements can be made in which elections are conducted in an atmosphere which is manifestly fair and in which all parties can participate.

Q. Do you see any role for the whites in Rhodesia?

A. Absolutely. I would hope to see them stay as full and equal citizens of an independent Zimbabwe, contributing their talent and skills in all areas to the development of the country. But keep in mind that barely five percent of Rhodesians are white; it just isn't realistic for them to hope to hold on to an effective monopoly of political power.

Q. What role should the US play in the crisis?

A. The US should continue to play the role it is playing now: trying to bring the parties to the negotiating table so that a peaceful and enduring transition to majority rule can be arranged. This isn't easy, but the alternatives are worse. If we are to continue to play this role, then we will have to remain an honest broker in the dispute and refrain from choosing sides.

A QUEST FOR A NEW STRATEGY ON SOUTHERN AFRICA[8]

The Carter administration is being dragged, kicking and screaming, toward a new policy for southern Africa. Events in Zaire last week forced American intervention jointly with French and Belgian troops. The White House has portrayed its participation as strictly humanitarian—to help rescue trapped Europeans and their families. But the invasion of mineral-rich Shaba province by antigovernment guerrillas from bases in Angola was more than just another episode

[8] Article by Sol W. Sanders, associate editor. *Business Week.* p 76+. Je. 5, '78. Reprinted from Business Week by special permission. © 1978 by McGraw-Hill Inc.

in the often violent politics of postcolonial Africa: It was a carefully mounted sabotage operation by the National Front for the Liberation of the Congo (FLNC) and another example of the Soviet Union's strategy to exploit the plethora of political opportunities for making mischief in a confused and ethnically complex region.

Just as in 1976, when the Soviet Union and Cuba went all out to back the People's Movement for Liberation of Angola, Moscow is on the lookout for political pawns. It is part of the Soviets' program for establishing a series of client relationships in southern and east Africa. If the Soviets were to succeed in Zaire and establish a belt of well-disposed states across central Africa, from Tanzania through Zaire to Angola, moderate states such as Zambia, Botswana, and Kenya would be in deep trouble. So would the US.

Washington's Tough Choices

. . . South of these states lies the Republic of South Africa, with its five million whites, the majority of whom are determined Afrikaners with a 300-year history in the region. A Soviet-supported campaign to bring white-dominated South Africa down would be a long and bitter struggle. It would pit black guerrillas, supported by Soviet and Cuban advisers, against an industrialized and powerful enemy. The conflict would pose an excruciating dilemma for the US. For, as UN Representative Andrew Young is fond of pointing out, Russia's influence in southern Africa is to some degree built on a reaction to racial policies in South Africa. But the South Africans, like their Rhodesian neighbors, are already engaged in "hot pursuit" of guerrillas across national borders. Pretoria also supported Jonas Savimbi's National Union for the Total Liberation of Angola. So it is clear that Young is wrong to dismiss the Cuban presence as a stabilizing influence in the region, invited in by African states, and to view African turbulence as unimportant in Soviet strategy around the world.

Moderate African leaders such as Kenneth D. Kaunda of Zambia are caught up in all this. Last week the FLNC passed through Zambian territory en route to Zaire from their Angolan bases. Kaunda could not prevent that. What is more, his support of the South West Africa People's Organization and the Zimbabwe African People's Union (ZAPU) has led to the establishment of guerrilla bases in Zambia that are rapidly getting out of hand. Both groups already have Cuban and Soviet support.

Kaunda was in Washington to tell his troubles to President Carter earlier this month. Zambia is suffering from a three-year-old recession in copper, and Kuanda needs Western aid. He also fears that unless Rhodesia and the guerrillas stop fighting soon, Zambia may be swamped with increasing Soviet aid to Rhodesian nationalists. Kuanda has therefore urged Washington and London to force Rhodesia's interim government to risk the political participation of ZAPU and its partner organization, the Zimbabwe African National Union, which is based mostly in Mozambique.

Moscow's Gains

The Soviets have an easier time designing their strategy. Offers of arms and military expertise have opened doors all over the continent. Moscow exploits local rivalries, secessionist impulses, and armed struggles against white-minority regimes. But no African state has yet joined the Communist bloc on the Eastern European model. In client states such as Somalia, Ghana, and Mali, the Soviet Union has found that the privileges it had been accorded could be revoked. But Moscow is apparently prepared to risk such fiascos in order to gain short-term strategic and military advantage over the US. Young and others who think like him in the Carter administration argue that the US does not have to react to Moscow's gains, which they believe will be temporary, and that Washington should instead put its weight behind long-term objectives, such as just settlements for blacks in Rhodesia and South Africa.

But in spite of internal disagreements on foreign policy matters, the Carter administration is inching closer to a new policy of stronger response to Soviet initiatives. One

faint hope: That Paris can organize its former colonies—
with whom it has been cultivating strong ties . . . —into
a kind of fire brigade, equipped with Western arms, as a
counter to Soviet-Cuban intrigue. At the same time, the
resolution of the independence issues in Rhodesia and
South West Africa would help cool off the area. And a
more liberal racial policy in South Africa itself would help
ease tensions and make it possible to harness South Africa's
economic power for regional development. To achieve that,
however, Young's rhetoric will have to be curbed. A far-
reaching bargain with Pretoria could then be explored.

THE SOVIET/CUBAN FACTOR IN THE NEW UNITED STATES POLICY TOWARD SOUTHERN AFRICA[9]

Africa in general, and southern Africa in particular, has
emerged as an important area for United States foreign
policy. The United States now strongly supports majority
rule in southern Africa, is attempting to find a peaceful
solution to conflicts in the area, and has repealed the controversial Byrd Amendment. Why the sudden interest on
the part of the United States in majority rule and civil
rights for blacks in southern Africa? This article analyzes
these new developments in the context of Soviet/Cuban
activities on the African continent, with special emphasis
on the countries of southern Africa—South Africa, Namibia
(South-West Africa), Zimbabwe (Rhodesia), Angola, and
Mozambique. The major contention is that the shift in US
policy, from one which favored minority rule and few
rights for the majority to one which advocates majority rule
and minority rights, is a direct response to political realities
in southern Africa which have been highlighted by Cuban
and Soviet intervention.

    [9] Article by Dr. Richard J. Payne, assistant professor, Illinois State Univer-
sity and visiting lecturer, University of Missouri, with research assistance of Hib-
bert Roberts and Denis Thornton. *Africa Today.* p 7-26. Ap./Je. '78. By permission of Africa Today Associates.

Contemporary foreign policies are not formulated in a vacuum. Events in one part of the world will affect those in another. Relations between Africa, the United States, Cuba, and the Soviet Union are part of "this great living web of action, reaction and interaction." The new United States policy toward southern Africa reflects the interdependency of actors in world politics.

The confrontation between the US and USSR in Africa is indicative of this interaction. Both nations are vying for the friendship (or the lessening of hostility) of African countries and trying to gain political, economic, military, and strategic advantages. However, to suggest that what is occurring in Africa is strictly US–USSR rivalry would be incorrect because it would ignore China's role. While this is an important aspect of great power rivalry and cannot be overlooked, it is beyond the scope of this article.

Despite the fact that in this paper the Soviets and Cubans are treated as one group, it should be clear that this does not mean that Cuba is simply acting on behalf of the Soviet Union. In addition to cooperating with the Soviet Union, Cuba is apparently pursuing an independent foreign policy. Cuba has been supporting liberation movements throughout the Third World, particularly Africa, and has recently strengthened its ties with a number of Latin American and Caribbean governments.

While one can argue that Cuba is economically dependent on the Soviet Union, one should also be aware of Cuba's expanding trade with Canada, Japan, and West European countries, and its efforts to reestablish trade relations with the United States. On Cuban foreign policy in relation to developing countries, Edward Gonzalez, an expert on Cuba, writes:

In his self-appointed role as a Third World spokesman, Fidel has time and again called for OPEC to unite with the less-developed countries to ease dependency and further swing the global balance against imperialism. [*Problems of Communism*. N./D. '77. p. 9.]

Cuban activities in Africa may be viewed as an effort to build and consolidate Cuban ties with the various countries. Furthermore, Cuba has strong racial and cultural ties with the African continent. Treatment of the Soviet Union and Cuba as one group can be justified by the fact that the US perceives them to be essentially the same in southern Africa and has responded accordingly.

In the 1960s the United States and the Soviet Union competed for influence in newly independent African countries. Today, this rivalry has returned to Africa with new vigor and intensity, despite outward appearances of détente. Several factors may account for this. First, the vacuum left by the European powers facilitated Soviet and US intervention in Africa. Second, the instability which characterizes many African governments and the socialist ideologies of some of them may have been a temptation to the Soviets to intervene while the US has supported regimes most open to capitalist penetration. Third, the Soviets, after several failures, are now more knowledgeable and confident of their ability to be successful in Africa. Finally, the Soviets have been influenced by the past US policy of neglect of African liberation movements and its support of white minority regimes in Angola, South Africa, Namibia, and Zimbabwe.

To a large extent, the West took Africa for granted. American policy toward Africa was intertwined with its relationship toward European allies, an alliance which obscured the dynamism characteristic of African politics and society. Africa presented an open invitation to the Soviets to intervene. Other areas such as southeast Asia and the Middle East became priorities of US foreign policy. African aspirations and problems were relegated to the bottom of the list because Africa was omitted from the balance-of-power equation.

The Soviet Union has been trying to influence African governments for over two decades. Until Angola in 1975, they could be described as awkward, inexperienced and certainly unsuccessful, with the exception of a few worthwhile connections made with Guinea, Somalia and unstable Congo-Brazzaville. Earlier, the Soviets had to compete with a massive, pervasive, and long-established Western presence. Furthermore, the new nations were heavily dependent on Western European advisers, technicians, and administrators.

Approximately 17 years ago, the United States was admired by Africa as a model. From 1960 to around 1965 it enjoyed more credibility than any other major power. This changed, due in part to the failure of the United States to realize the centrality of white minority rule in southern Africa as a unifying issue. Most influential African leaders are, even now, distrustful toward communism and do not want the intrusion of big power politics in Africa. However, they view white racism in southern Africa as a greater menace than communism, and welcome any help in the struggle against minority regimes. Thus, it is not surprising that African liberation movements which have Soviet/Cuban assistance are supported by the overwhelming majority of African governments. Majority rule throughout Africa is a major policy goal of African countries, individually and collectively (Organization for African Unity—OAU).

The United States' indifference, and sometimes opposition, to African liberation movements has been shaped by the conception of Africa as an extension of Europe, and by an overriding concern with communism rather than majority rule.

Alliances in Europe guided the American response to African problems. For example, concern over landing rights in the Portuguese Azores influenced the US position on the liberation struggles in Angola and Mozambique. The now infamous National Security Council Memorandum 39 clearly indicated a dramatic shift away from the professed Kennedy-Johnson concern for gradual peaceful transition to majority rule in southern Africa to intensified *de facto* support for continued minority control. Essentially, the memorandum stated that liberation groups were ineffective and, as a consequence, white minority governments were entrenched for the foreseeable future. Therefore, accommodation was actively sought with the minority governments of Angola, Mozambique, Zimbabwe, and South Africa in order to foster political stability, economic development, and, above all, the strategic global balance of power.

The strength of the liberation movements and widespread discontent and militancy on the part of blacks was seriously underestimated. Another factor, somewhat unpredictable, was the massive military assistance given to the liberation movements by the Soviet Union and Cuba, which emerged after the Portuguese collapse. It was only after the defeat of the so-called Western-oriented factions, the FNLA [Angolan National Liberation Front], and UNITA [National Union for Total Independence of Angola], by the Soviet/Cuban-backed MPLA [Popular Movement for the Liberation of Angola], that US policy started to change significantly. As Senator Dick Clark, Chairman of the Subcommittee on Africa of the United States Senate Foreign Relations Committee, stated:

> While we commend Henry Kissinger for changing basic American policy to favor peaceful transition to majority rule in southern Africa, we must lament . . . that it occurred only after the Soviet Union and Cuba were camped on southern Africa's doorstep.

Having supported minority rule, there are two obstacles confronting the United States as far as new policies are concerned. First, approaches to the achievement of peaceful transition to majority rule must be worked out. Second, African countries, especially those ruled by white regimes and the frontline states of Mozambique, Tanzania, Zambia, Angola and Botswana must be persuaded that America is genuinely interested in the future and well-being of Africans. In order to accomplish these objectives, concrete steps must be taken by the United States to redistribute wealth and political power in Zimbabwe, South Africa, and Namibia.

US southern African policy under the Nixon-Ford administrations was based on the balance of power advocated by then Secretary of State Kissinger and tended to concentrate on short-term advantages rather than long-term goals.

This expediency inevitably necessitated cooperation with minority regimes in southern Africa which, in turn, undermined US credibility in Africa. It also ignored basic American values of human dignity, political equality, and justice. As Arkhurst notes, American policy toward southern Africa has been a combination of pious pronouncements, to allay the anxieties of Africans, and massive economic and diplomatic support, through investments, technical assistance and cooperation for the white-minority regimes of southern Africa. This is especially true of the period from 1970–1974—when there was an obvious shift in US policy toward increased interaction with, and tolerance of, Portuguese colonialism and minority dominance in the southern African countries. But it continued even after the Portuguese collapse. When Donald Easum, in his brief term as Assistant Secretary of State for African Affairs, observed that the two crucial issues with which Africans are preoccupied are human dignity and racial equality, he was replaced by Nathaniel Davis, formerly US ambassador to Chile. This action showed a sensitivity to the white south due in part to US economic, political, and military-strategic interests there.

Minerals and Other Investments

The United States is becoming increasingly dependent on southern Africa for minerals, many of which are of key importance for an industrialized economy. This fact has helped to complicate its relationship with existing governments in southern Africa. Reliance on South Africa and Zimbabwe for chrome, and fear of becoming too dependent on the Soviet Union for a strategic metal, led to the adoption of the Byrd Amendment in 1971. This controversial amendment allowed the US to resume importation of chrome from Rhodesia despite US participation in the United Nations' economic embargo against that country. Violations of United Nations' sanctions continued until early 1977 when the Byrd Amendment was repealed. Zimbabwe together with South Africa, accounted for 47 percent of all chrome imported by the United States. Almost 100 percent of chrome consumed is imported. Dependence on Zimbabwe and South Africa is likely to continue for the foreseeable future because, together, they have more than 80 percent of the world's known reserves. Obviously, it is in the interest of the US to have access to these sources of chrome. In addition to chrome, Namibia and South Africa supply the US with a wide variety of minerals. These include vanadium, platinum, manganese, uranium, and copper.

There is considerable US investment in mining and manufacturing in South Africa. These investments constitute almost 40 percent of all American investments in Africa in 1974 when the value was nearly $1.5 billion. Approximately 350 US corporations have subsidiaries in South Africa, including many of the biggest and best known. Oil and automobile related industries predominate. For example, General Motors and Ford assemble motor vehicles there and are manufacturing an increasing number of automotive components, including engines. Other American corporations include Mobil Oil, Firestone, Goodyear, Union Carbide, Minnesota Mining and Manufacturing, IBM, Chase Manhattan, and Citibank. Dividends on investments in South Africa averaged 18 percent in 1974 against 16 percent on American foreign investments elsewhere.

These substantial investments have engendered strong economic and political ties to South Africa which, in turn, helped to complicate the choices available to foreign policymakers. Morally, at least on the surface, the US has been committed to basic civil rights for the majorities of South Africa. Yet, because of extensive economic ties, America has been reluctant to take meaningful action that would culminate in the eradication of apartheid or racial separation in South Africa. Such large investments created a major American interest in that country. Timothy H. Smith, Director of the Interfaith Center on Corporate Responsibility, stated that the US is somewhat mortgaged to

South Africa. "As in any mortgage relationship, the bank has considerable interest in the financial health and well-being of the person paying the mortgage, and in fact becomes a *de facto* partner in the project." [Smith. *Quarterly J. of Africanist Opinion*. Spr. '77.] It would be more accurate to say that South Africa is mortgaged to the United States. However, maintaining economic and social stability in South Africa was regarded as being in the US interest. This meant favoring the *status quo*, with some provisions for incremental changes in racial policies.

While investments in Angola have not been as large, American policy toward liberation movements was to some extent determined by the production of oil by Gulf Oil. Most of the oil produced in Angola came from Cabinda, the enclave between the Republic of the Congo and Zaire. Cabinda provided close to 160,000 barrels of oil a day from 120 wells during 1976. Despite the fact that it appears to be an insignificant oil producer when compared to Middle Eastern countries, it nonetheless represents the second largest operating field in black Africa (Nigeria being by far the largest). There was some speculation that Texaco, which received exploration rights to offshore areas of Angola proper, had discovered petroleum deposits much larger than those in Cabinda. In addition to oil, Angola is rich in diamonds. Since 1921, Diamond Angola or Diamong, a company under the joint ownership of Portuguese, Americans, and South Africans, has exploited diamond deposits under concession agreements covering an extensive area— approximately 45,000 square miles. It is estimated that these fields are the fifth largest in the world.

The evidence seems to suggest that the American position toward the liberation movements in Angola was partly influenced by these economic considerations. Continuation of Portuguese control seemed to ensure the safety of investments. Portuguese colonialism also provided a buffer zone between South Africa and black countries to the north. Memorandum 39 clearly demonstrated that supporting white minority regimes, and thus the *status quo,* was viewed as the only sensible alternative to guarantee the safety of investments in South Africa and Angola.

Given the growing dependence of the United States on foreign sources of minerals, southern Africa will become more important in its policy objectives. It is widely known that this is one of the world's richest areas of untapped mineral resources. Angola, Namibia, Botswana, South Africa, Zaire, and Zambia contain most of the valuable minerals on the continent. South Africa has more gold than any other country in the world, and the copper found in Zambia and Zaire is not only more widespread but also estimated to be 20 times richer than the richest deposits in the United States. Because the above-mentioned resources are essential to an industrialized economy, they assume strategic importance as well. Hence, it is in the US interest to lessen Soviet Union and Cuban influence in this area.

The Conflict in Angola: Strange Alliances

The primary political interest of the United States appears to be checking Soviet/Cuban advances. Because of this, South Africa, a staunch anti-communist country, is regarded, even though reluctantly, as an ally. However, many US policy makers would prefer to keep some distance between the US and South Africa for the fear of being labelled as pro-South Africa, and thus in favor of apartheid and white minority rule.

However, when the United States opposed the Soviet/Cuban-supported MPLA, it found itself in a strange alliance with China and South Africa, specifically because the Soviet Union and Cuba were on the other side. Senator Clark noted:

> Too often US policy has been determined solely by what the Soviet Union is doing. If the USSR intervenes on one side of a conflict, policymakers feel obliged to commit American resources and prestige to the other side.

Secretary of State Kissinger, in testimony before the Senate Subcommittee on African Affairs, confirmed this approach to foreign policy. He stated that United States policy in Angola had sought to help friends achieve a local balance of forces. He added:

Angola represents the first time since the aftermath of World War II that the Soviet Union has moved militarily at long distances to impose a regime of its choice. It is the first time that the US has failed to respond to Soviet military moves outside their immediate orbit.

In the overriding preoccupation with competition between the Soviet Union and the United States for political influence in southern Africa, what was overlooked was that Gulf Oil, a United States Corporation, was paying huge royalties, about $125 million, to the Angolan faction backed by the Soviets and Cubans in order to protect its investments. These payments, which were briefly suspended, amounted to more than was given through covert operations by the US to UNITA.

US strategic-military interests are intertwined with its political and economic interests in southern Africa. As has been previously indicated, most of the minerals in which US firms have invested in southern Africa are of crucial strategic importance. A strong military cannot exist independent of relatively abundant supplies of the above-mentioned minerals. Furthermore, political influence in southern Africa may readily be converted into military advantage. A friendly country may permit the building of military bases, make its ports available to warships or, conversely, prevent the other country's military aircraft from flying over its airspace or refusing permission to refuel.

Prior to 1975, the US strategic interests in southern Africa were perceived to be closely linked with those of Portugal and South Africa. However, US strategic concerns were relegated to supplying Portugal and South Africa with aircraft which were capable of being utilized for both military and civilian purposes. Chester Crocker, Director of African Studies at Georgetown University Center of Strategic and International Studies asserts:

The fact that its NATO allies enjoyed access to extensive African facilities no doubt played a part in reducing Washington's incentives to seek its own strategic presence: US Navy vessels in transit made regular use of Portuguese African ports.

This military relationship with Portugal placed the United States at a disadvantage in the long run. More important, continued support of Portuguese rule in Angola demonstrated the competition between the Soviet Union and the United States.

During the guerrilla warfare in Angola against Portuguese rule, the US opposed the liberation movements, although it has been revealed that it kept its hand in with FNLA through an annual CIA stipend of $10,000 to Roberto. However, the coup in Portugal on April 25, 1974, altered the situation significantly. By early 1975, limited aid was given to FNLA and UNITA, in order to defeat the MPLA and to gain the friendship of an independent Angola. In July, 1975, Moscow responded with a significant escalation of military assistance to MPLA. It is estimated that 150,000 tons of military equipment had been supplied by Moscow in the final stage of the Angolan conflict. This included automatic weapons, ammunition, explosives, armored personnel carriers, anti-aircraft guns, mortars, rockets, and ground-to-air missiles. This by far exceeded the scale of any previous Soviet assistance to an African liberation movement.

Angola was clearly different. Approximately 12,000 Cuban troops were flown to Angola to fight with the MPLA. Cuban intervention was largely responsible for the military superiority and victory by the MPLA. This was an unprecedented event in post-war history. Cuban troops had not been used on such a grand scale to fight anywhere—not even in neighboring Latin American countries. Tanzania and the Congo cooperated with the Soviets by allowing Dar es Salaam and Brazzaville, respectively, to be used as major transshipment points for military weapons to Angola.

In the wake of increased Soviet/Cuban aid to the MPLA, Secretary of State Kissinger asserted:

The Soviet Union's massive and unprecedented intervention in the internal affairs of Africa—with nearly $200 million of arms, and its military technicians and advisors, with 11,000 Cuban combat troops, and with substantial sea and airlift and naval cover in adjacent waters is a matter of urgent concern.

The Senate refused to approve any form of intervention in Angola, partly because of a certain degree of post-Vietnam paralysis and, more importantly, because by opposing the Soviets the US would be allying itself with South Africa. Alliance with South Africa could only help to strain relationships with black countries which are united in opposition to racism in South Africa. Nigeria, for example, the second largest supplier of oil to the US, was clearly in opposition to US involvement in Angola. Despite the temptation to resist Soviet/Cuban advances, the Senate managed to steer the country toward long-term objectives rather than immediate goals whose consequences would be detrimental to strategic and economic interests of the United States in southern Africa. By linking the US with minority regimes, the Soviet Union could enhance its relationships with Africa.

Indian Ocean Policy

In the long run, continued support of white rule in southern Africa also seemed inconsistent with the realization that the Indian Ocean is of paramount importance in the strategic balance between the super-powers. It is evident that Indian Ocean policy is connected with the great power rivalry between the US and USSR and the changes occurring in southern Africa. "The threat to US interests has been perceived . . . in terms of possible littoral state behavior, which an exclusive Soviet naval presence would tend to encourage." [Crocker. *Indian Ocean Policy*.] In other words, coastal states such as Mozambique and Tanzania could be influenced by the Soviet Union even more if the US continued to support minority rule—and if it were absent from the Indian Ocean. The Indian Ocean, due to its location and oceanographic characteristics which are conducive to hiding submarines, has become an area of intense Soviet-American air and naval competition. "Southern Africa enters the arcane calculus of the Soviet-American balance of terror principally through the possibility of stationary atomic missile-bearing submarines in the Indian Ocean." [Foltz. *Political Science Q.* Spr. '77.]

The Indian Ocean became increasingly important to the Soviets in 1967 after the development of Poseidon submarines made the central part of the Soviet Union vulnerable to missiles launched from them when stationed in the Indian Ocean. In response, the Soviet Union stepped up its activities in the Indian Ocean and along the east coast of Africa. It is estimated that between 17 and 34 Russian warships regularly cruise the ocean, calling at the dozen or more ports on the periphery where they are welcomed. Soviet air presence is also greater than that of the United States. Indian Ocean politics is closely connected with Soviet/Cuban activities on the African continent, especially in Mozambique, Zimbabwe and more recently the Ethiopia-Somali conflict on the Horn of Africa. There, the Soviet Union has shifted its support to Ethiopia in its war with the Somalis.

Soviet and Cuban Policies

The Soviet Union has managed to maintain friendly relations with Guinea since its independence from France in 1958. Soviet and Cuban military advisors are stationed there, and Soviet economic and military aid is substantial. Other African countries receiving Soviet aid, economic and military, are Mali, Ethiopia, Algeria, Nigeria, Libya, Uganda, Sudan, Mozambique, Angola, Tanzania, Zambia, Central African Empire, Upper Volta, Burundi, and Guinea-Bissau.

One should not construe the extensiveness of Soviet assistance to Africa to mean that the Soviet Union will involve itself in any conflict without calculating benefits and costs. For example, during the early part of 1977, there were reports that the Soviet Union and Cuba were backing

Katangans who invaded the Shaba province of Zaire. However, when Zaire obtained military support from France, Morocco, and Egypt, the Soviets and Cubans did not respond in kind.

Soviet/Cuban efforts in southern Africa are focused on cementing ties which already exist with Angola and Mozambique, and supporting the liberation movement in Zimbabwe. The overall objective seems to be continued political and military influence in those countries, and, in the long run, in the rest of Africa, including South Africa itself. The Soviets appear to be operating on the belief that the longer and more violent the struggle to gain independence, the greater the indebtedness of the liberation movements to them. For the time being, this theory seems valid in light of the progress they are making with the Angolan regime. The same is true of Guinea-Bissau and Mozambique.

Having gained a foothold in Angola and Mozambique, the Soviet Union and Cuba seem to be utilizing Mozambique, in particular, to gain greater influence in Zimbabwe in the event of majority rule. Zimbabwe, as part of the Soviet/Cuban camp, would provide them with a belt of friendly countries stretching from the Indian Ocean to the Atlantic. This would clearly have serious consequences for South Africa and the United States.

In early April, 1977, the Soviet Union sent substantial shipments of anti-aircraft weapons and artillery to Mozambique in an attempt to neutralize Smith's airpower and thwart retaliatory strikes into bases of the liberation movement on the extremely long Zimbabwe-Mozambique border. Simultaneously, Soviet military advisors in Mozambique were training members of the liberation movements. There was also speculation that a few hundred soldiers returned to Mozambique after several months training in the Soviet Union and Cuba. Nowhere else in the world is Moscow as openly bellicose as in southern African conflicts. It frequently reiterates its pledge to continue supporting "the peoples of Zimbabwe, Namibia, and South Africa who are selflessly fighting the racist regimes." [Osnos. Washington *Post*. Mr. 18, '77.]

In addition to supplying military aid, the Soviet Union is trying to consolidate its relationships with the frontline countries of Tanzania, Zambia, and Mozambique. This fact is demonstrated in part by the unprecedented 1977 visit of Nikolai Podgorny—then President of the Soviet Union. The timing of the visit was also significant because it coincided with the failure of American and British efforts to find peaceful solutions to the conflict in Zimbabwe. The Soviet Union has been generally critical of such attempts.

During Podgorny's visit, a Treaty of Friendship and Cooperation was signed between Moscow and Mozambique, which indicates growing Soviet influence and a greater commitment on the part of Samora Machel, Mozambique's president, to Marxist-Leninist ideology and practice. On the African continent, only Angola has a similar treaty with Moscow. Essentially, the arrangement provides Soviet military assistance for Mozambique, especially in the event of an attack by South Africa or the minority government of Zimbabwe. Thus, the treaty bespeaks possible Soviet military involvement in order to protect Mozambique.

While Podgorny's visit to Tanzania did not encounter the same degree of success as in Mozambique, it marks a turning point in Soviet-African relations. This was the first visit by a top Soviet official. On one hand, the visit could be seen as an attempt to chip away at Chinese influence. On the other hand, it could be regarded as an effort to allay the fears of Tanzanians concerning the construction of military bases in Eastern Africa. The Soviets were quick to point out that they have no intentions of maintaining a military presence there. They stressed that "the Soviet Union does not seek concessions or military bases or some special privileges, neither in African countries nor anywhere else." [Ottaway. Washington *Post*. Mr. 24, '77.] This assurance was necessary because African countries, which are highly nationalistic, tend to suspect Soviet as well as American intentions.

In Zambia, Podgorny promised that the Soviet Union would permanently support liberation struggles in southern Africa. This pledge appears to be designed to delay any peaceful solution to the conflict and to remind the frontline countries, where liberation movements operating in Zimbabwe are based, that the Soviet Union is committed to assisting independence movements. This ties in with a more comprehensive Soviet objective:

> The Soviets believe that the more sparks fly in Zimbabwe and Namibia, the more likely they are to ignite revolt in South Africa. A position of dominant influence over the whole southern Africa is the prize the Russians think is almost within their grasp. [*Economist.* Ja. 27, '77.]

Whether the Soviets are actually that optimistic is indeed debatable. What is clear is that southern Africa is of great importance to their foreign policy objectives.

In addition to the then Soviet President, the Cuban Prime Minister, Fidel Castro, visited Africa at almost the same time to meet with leaders of several countries, including Angola, Somalia, Mozambique, Libya, and Ethiopia. While this personal diplomacy could be analyzed in terms of Cuba's aim to play a greater and more independent role in international politics, it is most likely part of a joint Soviet/Cuban effort to influence African politics. Of the two communist powers, Cuba is regarded as the more trustworthy. This is evidenced partly by the warmer welcome accorded Fidel by Tanzania's Nyerere, as compared to the formal reception of the Soviets. Cuba is regarded as genuinely interested in Africa's economic development and, due to the large number of Cubans of African descent, Cuba can boast of cultural ties with Africa. Furthermore, unlike the Soviet Union, Cuba is a Third World nation—a factor which tends to foster greater solidarity with Africa. Despite these differences, it is obvious that Soviets and Cubans are collaborating in southern Africa, especially in light of Cuba's great reliance on Soviet aid.

Together, Cuban advisors and troops and Soviet military assistance have made the racial situation in southern Africa more explosive. Already they have significant political and military ties with Angola and Mozambique, and are helping Namibia's liberation movement, the South-West

Africa Peoples' Organization (SWAPO), to engage in guerrilla warfare against South African rule. With independence now scheduled for both Zimbabwe and Namibia at the end of 1978, South Africa will be the only country where the minority determines the political, economic, and social destiny of the majority under apartheid, even though the regimes installed may be accommodationist rather than revolutionary. The buffer which the Portuguese colonies once provided is no longer there. Instead of friendly troops across the border between Angola and Namibia, Cuban and MPLA soldiers are currently in control. South African blacks are isolated now, in the same sense that they, along with blacks in Zimbabwe, are the only majority not in leadership positions on the continent. Furthermore, violence and freedom tend to be contagious, and the repression emanating from apartheid fuels feelings of frustration and bitterness, the ingredients from which revolutions are made.

The South African government is relying primarily on force to continue its grasp on power. This, coupled with the growing militancy of the young black Africans, as demonstrated by the Soweto Riots of 1976 and summer, 1977, creates a climate conducive to Soviet/Cuban involvement. Unlike Mozambique and Angola, South Africa has sophisticated military weapons, and there are speculations that it has nuclear capability. In the event of Soviet/Cuban involvement, South Africa will undoubtedly be prepared to fight a full-scale war in order to protect minority dominance. It is in the interest of both South Africans and the United States to prevent such a tragedy from taking place by working out a peaceful solution to racial problems.

Implications for United States Policy

What is the American response to this unprecedented Soviet/Cuban intervention in southern Africa? While the Soviet Union and Cuba see southern Africa as an opportunity to "unmask the democratic pretensions of the US and for identifying their own policies with the aspirations of the Third World, the United States is faced with a problem

that challenges the political ideals which it symbolizes"
[Ottaway. Washington *Post,* Mr. 24, '77.] and on which its
international prestige is partly based. What, then, is America doing to regain the trust of Africa and counter So-
viet/Cuban influence in southern Africa? What is the new
United States policy?

As discussed previously, the new United States policy
toward southern Africa is in direct response to Soviet/Cu-
ban activities in the area. In fact, Soviet/Cuban activities
may have simplified the alternatives available to the US,
providing the US an opportunity to implement foreign policy more consistent with its democratic philosophies, without sacrificing its political, economic and strategic interests.
Soviet/Cuban presence on the doorstep of South Africa
and Zimbabwe makes it easier for the United States to con-
vey to these countries the serious consequences of continued
minority rule.

The shift in US policy toward Zimbabwe was initiated
by President Ford and Secretary of State Kissinger, and is
being continued and expanded by President Carter, Vice
President Mondale, Secretary of State Vance, and UN Ambassador Young. The Carter administration is clearly more
committed to majority rule not only in Zimbabwe but also
South Africa. In fact the Ford-Kissinger policy left South
Africa virtually untouched. Essentially, US policy seeks (1)
an African solution to the problem, thus diminishing the
possibility of Soviet/Cuban intervention; (2) peaceful
transition to majority rule—which would lessen the Soviet/
Cuban influence; and (3) racial and political equality. As
Carter's Under Secretary of State, Philip Habib, asserts:

> The general thrust of our policy review has been to find ways
> of strengthening the commitment of the US to social justice and
> racial equality in southern Africa and of demonstrating that com-
> mitment in tangible and meaningful ways

Despite the genuine concern for majority rule in southern
Africa, the central objective of the new policy appears to
be to undermine Soviet/Cuban influence in southern Africa. By emphasizing human rights, supporting majority

rule, and favoring peaceful transition to it rather than a protracted war, the new policy is designed to shortcircuit the Soviet/Cuban strategy of trying to identify the US with minority regimes. And, as mentioned earlier, a prolonged, violent struggle would be in the interest of the Soviet Union and Cuba. This new approach can be best demonstrated by two cases: Rhodesia and South Africa.

Zimbabwe

Zimbabwe is governed by a minority of 270,000 whites out of a total population of approximately six and a half million. This fact was brought into sharper focus because of the Soviet and Cuban support of nationalist guerrilla movements, and subsequent US-British efforts to achieve a peaceful settlement. Zimbabwe best illustrates the rivalry between the Soviet Union and the United States and the changing American policy.

It was subsequent to Angola and during growing conflict in Zimbabwe that the Ford Administration announced a major change in US policy toward southern Africa. Secretary of State Kissinger elaborated on the particulars of the US position in a speech delivered in Lusaka, Zambia, on April 27, 1976. The Lusaka speech is a landmark in US-African relations. It symbolizes a new era in American policy in Africa. In his speech, Kissinger outlined the shift in US policy toward Zimbabwe: majority rule in the near future, no US support for the minority regime, repeal of the Byrd Amendment, and consultation with the frontline states. It is obvious that this move was intended to enhance the US position throughout Africa and to be a diplomatic setback for the Soviet Union and, to a lesser extent, Cuba.

While past US policy theoretically supported majority rule in Zimbabwe, little was done to help Africans achieve it. In 1976 this was no longer the case. Secretary of State Kissinger in his Lusaka speech made it abundantly clear that majority rule should be achieved within two years and that the US does not recognize the minority government. In order to promote peaceful transition to majority rule, the US (during the Ford administration) proposed giving $100 million for a Zimbabwe Development Fund. Essentially, this program would assist the economic and social development of Rhodesia. While most of the funds would be allocated to education and economic opportunities for blacks, it is anticipated that this aid would also be instrumental in maintaining confidence among whites in the future economic prospects of the country. Thus, the new policy seeks to accommodate majority rule as well as minority rights. It strives to be more consistent with the basic democratic and moral values of the American society. Carter's avowed commitment to human rights as a foreign policy objective supports this.

While US concern with human rights is an integral part of efforts to achieve majority rule, it is also designed to enhance its position and simultaneously lessen Soviet/Cuban influence in Africa. The appointment of Andrew Young, long an advocate of civil rights in America, as UN Ambassador, can be construed as an attempt by the Carter administration to improve its credibility in Africa. Another aspect of the new United States policy is close consultation with leaders of the frontline countries of Mozambique, Zambia, Tanzania, and Botswana, and a clear indication that the minority government of Zimbabwe cannot expect US support at any stage in its conflict with African states and the liberation movements. Kissinger stressed that, "On the contrary, it will face our unrelenting opposition until a negotiated settlement is achieved." The US government has also informed Americans that they cannot be assisted or protected while in Zimbabwe. American travellers are advised against entering the country and American residents have been urged to leave. This marks a dramatic departure from past policy. Americans had been moving to and visiting Zimbabwe in large numbers previously without any official warnings.

Under the Carter administration, the shift is also evidenced by closer consultations with the frontline countries, all of which support the liberation movements. These countries also receive Soviet aid, especially Mozambique. But instead of being on the side opposing the Soviets, the US has now joined African leaders who turned to the Soviet Union partly because of previous American neglect of or lack of interest in African liberation movements. (It should be clear that African leaders pursue their own national interests, which may coincide with that of the Soviet Union.) To augment its position on majority rule the Carter administration invited Tanzania's President Nyerere to Washington in early August 1977. Nyerere is regarded as one of Africa's outstanding and most respected leaders. Like Carter, he is concerned with basic human rights and favors a peaceful solution. He, too, is distrustful of the Soviets and has established closer ties with the Chinese. The important point here is that Carter is attempting to diminish Soviet influence by helping Africans to work out their own problems and not rely on the Soviets and Cubans.

A final component of the new US policy toward Zimbabwe is the implementation of United Nations economic sanctions by repealing the controversial Byrd Amendment. Much of the criticism from African countries centered on the US importation of chrome, authorized by the Byrd Amendment. Early in 1977 the Carter administration succeeded in persuading Congress to repeal the amendment. Secretary of State Vance had asked Congress to support the bill repealing the amendment because "to do so would strengthen the hand of the US and others who are working for a peaceful solution to the problem." This action is indicative of a US effort to disentangle itself from the minority regime in Zimbabwe. Furthermore, Congress and the Executive branch are working together to present a unified American position as a signal to the Soviet Union and Cuba. When the Senate and President Ford disagreed about US involvement in Angola, the Cubans and Soviets seemed to interpret this as a green light for them to intervene to the extent they did. It is believed that a unified American position is likely to influence the Soviets to reconsider repeating their Angolan experiences in Zimbabwe.

South Africa

The shift in US policy toward South Africa is almost as significant as in the case of Zimbabwe. Unlike Ford and Kissinger, the Carter administration has warned Vorster that the US will not continue to pay only lip service to democratic principles in its relations with South Africa. Despite genuine concern in the US about majority rule and elimination of blatant discrimination in South Africa, the new policy has been influenced more by Soviet/Cuban advances in Africa than anything else. Vice President Mondale's discussion with Vorster in Geneva in May 1977 confirms this view. Mondale told Vorster that "the United States believes it is South Africa's racial policies that represent the greatest opportunity for increased Communist-bloc influence in South Africa." [Mohr. NY *Times,* My. 29, '77.] In other words, support of South Africa's racial policies would benefit the Soviets and Cubans. The new policy is designed to prevent this.

The primary immediate US policy goal as far as South Africa is concerned is independence for Namibia, the UN mandate which is effectively under South African control. Numerous resolutions have been adopted in the UN condemning South African domination of Namibia and supporting SWAPO, the national liberation movement. Due in part to increasing US pressure and discouragement of investments in Namibia, South Africa has agreed to give Namibia its independence by December, 1978. Mondale, however, admonished Vorster that independence for Namibia does not free South Africa of its responsibility to end racial discrimination and "separate development" at home. This message has been reiterated by Young to South African Ambassador R. F. Botha. This clearly distinguishes the Carter administration from the Nixon-Ford administration.

Another aspect of the new policy toward South Africa enunciated by Mondale at Vienna is opposition to the balkanization of the black community in South Africa through the creation of homelands for each ethnic or linguistic group. Under this system, blacks would continue to work in South Africa but would have no political rights there. Technically, they would be foreigners. This approach to the country's racial problems is repudiated by the US. The new US policy is that only full political and social participation in a unitary South Africa is acceptable. Consistent with its new policy, the US has not recognized the newly created homelands, the Transkei and Bothuputswana. Recognition of these entities and future ones would be tantamount to condoning apartheid and supporting minority rule. Finally, Mondale has unequivocally stated that South Africa should not entertain the illusion that the US will intervene to prevent South Africa from experiencing the consequences of its racial policies. The US is dedicated to pursuing a policy true to its beliefs and values. It was the discrepancy between beliefs and actual practice in past American-African policy that the Soviet Union exploited. Thus the warning to Vorster is also a message to the Soviets, namely, America will not facilitate Soviet intervention and influence in Africa by collaborating with minority regimes.

Conclusion

The new United States policy toward southern Africa has been strongly influenced by Soviet/Cuban activities in Angola, Mozambique, Zimbabwe, and the Indian Ocean. It is not coincidental that major changes in US policy came immediately following the victory of the Soviet and Cuban supported MPLA in Angola. Just a few months before, President Ford and Secretary of State Kissinger wanted the US to step up its aid to opposing factions. The new policy is an outcome of the Angolan conflict. It is an indication of the realization that being on the side opposing the Soviets and Cubans can be disastrous for US relations, not only with southern Africa but throughout the continent. It is also a recognition (1) of the dynamics of internal African politics and (2) that American economic, political and strategic interests can best be protected in the long run by supporting majority rule.

Africa, and southern Africa in particular, has become an area of US-USSR/Cuban confrontation and competition for influence. This fact, while not the sole reason for the new policy, is the major one. It is apparent from policy statements by officials in the Ford and Carter administrations that diminishing Soviet/Cuban influence in Africa is an overriding concern. There is too much at stake in southern Africa for the US not to react to Soviet/Cuban activities there. However, the United States should bear in mind that African leaders are concerned about economic inequalities, particularly in South Africa. Thus the Carter administration, if it is to gain the support of Africans, must be prepared to take necessary economic measures to force South Africa and American companies there to redistribute wealth and economic and political opportunities on a more equal basis, if persuasion proves ineffective. Furthermore, in the process of trying to find a peaceful solution to the conflicts in Zimbabwe and Namibia, one pitfall that should be avoided is the acceptance of majority rule in Zimbabwe without the Patriotic Front or in Namibia without SWAPO. Exclusion of these groups will not result in a meaningful solution.

BIBLIOGRAPHY

An asterisk (*) preceding a reference indicates that the article or part of it has been reprinted in this book.

BOOKS, PAMPHLETS, AND DOCUMENTS

Adam, Heribert. Modernizing racial domination: the dynamics of South African politics. University of California Press. '71.

Arnold, Millard, ed. Steve Biko: black consciousness in South Africa. Random House. '78.

Austin, Dennis. Politics in Africa. University Press of New England. '78.

Barton, Frank. The press of Africa; persecution and perseverance. Africana Publishing Company. '79.

Biko, Steve. I write what I like. Adrian Stubbs, ed. Harper and Row. '78.

Bissell, Richard E. Apartheid and international organizations. Westview Press. '77.

Blake, Robert. A history of Rhodesia. Knopf. '78.

Boateng, E. A. A political geography of Africa. Cambridge University Press. '78.

Bowman, Larry W. Politics in Rhodesia: white power in an African state. Harvard University Press. '73.

Brink, André. Rumours of rain. Morrow. '78.

Brown, Leslie. Africa: a natural history. Random House. '65.

Burchett, Wilfred. Southern Africa arises: Angola, Mozambique, Namibia and South Africa. Michael Roloff, ed. Urizen Books. '78.

Butler, Jeffrey and others. The black homelands of South Africa: the political and economic development of Bophuthatswana and Kwazulu. University of California Press. '77.

Callinicos, Alex. Southern Africa after Soweto. Pluto Press. '77.

Carter, Gwendolen M. and Patrick O'Meara, eds. Southern Africa in crisis. Indiana University Press. '77.

Cervenka, Zdenek and Barbara Rogers. The nuclear axis: secret collaboration between West Germany and South Africa. Times Books. '78.

Chanock, Martin. Britain, Rhodesia and South Africa, 1900-1945: the unconsummated union. Totowa, NJ: Frank Cass. '77.

Davenport, T. R. H. South Africa: a modern history. University of Toronto Press. '77.

Davidson, Basil. Let freedom come: Africa in modern history. Atlantic-Little Brown. '78.

Davidson, Basil, Joe Slovo and Anthony R. Wilkinson. Southern Africa: the new politics of revolution. Penguin. '76.

De St. Jorre, John. A house divided: South Africa's uncertain future. Carnegie Endowment for International Peace. '77.

De Villiers, André. English-speaking South Africa today. Oxford University Press. '76.

Dugard, John. Human rights and the South African legal order. Princeton University Press. '78.

Du Toit, Brian M., ed. Ethnicity in modern Africa. Westview Press. '78.

Editorial Research Reports. Jl. 14, '78. V. 2, No. 2. African policy reversal. Richard C. Schroeder.

Fage, J. D. A history of Africa. Knopf. '78.

Finger, Seymour M. and Joseph R. Harbert, eds. U.S. policy in international institutions: defining reasonable options in an unreasonable world. Westview Press. '78. (Section on southern Africa, p 79ff.)

Foreign Policy Association. Great decisions 1979. Section 6 on Black Africa. The Association, 345 E. 46th St., NY 10017. '79.

Gann, Lewis H. and Peter Duignan. South Africa: war, revolution, or peace? Hoover Institution. '78.

Gerhart, Gail M. Black power in South Africa: the evolution of an ideology. University of California Press. '78.

Good, Robert C. U.D.I.: the international politics of the Rhodesian rebellion. Princeton University Press. '73.

Grundy, Kenneth W. Confrontation and accommodation in southern Africa. University of California Press. '73.

Gutkin, Peter C. W. and Immanuel Wallersteins, eds. The political economy of contemporary Africa. Sage. '76.

Hance, William A. The geography of modern Africa. Columbia University Press. '75.

Hartland-Thunberg, Penelope. Botswana: an African growth economy. Westview Press. '78.

Horrell, Muriel, compiler. Laws affecting race relations in South Africa, 1948–1976. South African Institute of Race Relations. '78.

Huet, Michel and others. The dance, art and ritual of Africa. Pantheon. '78.

Johnson, R. W. How long will South Africa survive? Oxford University Press. '77.

Kahn, Ely J. Jr. The separated people: a look at contemporary South Africa. Norton. '68.

Konczacki, Z. A. and Konczacki, J. M., eds. An economic and social history of southern Africa (Vol. 3). Frank Cass. '78.

Kowet, Donald Kalinde. Land, labour migration and politics in southern Africa: Botswana, Lesotho and Swaziland. Scandinavian Institute of African Studies (Uppsala) . '78.

Lake, Anthony. The "tar baby" option: American policy toward southern Rhodesia. Columbia University Press. '76.

Lee, Marshall, photographed by Peter Magubane. Soweto. Don Nelson, publisher (Cape Town) .

Legum, Colin, ed. Africa contemporary record VIII: Annual survey and documents, 1975–76. Africana Publishing Co. '76.

Legum, Colin and others. Africa in the 1980s; a continent in crisis. McGraw-Hill. '79.

Lemarchand, Rene, ed. American policy in southern Africa: the stakes and the stance. Washington, University Press of America. '78.

Luthuli, Albert. Let my people go. McGraw-Hill. '62.

Magubane, Peter. Magubane's South Africa. Knopf. '78.

Markovitz, Irving L., ed. African politics and society. Free Press. '70.

Mathews, Anthony. The darker reaches of government: access to information about public administration in United States, Britain and South Africa. University of California Press. '79.

Matthiessen, Peter and Eliot Porter. The tree where man was born: the African experience. Dutton. '72.

Mazrui, Ali A. Political values and the educated class in Africa. University of California Press. '78.

Mittlebeeler, Emmet V. African custom and western law: the development of the Rhodesian criminal law for Africans. Holmes & Meier. '76.

Muzorewa, Bishop Abel T. Rise up and walk: an autobiography. Abingdon. '78.

Newlon, Clarke. Southern Africa—the critical land. Dodd. '78.

Price, Robert M. US foreign policy in sub-saharan Africa: national interest and global strategy. Institute of International Studies. '78.

Raeburn, Michael. We are everywhere: narratives from Rhodesian guerrillas. Random House. '79.

Robertson, Ian and Phillip Whitten, eds. Race and politics in South Africa. Transaction Books. '78.

Russell, Margo and Martin. Afrikaners of the Kalahari; white minority in a black state. Cambridge University Press. '79.

Shamyurira, Nathan. Liberation movement in southern Africa. African Studies Program, Indiana University. '78.

Stevens, Christopher. The Soviet Union and black Africa. Holmes and Meier. '76.

Strack, Harry R. Sanctions: the case of Rhodesia. Syracuse University Press. '78.

Tarabrin, E. A. and others. Neocolonialism and Africa in the 1970s. Chicago: Imported Publications. '78.

Updike, John. The coup. Knopf. '78.

U. S. House of Representatives. Subcommittee on Africa. S. 7, '77. United States policy toward Rhodesia. Washington. '77.

U. S. House of Representatives. Subcommittee on Africa. Ja. 31, '78. United States policy toward South Africa. Washington. '78.

U. S. House of Representatives. Subcommittee on Africa. Je. 30– Jl. 12, '78. United States–South Africa relations: nuclear cooperation. Washington. '78.

U. S. Senate Committee on Foreign Relations. My. 12, '78. United States policy toward Africa. Washington. '78.

U. S. Senate Committee on Foreign Relations. Je. '78. A Rhodesian settlement? Washington. '78.

West, Richard. The white tribes—revisited. Private Eye/Andre Deutsch. '78.

Whitaker, Jennifer Seymour. Africa and the United States: vital interests. New York University Press. '78.

Whitaker, Jennifer Seymour. Conflict in southern Africa. Foreign Policy Association, Headline series 240. '78.

Woods, Donald. Biko. Paddington Books. '78.

PERIODICALS

AEI Defense Review. 2:2–43. N. 6, '78. U.S. security interests and Africa south of the Sahara. Bruce Palmer Jr. (American Enterprise Institute)

African Affairs. 77:197–213. Ap. '78. A case for Rhodesia. V. J. Belfiglio.

Africa Report. 23:50–3. Jl. '78. Banking on apartheid. Richard Deutsch.

Africa Report. 23:54–8. Jl. '78. Invest in peaceful change. Harry Oppenheimer.

Africa Report. 23:18–22. S. '78. Campaigning for divestment. Shelly Pitterman and David Markun.

*Africa Today. 25:7–26. Ap. '78. Soviet/Cuban factor in the new United States policy toward southern Africa. R. J. Payne.

Africa Today. 25:27–44. Ap. '78. Political economy of Zimbabwe: implications for the internal settlement. Galen Hull.

Africa Today. 25:57–68. Ap. '78. United States economic relations with the Republic of South Africa. V. J. Belfiglio.

Atlantic. 240:43–51. O. '77. Asking for trouble in South Africa. George W. Ball.

Black Scholar. 10:2–10. S. '78. Internal political settlement in Zimbabwe; a sell-out or an advancement to African majority rule. Tendai Mutunhu.

*Business Week. p 76. Je. 5, '78. Quest for a new strategy on South Africa. Sol W. Sanders.

*Business Week. p 23. O. 9, '78. New deal for blacks. Connie Mulder.

*Business Week. p 27–8. O. 9, '78. Investment not violence. Harry Oppenheimer.

Business Week. p 45–6. N. 13, '78. Much-needed boost from the gold bonanza.

*Business Week. p 24B–F. D. 25, '78. A healthy Namibia has some problems. Jonathan Kapstein.

Business Week. p 52. D. 25, '78. Opportunity to begin dismantling apartheid. Jonathan Kapstein.

Business Week. p 35. Ja. 29, '79. Big US stake in South Africa's minerals. D. I. Fine.

Business Week. p 39. F. 19, '79. Strained economy is sinking still lower.

Change. 11:26–30. F. '79. Showdown over South Africa. Marc Fisher.

Christian Century. 95:1253–4. D. 27, '78. Turning point in Namibia. George M. Houser.

*Christian Science Monitor. p 23. O. 26, '78. Old enemies meet again in Africa. Joseph C. Harsch.

Christian Science Monitor. p 23. Ja. 3, '79. The queen could prevent armageddon in Rhodesia. Robert I. Rotberg.

Christian Science Monitor. p 7. Ja. 4, '79. A new leader for South Africa's colored. Humphrey Tyler.

Christian Science Monitor. p 24. Ja. 5, '79. South Africa: whites vs. apartheid.

Christian Science Monitor. p 9. Ja. 22, '79. Rhodesia looks to US as possible ally. Tony Hawkins.

Christian Science Monitor. p 22. Ja. 24, '79. Suddenly some *good* news for Namibia. Robert I. Rotberg.

Christian Science Monitor. p 12–13. Ja. 25, '79. A "born again" Christian as interrogator. June Goodwin.

Christian Science Monitor. p 24. F. 1, '79. Rhodesia's step toward the future. (Editorial)

Christian Science Monitor, p 8. F. 5, '79. South African blacks flexing economic muscles. Humphrey Tyler.

Christian Science Monitor. p 12. F. 13, '79. US "guide" offends S. Africa blacks. Gary Thatcher.

Christian Science Monitor. p 23. F. 14, '79. South Africa and the free world. George McGovern.

Christian Science Monitor. p 8, F. 20, '79. Race relations in South Africa—an unusual calm. Gary Thatcher.

Christian Science Monitor. p 3. F. 27, '79. Indians: caught in apartheid's web. Gary Thatcher.

Christian Science Monitor. p 5. F. 28, '79. Decision ordered by UN on Namibia settlement. Louis Wiznitzer.

Christian Science Monitor. p 23. Mr. 7, '79. South Africa's remarkable conference on rights. Robert I. Rotberg.

*Chronicle of Higher Education. 17:11. S. 25, '78. White students' union struggles to define role in divided South Africa. Helen Zille.

*Chronicle of Higher Education. 17:9. N. 6, '78. Colleges face greater pressure to bar South Africa investments. Jack Magarell.

Columbia Journalism Review. 17:32–4. Mr./Ap. '79. Reporting the race war in Rhodesia. Roger Morris.

Commonweal. 105:713–22. N. 10, '78. On the brink in South Africa; symposium.

Commonweal. 105:713–17. N. 10, '78. Investment or disengagement. Peter Walshe.

Commonweal. 105:714–15. N. 10, '78. Why I stay in South Africa. Alan Paton.

*Commonweal. 105:718–20. N. 10, '78. Are black unions the key? William B. Gould.

*Commonweal. 105:721–2. N. 10, '78. Justice under apartheid. Thomas J. Downey.

Current Biography. p 22–5. Mr. '79. Abel Tendekai Muzorewa.

Current Biography. p 24–7. Ap. '79. Robert Gabrial Mugabe.

*Current History. 73:193–5+. D. '77. United States policy in Africa. Richard E. Bissell.

Current History. 73:209–13+. D. '77. South Africa and Namibia. Richard Dale.

Current History. 73:218–22+. D. '77. Rhodesia and her neighbors. Richard W. Hull.

Current History. 76:97–100+. Mr. '79. United States policy in Africa. Russell Howe.

Current History. 76:101–4+. Mr. '79. South Africa and Namibia: changing the guard and guarded change. Richard Dale.

Current History. 76:105–9+. Mr. '79. Rhodesia in crisis. Richard W. Hull.

Ebony. 32:88–90. D. '76. The African-American manifesto. The Congressional Black Caucus.

*Ebony. 34:124–8. D. '78. Sir Seretse Khama of Botswana. Hans J. Massaquoi.

Economist. 268:45–6. Ag. 12, '78. Alternative voice speaks up in Africa.

*Economist. 269:32–3. D. 30, '78. Positive thinking.

*Esquire. 90:98–107. N. 21, '78. Rhodesia: the storm before the storm. Geoffrey Norman.

Forbes. 122:33–5. N. 27, '78. South Africa: US don't go home; interview, ed. by John Train. Gatsha Buthelezi.

*Foreign Affairs. 56:521–8. Ap. '78. South Africa's face to the world. Donald Woods.

Foreign Affairs. 57:633–51. No. 3. Extra Issue. '79. The African crisis. Colin Legum.

Foreign Policy. 33:31–44. Winter '78. Rhodesia is not Kenya. Gary Wasserman.

*Fortune. 97:60–4+. Je. 19, '78. The case for doing business in South Africa. Herman Nickel.

Fortune. 98:132–140. Ag. 14, '78. A sharper focus for US policy in Africa. Herman Nickel.

Freedom At Issue. No. 49:30–2. Africa: black nationalism intensifies. Leslie Rubin.

*In These Times. 3:8–9. D. 6–12, '78. Independence for black bantustans a curse, not cure.

*Inquiry. 1:7–10. O. 30, '78. Carter's nuclear deal with South Africa. Robert A. Manning and Stephen Talbot.

Interdependent. 5:1 and 7. D. '78. Gold: double-edged sword for South Africa. Michael R. Gordon.

Journal of Current Social Issues. 15:93–5. Summer '78. An effective course of action. George M. Houser.

Journal of Current Social Issues. 15:96–8. Summer '78. Let go our fears. Interview with Alan Paton.

Journal of Modern African Studies. 16:1–32. Mr. '78. The political economy of resources: Africa's future in the global environment. T. M. Shaw and M. J. Grieve.

Life. 1:107–12. N. '78. Rising terror in Rhodesia. Steve Robinson.

Listener. 100:386–7. S. 28, '78. Africa after Vorster. Keith Kyle.

Listener. 100:706–8. N. 30, '78. Apartheid, law and justice. Sydney Kentridge.

*Los Angeles Times. p 2V. D. 17, '78. In Namibia, they've counted votes, but the verdict is undecided. Richard L. Sklar.

Los Angeles Times. p 1 and 4. D. 31, '78. Africans find independence a hard road. David Lamb.

Macleans. p 32–4. O. 2, '78. Namibia: more than a sacred trust profaned. Dan Turner.

Midwest Quarterly. 22:137–46. Winter. '79. The civil religion of apartheid: Afrikanerdom's covenant. Ronald Christenson.

Military Review. 59:26–39. Mr. '79. Counterinsurgency in Rhodesia. James K. Burton Jr.

Nation. 227:564–5. N. 25 '78. Namibian soufflé. Patrick Lawrence.

*Nation. 227:725–6. D. 30 '78. Namibia—Rhodesia again? Christopher Hitchens.

National Geographic. 147:641–70. My. '75. Rhodesia, a house divided. Allan C. Fisher Jr. and Thomas Nebbia.

National Geographic. 151:780–819. Je. '77. South Africa's lonely ordeal. William S. Ellis and James P. Blair.

New Leader. 61:5–8. N. 6, '78. Southern Africa vs. the world. Russell Howe.

New Republic. 179:6–8. O. 21, '78. Killing for Christ. Stephen Chapman.

New Republic. 179:12–15. O. 21, '78. Mr. Smith's visit. Tad Szulc.

*New Republic. 179:5–8. O. 28, '78. An African tragedy. Editorial.

New Republic. 180:17–21. F. 3, '79. American oilgate. Stan Luxenberg.

New Scientist. 80:168–70. O. 19, '78. Nuclear South Africa. Frank Barnaby.

*New Society. 45:610. S. 21, '78. Rhodesia in turmoil. Colin Legum.

New Society. 46:6–7. O. 5, '78. South Africa on a collision course. R. W. Johnson.

*New Statesman. 95:808–11. Je. 16, '78. Will the Afrikaners fight it out? Roger Omond.

New Statesman. 95:868–70. Je. 30, '78. Rhodesia: sanctions busters' secrets revealed. Martin Bailey and Bernard Rivers.

New Statesman. 96:4–5. Jl. 30, '78. Sanctions busting: the coverup.

New York Review of Books. 25:24–31. O. 26, '78. Rhodesia: the coming chaos. Xan Smiley.

*New York Times. p A2. N. 24, '78. Rhodesia finds tribal loyalties on the increase. Michael T. Kaufman.

*New York Times. p A23. N. 28, '78. Dependent democracy. Tom Wicker.

*New York Times. p A33. D. 22, '78. A measure of apartheid. Tom Wicker.

*New York Times. p A19. D. 26, '78. This country is ours. Tom Wicker.

New York Times. p A1 and A7. Ja. 3, '79. Aid for guerrillas splits church unit. Kenneth A. Briggs.

New York Times. p A21. Ja. 22, '79. No end of torment: I. Anthony Lewis.

New York Times. p 18. Ja. 23, '79. The white hyphen in Rhodesia. (Editorial)

New York Times. p A19. Ja. 25, '79. No end of torment: II. Anthony Lewis.

New York Times. p A25. Ja. 26, '79. US oil and the embargo on Rhodesia. Tami Hultman and Reed Kramer.

New York Times. p E5. Ja. 28, '79. Among Afrikaners, liberal means only less conservative. John F. Burns.

New York Times. p A17. Ja. 29, '79. No end of torment: III. Anthony Lewis.

New York Times. p A19. Ja. 30, '79. African policy's big test. Dick Clark.

New York Times. p A3. Ja. 31, '79. Whites in Rhodesia vote over-whelmingly to accept limited rule by black majority. John F. Burns.

New York Times. p A23. Ja. 31, '79. Besieged white Africans. Richard West.

New York Times. p A3. F. 1, '79. Rhodesia's whites look to US for aid. John F. Burns.

New York Times. p A23. F. 1, '79. No end of torment: IV. Anthony Lewis.

New York Times. p 4. F. 2, '79. In South Africa, rights parley offers paradox. John F. Burns.

New York Times. p 3. F. 3, '79. Rhodesia's new antidiscrimination laws get unenthusiastic reception. John F. Burns.

New York Times. p E3. F. 4, '79. Rhodesia fearful of a descent into chaos. John F. Burns.

New York Times. p A19. F. 5, '79. Reason for hope. Anthony Lewis.

*New York Times. p A10. F. 7, '79. Mugabe, sensing victory, declares he ought to rule Rhodesia alone. Anthony Lewis.

New York Times. p A19. F. 8, '79. Talking with Mr. Mugabe. Anthony Lewis.

New York Times. p A2. F. 9, '79. Ian Smith says US and Britain appease guerrillas. John F. Burns.

New York Times. p 15. F. 11, '79. Rhodesian disputes view of guerrillas. John F. Burns.

New York Times. p A27. F. 15, '79. Down the sluices. Anthony Lewis.

New York Times. p E2. F. 18, '79. Suspicion, time—key Namibian factors. Anthony Lewis.

New York Times. p A15. F. 19, '79. South Africa: in an uncertain state. Anthony Lewis.

New York Times. p A2. F. 21, '79. New battle in Rhodesia is for the votes of blacks. John F. Burns.

New York Times. p 1. Mr. 22, '79. US citizens bribed, South African says. R. W. Apple Jr.

New York Times. p 1. Mr. 26, '79. Misleading statement ttributed to Vorster in information case. John F. Burns.

New York Times. p A7. Mr. 27, '79. Black Rhodesian leader rejects talks with rebels.

New York Times. p A20. Mr. 29, '79. Rhodesia's future and US: Carter is pressed on policy. Graham Hovey.

New York Times. p A4. Ap. 3, '79. House panel kills move to send observers to Rhodesian election. Graham Hovey.

New York Times. p 1. Ap. 8, '79. Pretoria is pressing secret trade with its black Africa opponents. John F. Burns.

New York Times. p 1 and A11. Ap. 18, '79. Rhodesia reports a fifth of blacks voted on first day of the election. John F. Burns.

New York Times. p 1. Ap. 23, '79. Some tallies in Rhodesia vote raise question on the turnout. John F. Burns.

New York Times. p A8. Ap. 23, '79. Congress is opening a drive to end trade sanctions against Rhodesia. Graham Hovey.

New York Times. p 1. Ap. 24, '79. Rhodesian election called a fraud by black leader seeking top post. John F. Burns.

New York Times. p 1. Ap. 25, '79. Muzorewa party wins in Rhodesia with bare majority in parliament. John F. Burns.

New York Times. p 1. Ap. 28, '79. South Africans are said to offer all-out aid to Bishop Muzorewa. John F. Burns.

New York Times. p A6. My. 2, '79. Altered Africa union laws could aid blacks. John F. Burns.

New York Times. p 1. My. 17, '79. Rhodesia, South Africa hail move in Senate to end curb on Salisbury. John F. Burns.

Newsweek. 92:41–2. O. 30, '78. Let's make a deal. Kim Willenson and others.

Newsweek. 92:49–50. D. 25, '78. State of siege. Russell Watson.

Political Quarterly. 49:181–90. Ap.–Je. '78. South African realities and realpolitik. R. Horwitz.

Political Science Quarterly. 93:443–64. Fall '78. US foreign policy in a changing Africa. Henry Bienen.

*Progressive. 43:42–4. F. '79. Friends of apartheid. Stephen Zunes.

Review of International Affairs. 30:6–7. F. 5, '79. The struggle until final victory. Joshua Nkomo.

*Saturday Review. 5:14–21. S. 30, '78. American business should stay in South Africa. Roger M. Williams.

Saturday Review. 5:14. N. 25, '78. Mr. Smith goes to Washington. Tad Szulc.

Time. 112:63–8. S. 18, '78. America's South African dilemma.

Time. 112:76. O. 16, '78. Gift from a hardship case; reopening of Zambian border in defiance of economic sanctions.

Time. 112:52. O. 30, '78. Pinning an elusive prime minister.

Time. 112:52+. O. 30, '78. Buying time; Namibia question.

Time. 112:46. D. 18, '78. Desert mirage.

Time. 113:69+. Ja. 1, '79. White theology's last bastion.

*Time. 113:52. F. 12, '79. One step closer to black rule.

*Time. 113:36–9. Ap. 30, '79. Now, Zimbabwe-Rhodesia.

*To the Point. 7:37–8. O. 13, '78. Rise of anti-whiteism threatens multiracial haven.

To the Point. 8:6–9. Ja. 5, '79. Tensions in southern Africa: what lies ahead.

To the Point. 8:31. Ja. 5, '79. Windhoek leaves door open.

*To the Point. 8:38–9. Ja. 5, '79. Accelerating into the unknown. Jan Hupkes.

To the Point. 8:22–3. F. 2, '79. The country the world turned its back on (Transkei).

To the Point. 8:8–9. F. 9, '79. Now back to the drawing board.

To the Point. 8:31. F. 9, '79. Perilous road ahead for black moderates. (Rhodesia)

UN Chronicle. 15:22–3. Ag. '78. Committee of 24 declares Rhodesia internal settlement unacceptable.

UN Chronicle. 15:5–16+. O. '78. Namibia plan approved as Secretary-General states importance of credible UN presence.

U.S. News & World Report. 85:38–40. S. 25, '78. Time running out for Rhodesia's whites. William D. Hartley.

U.S. News & World Report. 85:44. O. 9, '78. Another hard-liner to run South Africa; election of P. Botha.

U.S. News & World Report. 85:43. O. 23, '78. If race war comes, will Cubans be far behind?

U.S. News & World Report. 85:29. O. 30, '78. Southern Africa– testing ground for Carter's diplomacy.

*U.S. News & World Report. 85:31–2. O. 30, '78. Shift US policy on Rhodesia? No. George McGovern.

*U.S. News & World Report. 85:31–2. O. 30, '78. Shift US policy on Rhodesia? Yes. S. I. Hayakawa.

U.S. News & World Report. 85:37–8. D. 18, '78. War creeps a step nearer in Rhodesia.

U.S. News & World Report. 85:38. D. 18, '78. Ian Smith to US: get off our backs and give us a clear run; interview edited by W. D. Hartley.

Wall Street Journal. p 1 and 29. S. 11, '78. As majority rule in Rhodesia nears, white exodus grows. Richard R. Leger.

Wall Street Journal, p 1 and 34. Ja. 9, '79. Fleeing Rhodesians are refining the art of smuggling assets. Richard R. Leger.

Wall Street Journal. p 24. Ja. 16, '79. The Afrikaners and "infogate." Stephen Mulholland.

Washington Post. p A21. Ag. 18, '78. Church group's aid to Rhodesian rebels widely assailed. Marjorie Hyer.

Working Papers for a New Society. 6:25–43. Mr./Ap. '79. South Africa's future: "no easy walk to freedom." Lindsey Phillips.

World Issues. 3:3–10. O./N. '78. Africa and the superpowers. Gerald J. Bender and Richard L. Sklar.

*World Today. 34:417–25. N. '78. South African foreign policy: changing perspectives. J. E. Spence.